BOSTON SPA COMPREHENSIVE SCHOOL

REVISE FOR
SCIENCE GCSE

MEG COORDINATED

GILL ALDERTON
DAVID BERRINGTON
MICHAEL BRIMICOMBE

HIGHER

Heinemann Educational Publishers
Halley Court, Jordan Hill, Oxford, OX2 8EJ
a division of Reed Educational & Professional Publishing Ltd

Heinemann is a registered trademark of Reed Educational & Professional Publishing Ltd.

OXFORD   MELBOURNE   AUCKLAND
JOHANNESBURG   BLANTYRE   GABORONE
IBADAN   PORTSMOUTH NH (USA)   CHICAGO

© Gill Alderton, David Berrington, Mike Brimicombe, 1999

Copyright notice

All rights reserved. No part of this publication may be reproduced, stored in a retrieval system, or transmitted in any form or by any means, electronic, mechanical, photocopying, recording, or otherwise without either the prior written permission of the Publishers or a licence permitting restricted copying in the United Kingdom issued by the Copyright Licensing Agency Ltd, 90 Tottenham Court Road, London W1P 9HE.

First published 1998

ISBN 0 435 57866 9

02 01 00 99 98

10 9 8 7 6 5 4 3 2 1

Edited by June Thompson

Designed and typeset by Ken Vail Graphic Design

Illustrated by Graham-Cameron Illustration (Virginia Gray), Graeme Morris, Sam Vail (Ken Vail Graphic Design)

Cover artwork by Stephen May

Printed and bound in the UK by Bath Press

Contents

How to use this book iv

AT2 Life Processes and Living Things 1

Human life processes 2
Communication and control 10
Living things in their environment 16
Plant life processes 24
Keeping a healthy body 30
Inheritance and evolution 36
Concept map 44
Exam questions 45

AT3 Materials and their Properties 49

Introducing chemistry 50
Earth and geological changes 58
Using the Earth's resources 66
Carbon chemistry 72
Using chemical equations 78
The Periodic Table 84
Concept map 90
Exam questions 91

AT4 Physical Processes 95

Electric circuits 96
Using electricity 102
Energy transfer 110
Forces, energy and motion 114
Waves 124
Earth in space 130
Concept map 134
Exam questions 135

Answers 139

Now Do This answers 139
Exam answers 148

Index 155

How to use this book

This book is divided into three sections:
- AT2 (biology)
- AT3 (chemistry)
- AT4 (physics)

Helping you revise

1 At the end of each chapter is a *Concept map*. This will help you check that you remember everything you need to know and will help you see the connections between topics more clearly.

   The best plan is to make your own personal map of the subject which makes your own connections between topics.

2 The words in **bold** are all key words you need to know. A useful revision idea would be to build up your own glossary of these as you work through the book. For quick reference to a word or topic use the *Index* at the back of the book.

3 There are lots of questions in the book and they are an important part of your revision. There are:

   - simple questions to help you stop and think about the subject as you read.
   - questions at the end of each section to help you practise for the exam.

   The answers to all these are at the back of the book so you will never get stuck.

Good luck with your exams!

AT2

Life Processes and Living Things

Human life processes	2
Communication and control	10
Living things in their environment	16
Plant life processes	24
Keeping a healthy body	30
Inheritance and evolution	36
Concept map	44
Exam questions	45

The basics of life

The seven signs of life

All living things carry out the following seven activities. This makes them different from non-living things.

1 **M**ovement – animals move their whole bodies, plants move as they grow.
2 **R**eproduction – they make new individuals like themselves.
3 **S**ensitivity – they are aware of, and can respond to, changes in their surroundings.
4 **G**rowth – they all get bigger.
5 **R**espiration – they release energy from their food.
6 **E**xcretion – they get rid of waste products they have made.
7 **N**utrition – animals eat, plants make their own food by photosynthesis in their leaves.

Now do this

1 The first letters of each activity make the words 'Mrs Gren'. Cover up the list and use 'Mrs Gren' to help you write down all of the activities.
2 Which of the following are living things: coal, wood, plastic, maggots, grass, feathers, an oak tree and a sausage?

Cells – the building blocks of life

All living things are made of cells. The cells are so tiny that you can only see them using a microscope.

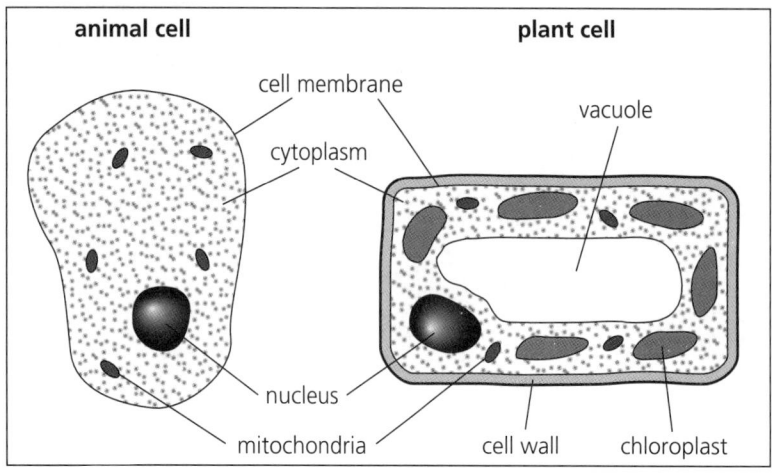

Cells contain:
- a **nucleus** to control everything a cell does
- **cytoplasm** – a watery jelly in which most of the cell's reactions occur
- a **cell membrane**, which controls what goes in and out of the cell
- **mitochondria**, which release energy from food (respiration).

Plant cells also have a few extras:
- a **cellulose cell wall** to help support the plant – think of the size of tall trees, and remember they don't have any bones to hold them up
- **chloroplasts** to contain the chlorophyll needed for photosynthesis
- large **cell vacuole**, a space filled with a fluid called cell sap.

The main chemical in cells is water.

The right cell for the job

Cells contain the same basic parts, but they also have important differences. They are specialised to do different jobs. These are examples:

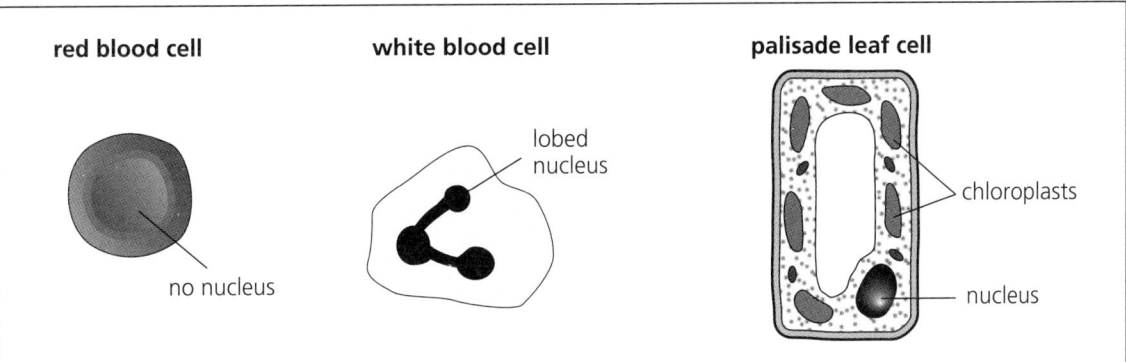

Red blood cells carry oxygen. They have no nucleus, to make more space for oxygen. White blood cells fight infection, and they can change their shape to engulf microbes. Palisade leaf cells near the surface of leaves are long and thin with lots of chloroplasts to trap light for photosynthesis.

Cells, tissues and organs

Tissues are groups of cells which do the same job, e.g. muscle cells make up muscle tissue.

Organs are different types of tissues grouped together to do one job, e.g. muscle and gland tissues make up the stomach.

Organs working together form an **organ system**, e.g. the stomach and several other organs are part of the digestive system.

Now do this

3 Which part of a plant cell
 a is needed for photosynthesis
 b controls what moves in and out of the cell
 c supports the plant?

4 A red blood cell is peculiar because it does not have a nucleus. Why?

Life Processes and Living Things

Digestion

The food you eat has to reach all your cells to release the energy needed to keep you alive. Food also provides the raw materials for growth and maintenance.

So that it reaches the cells, food has to be broken down into small enough pieces to be carried in the blood to the cells. This breaking down is called **digestion**, and it occurs in the **digestive system**.

Digesting what you eat

This is what happens:
- **digestion** is the breakdown of large, insoluble pieces of food into small, soluble pieces
- digestion is helped by the production of **digestive juices** by parts of the digestive system
- digestive juices contain special chemicals, called **enzymes**, which speed up digestion
- there are many different enzymes. Each one has its own type of food to break down
- **bile** is produced in the liver and stored in the **gall bladder**. It is *not* an enzyme. It helps to break down lipids (fats) by **emulsifying** them. This means breaking large droplets of fat into much smaller droplets, thereby increasing the surface area for the enzyme, lipase, to attack
- bile is alkaline, and therefore helps to neutralise the acids coming out of the stomach.

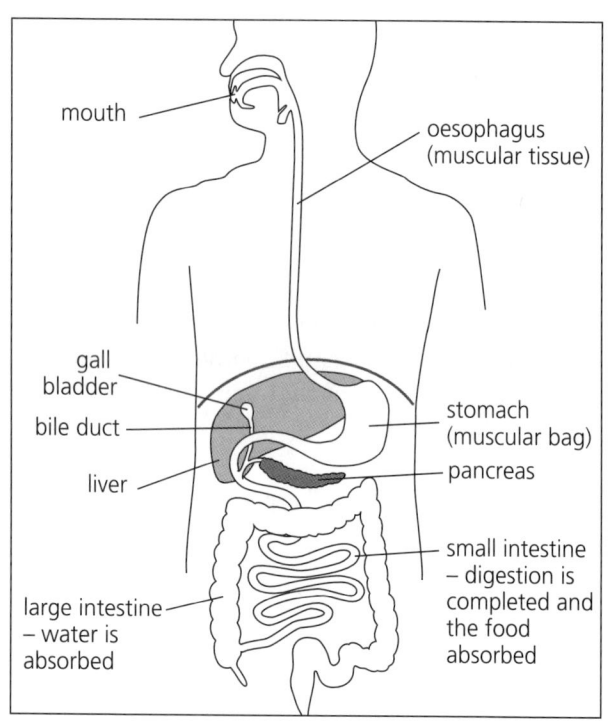

 **Now do this**

1. Explain what digestion is.
2. Where in the body is bile produced, and what does it do in the digestive system?
3. Explain how enzymes help with digestion.

Enzyme	Job	Location
amylase	starch to maltose (sugar)	mouth and small intestine
protease	proteins to amino acids	stomach and small intestine
lipase	fats to fatty acids and glycerol	small intestine

Digestive juices

The stomach makes an enzyme to digest certain foods. This enzyme needs acid conditions for it to work well. Therefore the stomach also makes an acid to provide the enzyme with the right conditions to work well. An added
bonus is that the acid kills any germs on the food!

The pancreas makes other enzymes which digest food. These enzymes are released into the small intestine together with juices from the liver. These juices neutralise the acid from the stomach so that the enzymes from the pancreas can work.

Human life processes

Enzymes are proteins which speed up (catalyse) reactions in living things. They will only work at the correct pH, and are also affected by temperature:
- too cold, movement is slow – the enzyme and food do not collide often enough for a fast reaction
- too hot – enzymes are destroyed.

Now do this
4. Give **two** uses of stomach acid.
5. Name **two** parts of the digestive system that produce enzymes.
6. Explain how all enzymes are affected by temperature.

Absorption and the small intestine

The small intestine has lots of finger-like projections called **villi**, which increase the surface area for the absorption of digested food.

The small intestine is adapted for food absorption:
- it is very long
- the villi give a huge surface area
- the walls are very thin and permeable
- it has a good blood supply to transport digested food.

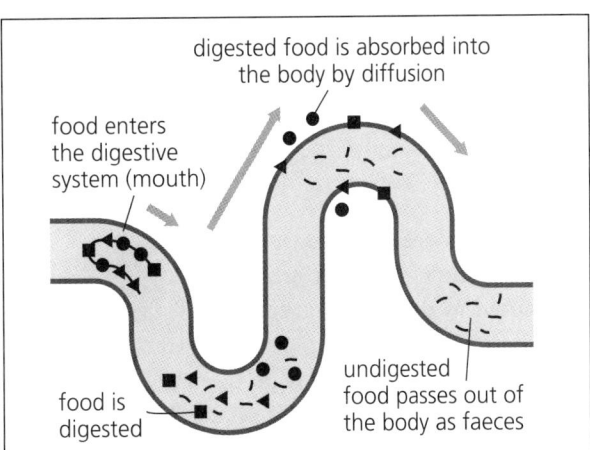

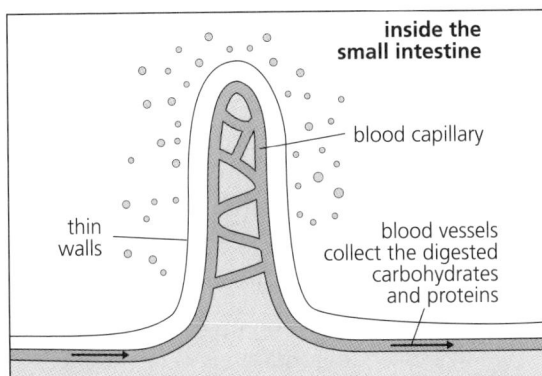

Food	Test	Result
starch	add iodine solution	a blue–black colour shows starch
protein	add biuret solution	a mauve colour shows protein
simple sugars	add Benedict's solution and warm	a brick red colour shows a simple sugar
fats	• rub on a piece of paper • add ethanol to the food and the same amount of water, shake well	• look for a grease spot • look for a cloudy white colour

Peristalsis

Food is squeezed through the digestive system by the muscles in the walls of the oesophagus, stomach and intestines. This squeezing action is called **peristalsis**.

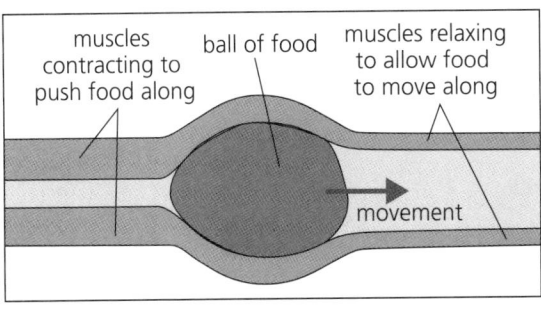

Now do this
7. Explain how the small intestine is adapted for the absorption of food.
8. What is peristalsis, and why is it so important?

Life Processes and Living Things

Circulation and transport

Your body needs a transport system to carry materials such as oxygen and food to all the body cells. The transport system has three main parts: **blood** to carry the materials; a network of tubes called **blood vessels** for the blood to pass through; and a pump called the **heart**.

Blood

Blood is made up of the following components:
- **plasma** is a watery fluid, which transports digested foods, water, hormones, and waste products such as urea and carbon dioxide
- **white blood cells** defend the body against disease

- **platelets** help with blood clotting

- **red blood cells** transport oxygen around the body. They are adapted to do this because:
  1. they do *not* contain a nucleus and therefore there is more room inside them
  2. they have a large surface area
  3. they contain haemoglobin, which combines reversibly with oxygen

$$\text{oxygen} + \text{haemoglobin} \rightleftharpoons \text{oxyhaemoglobin}$$

In areas where there is lots of oxygen, e.g. the lungs, oxyhaemoglobin is formed, but in areas where there is little oxygen, e.g. actively respiring cells, oxyhaemoglobin breaks down to release the oxygen.

Now do this

1. Name **three** materials transported by plasma.
2. Explain how red blood cells are adapted to transport oxygen.
3. Where do the following materials enter and leave the blood: oxygen, carbon dioxide, food?
4. The formation of oxyhaemoglobin is reversible. Why is this important?

Blood vessels

Blood is carried throughout the body in blood vessels. There are three different types of blood vessel.

Arteries

Carry blood at high pressure away from the heart..

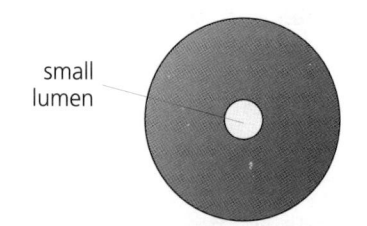

small lumen

Thick elastic muscular wall to withstand high blood pressure.

Capillaries

Link arteries and veins, allowing materials to be exchanged with surrounding tissues.

Walls only one cell thick to allow materials to diffuse in and out. Materials moving out form tissue fluid.

Veins

Carry blood at a lower pressure back to the heart.

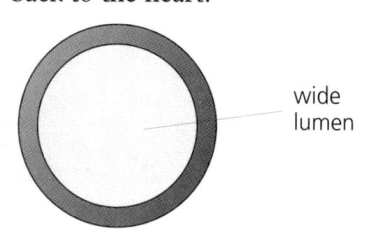

wide lumen

Thin muscular walls because the blood is no longer at high pressure. Contain valves to prevent blood flowing backwards.

Human life processes

Double circulatory system

A double circulatory system means that one blood cell passes through the heart twice on each complete trip around the body.

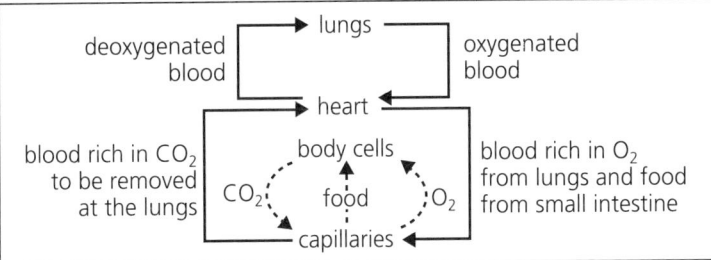

 **Now do this**

5 Give **two** differences between an artery and a vein.

6 What is the advantage of a double circulatory system?

The advantage is that oxygenated blood returns to the heart so it can be sent out around the body at higher pressure. This means that more blood flows around the body to all tissues.

Heart

Blood has to be pumped around the body, and this is the job of the heart. The heart is made of muscle. It has four chambers and four valves.

The four chambers are the right and left atria, which collect incoming blood from the veins, and the very muscular right and left ventricles, which contract to squirt blood out into the arteries at high pressure. It needs the pressure because some of the blood has a long way to go!

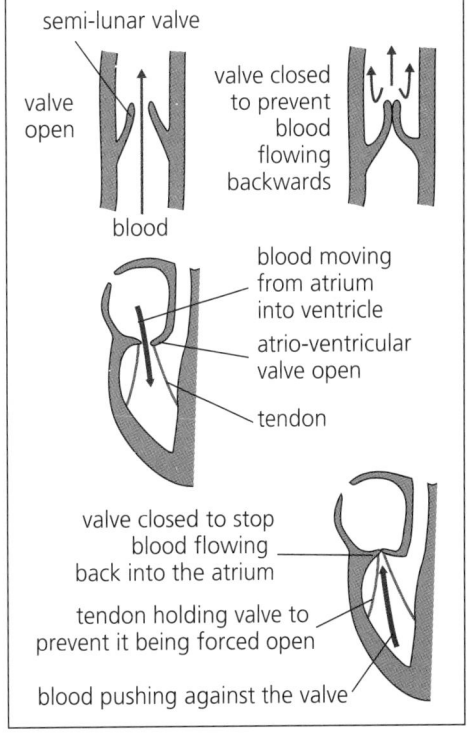

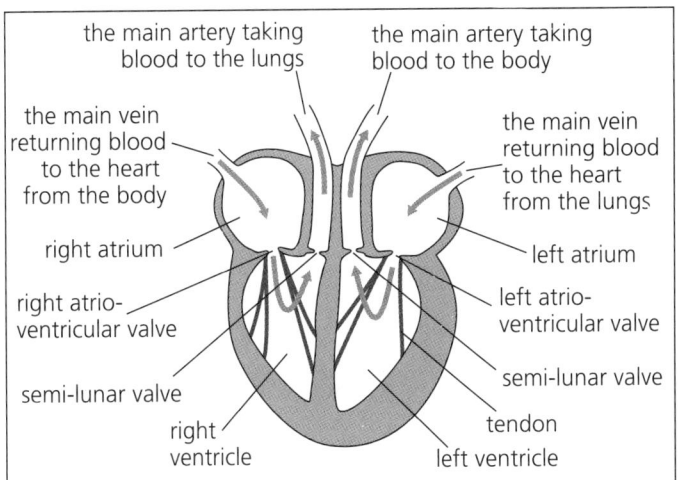

Look at the arrows in the heart. They show the direction the blood flows. The valves stop the blood flowing backwards. The valves that stop blood flowing back into the atria from the ventricles are named after their position between the atria and ventricles. They are called the **atrio-ventricular valves**. The other valves are called the **semi-lunar valves**. These are named after their shape. They guard the entrance to the arteries leaving the heart and they are the shape of a half moon.

 **Now do this**

7 Name the thick muscular chambers of the heart.

8 Why is it necessary to have valves between the chambers of the heart?

9 Name **one** other part of the body where there are valves, and explain their function.

Life Processes and Living Things

Breathing

You breathe in air to take oxygen into your body to be used in respiration (to release energy from your food). Releasing energy from food produces carbon dioxide, which needs to be removed from the body. Therefore **breathing** is **gas exchange**. Gas exchange occurs in the **lungs**, which are in the chest, protected by the **ribs**.

Gas	Air in	Air out
O_2	21%	16%
CO_2	0.04%	4%
N_2	78%	78%
H_2O vapour	variable	saturated

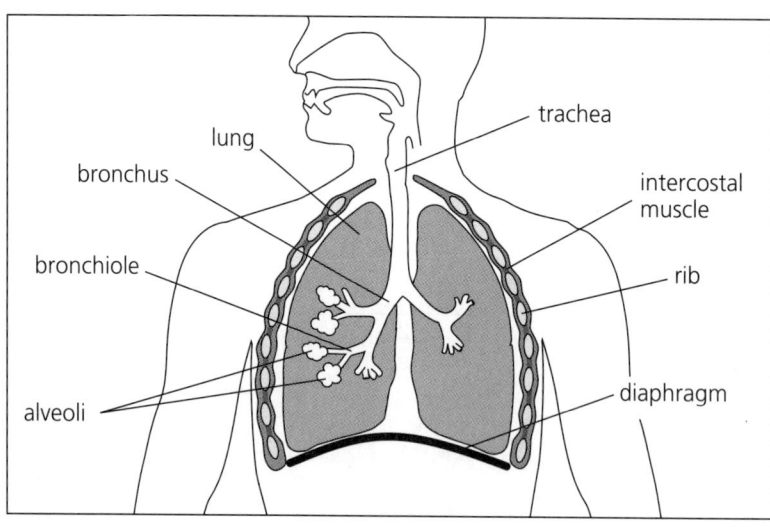

Gas exchange

The **bronchus** and **bronchioles** carry air into the lungs. At the end of the bronchioles are lots of little air sacs called **alveoli**. The alveoli are where gas exchange occurs.

One alveolus, lots of alveoli

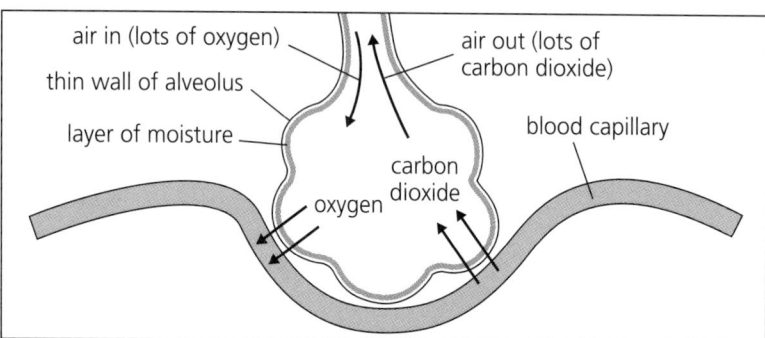

The alveoli are good at gas exchange because they have:
- a large surface area (there are thousands of alveoli)
- moist surfaces which make diffusion faster
- thin walls, which make diffusion faster
- lots of blood capillaries to carry the gases.

In the alveolus oxygen moves from a high concentration (lots of oxygen) through the thin wall into the blood capillary where there is a low concentration of oxygen (very little oxygen). Movement from a high to a low concentration like this is called **diffusion**. There is a high concentration of carbon dioxide in the blood, so carbon dioxide diffuses out of the blood into the alveolus.

 **Now do this**

1. Why do we need oxygen?
2. Explain why oxygen diffuses from the alveoli into the blood.
3. Give **three** ways in which alveoli are adapted for gas exchange.

Human life processes

Breathing in and breathing out

When we breathe in (inhale), the lung volume increases and therefore the air pressure decreases. When we breathe out (exhale) the lung volume decreases and the air pressure increases. Therefore the air pressure in the lungs is continuously changing. The bronchi and larger bronchioles have pieces of cartilage in their walls to support them and prevent them from collapsing as the air pressure changes.

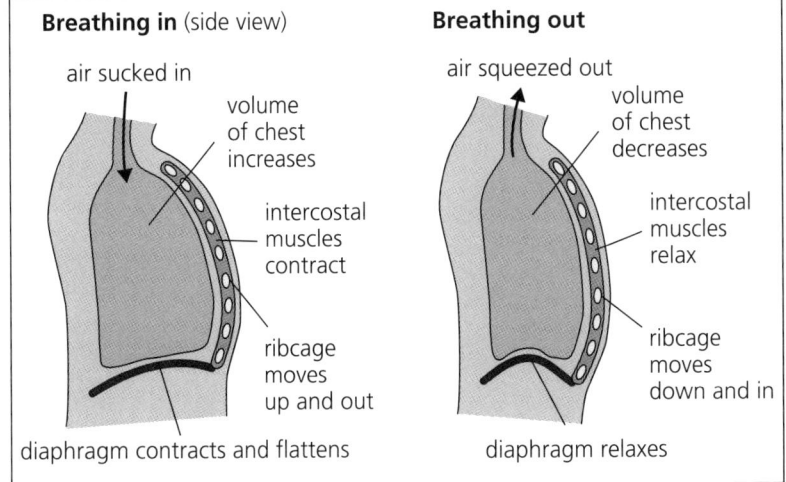

Now do this

4 Describe the changes in the position of the ribs and diaphragm that cause inhalation and exhalation.

5 Explain why the bronchi and larger bronchioles contain pieces of cartilage.

If the blood becomes more acidic due to increased carbon dioxide, or lactic acid (from anaerobic respiration), dissolving in the blood, the brain detects the change and causes the breathing rate to increase.

Keeping the lungs clean

Air often contains germs and dust. To help keep the lungs clean the trachea produces a sticky **mucus** to trap invaders. It also has small hairs called **cilia** which beat together to move the mucus away from the lungs.

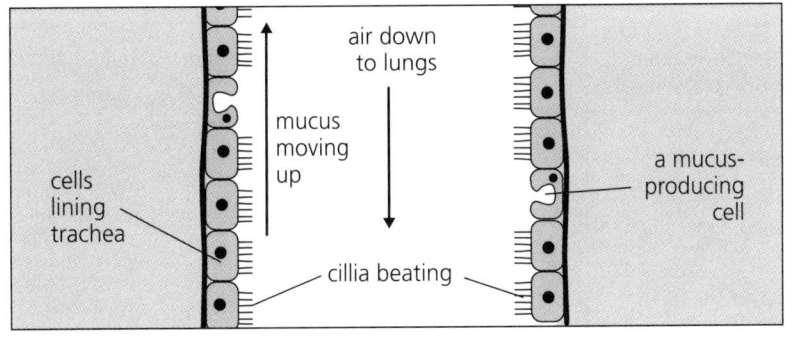

Smoking stops the cilia beating. This allows germs and mucus into the lungs. The germs increase the risk of infection, e.g. bronchitis. The mucus irritates the lungs causing coughing, e.g. smokers' cough. Chemicals in the smoke destroy alveoli. This makes gas exchange more difficult and may cause the disease emphysema. Some of the chemicals cause lung cancer.

Now do this

6 Explain the link between irritating chemicals in cigarette smoke and lung damage.

Life Processes and Living Things

Nervous system

Sense organs

We are aware of and can respond to changes in our surroundings. These changes are called **stimuli** and they are detected by parts of the body called **receptors**. Receptors often form part of a **sense organ**.

- The eye is a sense organ and responds to the stimulus light.
- The ear detects sound and balance.
- The nose detects chemicals (smell and taste).
- The tongue detects chemicals (taste).
- The skin detects touch, pressure and temperature change.

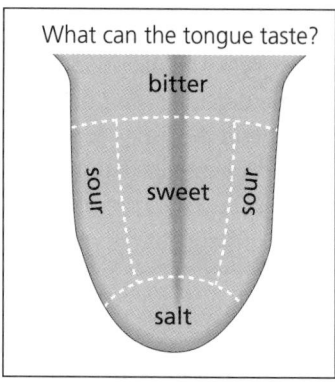

The eye

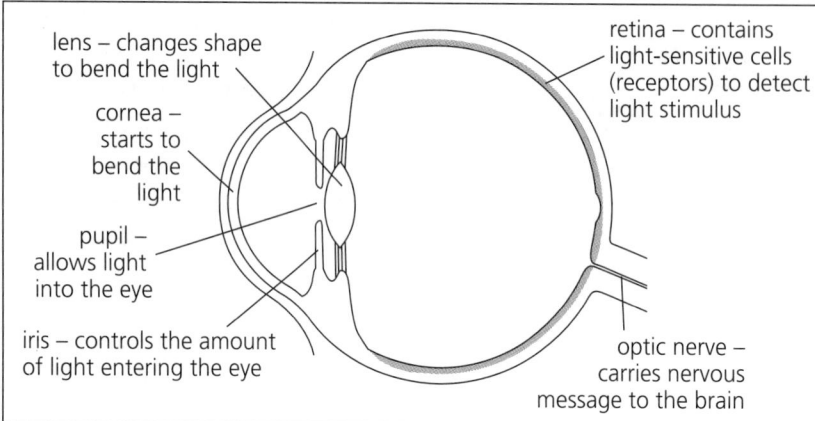

This is how we see things.

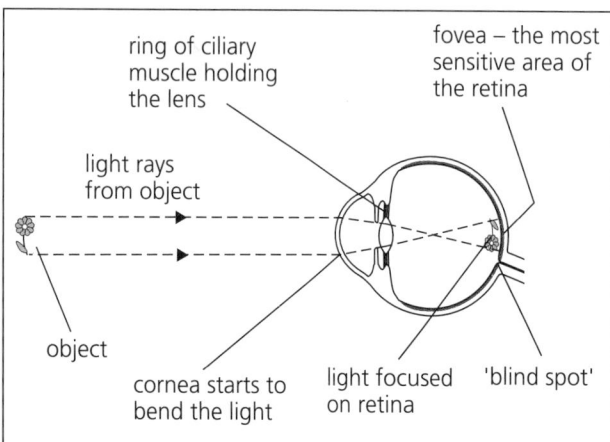

1. Light from the object reaches the cornea.
2. The cornea bends the light as it passes through.
3. The lens bends the light a little more to produce a clear focused image on the retina.
4. The retina contains two types of light-sensitive cells: **cones**, which are sensitive to colour and details, and **rods**, which function in dim light.

The iris is the coloured bit of your eye.

In dim light the pupil is large and the iris becomes smaller. This allows more light in.

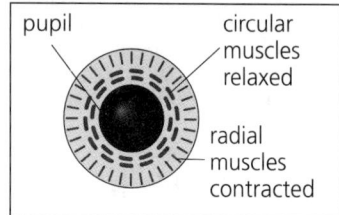

In bright light the pupil is small and the iris becomes larger. This prevents too much light damaging the retina.

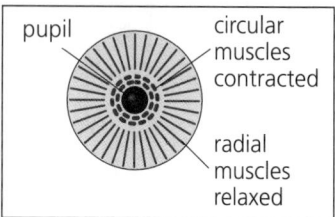

 **Now do this**

1. Which of the body's receptors gather information about the following: touch, smell, light, sound and balance?
2. What are the functions of the following parts of the eye: retina, iris, optic nerve and lens?
3. Describe how the muscles in the iris change to prevent too much light damaging the retina.

Communication and control

The nervous system

To enable us to respond to stimuli quickly, the receptors and sense organs need to be able to communicate with other parts of the body. This is the job of the **nervous system**. The nervous system is made up of two parts:

1 the **central nervous system**, which is the spinal cord and brain
2 the **peripheral nervous system**, which is the network of nerve cells (**neurones**) connecting all parts of the body to the central nervous system.

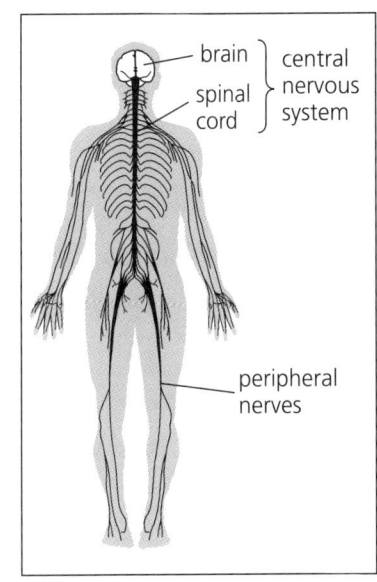

Sending a message

There are two types of neurones and they are named after the messages they carry. Messages come into the central nervous system from receptors via neurones called **sensory nerve cells** or **sensory neurones**. Neurones carrying messages away from the central nervous system are called **motor neurones**.

The diagram shows the structure of a motor neurone.

The end of one neurone is not connected to the next one. There is a little gap between them. This is called the **synapse**. Messages passing along a neurone are electrical but when they reach the synapse they release a chemical which diffuses across the synapse and spreads the message to the next neurone. Only one side of the synapse can make the chemical messenger. This ensures that nervous messages only go in one direction.

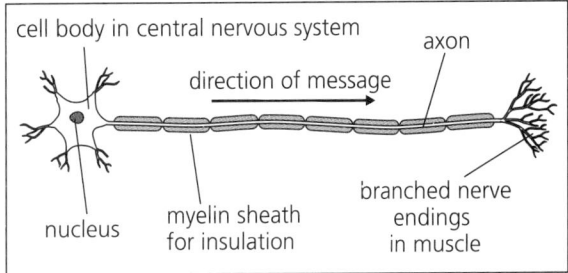

A motor neurone

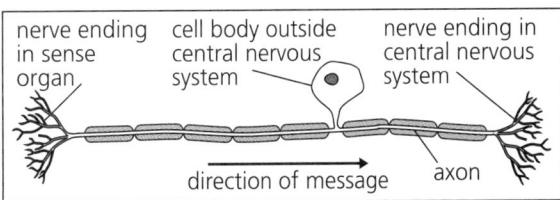

A sensory neurone

Reflex actions

What happens when you touch something hot?

1 Temperature receptors detect the hot stimulus.
2 The receptors send the message along a sensory neurone to the central nervous system.
3 The central nervous system sends the message along a motor neurone to a muscle (an **effector**).
4 The muscle contracts moving your hand away from the hot object.

A receptor **transduces** (converts) energy from a stimulus into an electrical nervous message.

> stimulus → receptor → sensory neurone → central nervous system → motor neurone → effector(muscle) → response (hand moves)

This is called a **reflex action**.

Reflex actions are:
- fast
- automatic (without thinking)
- protective.

Examples include blinking, swallowing and sneezing.

Now do this

4 Give **three** ways in which motor neurones are adapted to do their job.
5 What is a synapse? Suggest one advantage of synapses.
6 Describe the paths taken by a nervous message in the reflex action resulting from a dog biting your hand.

Hormones

Alongside the nervous control in your body, some activities are also controlled by **hormones**. These are chemical messengers produced by groups of cells called **glands**. Hormones travel in the blood plasma and work on groups of cells in the body. Each hormone acts in a particular way, on a particular group of **target cells**.

Controlling sugar (glucose) levels

All cells need glucose for energy. But you need to have the right amount of glucose available in your blood. Too much or too little can be fatal.

The hormone that controls the amount of glucose is called **insulin**. This is produced by the pancreas. When there is too much glucose in the blood, the pancreas releases insulin. Insulin lowers the level of glucose by:
- making cells take up more glucose
- making **liver** cells change glucose to **glycogen**. This is then stored in the liver.

Some people do not make any insulin, or do not make enough. This means they suffer from **diabetes**. In these cases the level of glucose in the blood can go up and down wildly. Many diabetics control their blood glucose level by injecting themselves with insulin. The amount of insulin a diabetic needs depends on their diet and activity.

Controlling sexual development

The changes which take place during adolescence (the stage of children growing into adults) are controlled by hormones.

As girls grow older their ovaries start to produce the hormone **oestrogen**. Oestrogen causes a number of changes in girls. They:
- start their menstrual cycle (have periods)
- develop breasts
- grow pubic and underarm hair
- grow taller.

These are called **secondary sexual characteristics**.

In boys, the development of secondary sexual characteristics is controlled by the hormone **testosterone**, which is produced by the testes. The effect is that boys:
- grow taller
- develop a longer penis
- grow pubic, underarm and facial hair
- develop a deeper voice.

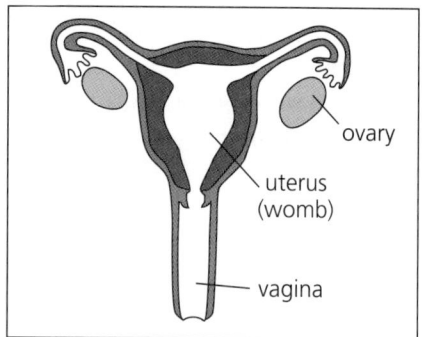

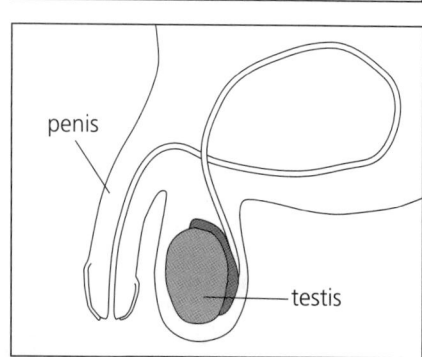

 **Now do this**

1. Give **three** female secondary sexual characteristics.
2. Explain why hormones (chemical messages) are likely to take longer to affect the body than nervous messages.

Controlling the menstrual cycle

Two hormones control a woman's menstrual cycle, **oestrogen** and **progesterone**.

What these hormones do:
- oestrogen repairs the uterus wall
- progesterone keeps the uterus wall thick and in position
- oestrogen and progesterone together control **ovulation** (ovaries releasing eggs).

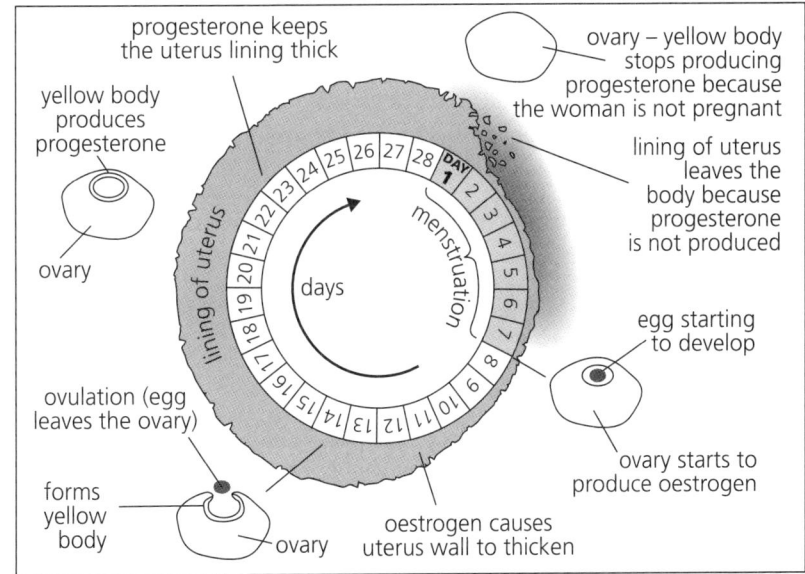

Preventing pregnancy ...

Hormones can be used in **contraceptive pills** to prevent ovulation and make the body think it is pregnant. This means that a woman will not release eggs and therefore cannot get pregnant.

... and helping pregnancy

Some women have difficulty in getting pregnant. Hormones can be used to help them produce more eggs, which will increase their chances of getting pregnant.

Controlling growth

Growth is controlled by **growth hormone**. This is produced by the **pituitary gland** in the brain. Too little growth hormone causes **dwarfism**. This is when a person does not grow enough. Too much growth hormone produces a giant. This is when a person grows too much.

Fight or flight

The hormone **adrenaline** prepares the body for action. It is produced by the two **adrenal glands**. It makes the heart beat faster. This forces blood around the body more rapidly, delivering more oxygen and glucose to the muscles to release more energy.

Now do this

3. Explain why a pregnant woman will not menstruate.
4. How do contraceptive pills work?
5. What part does oestrogen play in the menstrual cycle?

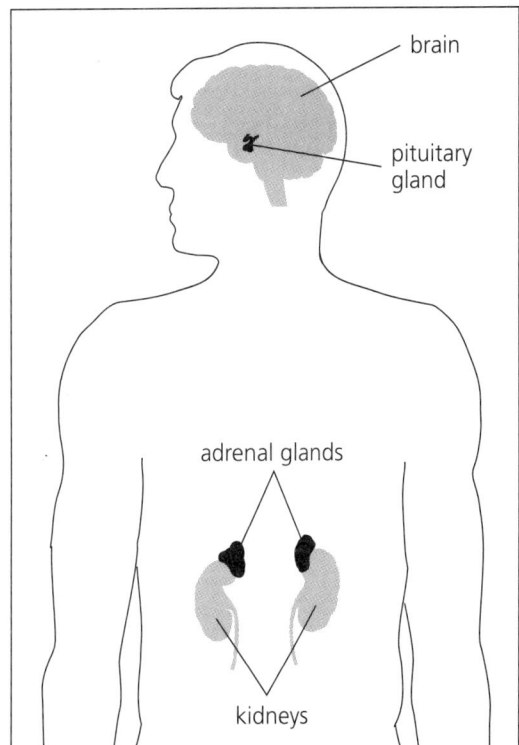

Control in plants

Plants do not have a nervous system and so usually cannot respond as quickly as animals. They react to stimuli more slowly. Their reactions are controlled by hormones called **auxins**, which are produced in shoot and root tips. The auxins dissolve in water and are then transported through the plant.

Auxins regulate cell growth and development to control:
- growth of shoots and roots
- flowering
- ripening of fruit.

How do plants grow?

The shoots of a plant always grow towards the light. They do this because leaves need the light to make the food needed for plants to grow. They make their food by photosynthesis (see page 24).

Growing towards the light is called **phototropism**. 'Photo' means light and 'tropism' means growth.

Plant roots always grow downwards in the direction of gravity. They need to do this to find the water the plant needs, and to anchor the plant in the ground.

Shoots are **positively phototropic** because they grow towards light.

Roots are **positively geotrophic** because they grow towards gravity.

 **Now do this**

1. Give **two** uses of auxins in plants.
2. Explain how auxins travel around a plant.

Auxins control the direction plants grow by making different parts grow at different speeds. To make a shoot grow towards the light, auxins make its shaded side grow faster, resulting in the tip bending over towards the light. To make a root grow downwards, auxins make the top side of the root grow faster, resulting in the tip curving downwards.

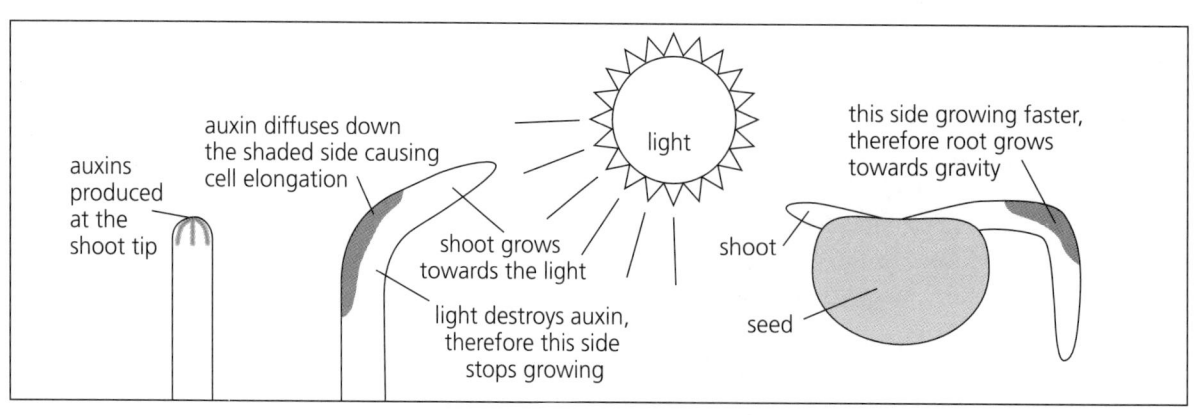

Using plant hormones

We use synthetic auxins to trick plants and make them behave in ways which are more convenient for us.

Making more plants

It can take some time for plants to produce young new plants naturally. Cutting shoots off plants and dipping them in auxins makes them grow roots. Gardeners use auxins, known as rooting powder, to make new plants.

Ripening fruit

Auxins can also be used to slow down fruit ripening. This is useful for farmers who have a long way to take their fruit to the shops. If they treat it in this way it stops the fruit getting overripe before it gets to the customers.

Selective weedkillers

Selective weedkillers contain auxins which speed up the growth of selected plants. This makes them grow too fast and die. For example, if there are weeds with broad leaves growing in a lawn, a weedkiller can be used which will kill only those weeds and not the grass.

> Have you ever thought how seedless grapes and oranges are made? If you apply auxins to flowers before they are pollinated they will grow into a fruit without any seeds.

> Shoot tips produce substances that inhibit side shoot growth. Therefore, if the tips are removed lots of side shoots will grow. This is why cutting a hedge makes it grow bushier.

broad-leaved weeds growing faster than the grass will die

grass

Now do this

3. Name **two** stimuli plants respond to. Explain why it is important that plants can respond to these stimuli.
4. Describe **two** commercial uses of auxins in agriculture.
5. Explain what is meant by a 'selective' weedkiller.
6. Explain how a bulb planted upside down manages to grow.

Life Processes and Living Things

Ecosystems

Ecology is the study of living things and the way they react with each other and with their surroundings (**environment**). To make it easier to study, the environment is divided into lots of smaller areas called **ecosystems**.

For example, a rock pool is an ecosystem.

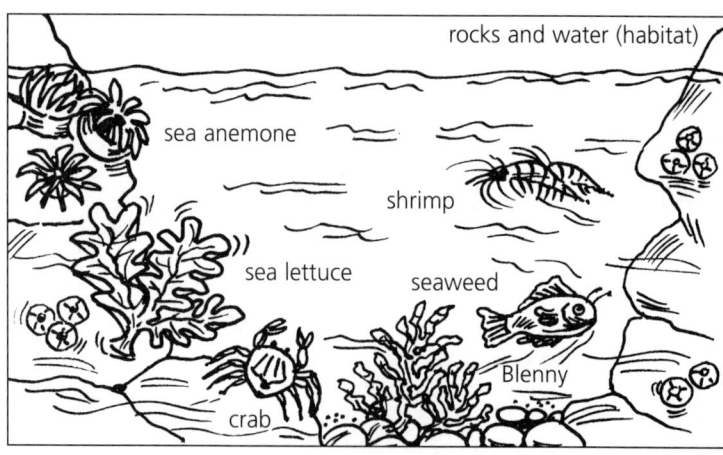

Every ecosystem is made up of **two** parts:
- the **habitat**, which is the non-living part, e.g. the water and rocks in the rock pool
- the **populations** of plants and animals, which are the living part. A population includes all members of the same species. In the rock pool would be a population of crabs, a population of sea lettuce, a population of sea anemone and many more. All the populations make up the **community**.

Using keys

There is such a wide variety of different living things that scientists have divided them into smaller groups to study them. Scientists then use **keys** to identify where each living thing belongs.

A key consists of a set of questions. The questions are based on visible features. You have to look at the first question and compare it with your living thing. Answer the question yes or no, and do what the key tells you.

 **Now do this**

1 Describe the two parts of an ecosystem.
2 What is a key used for?

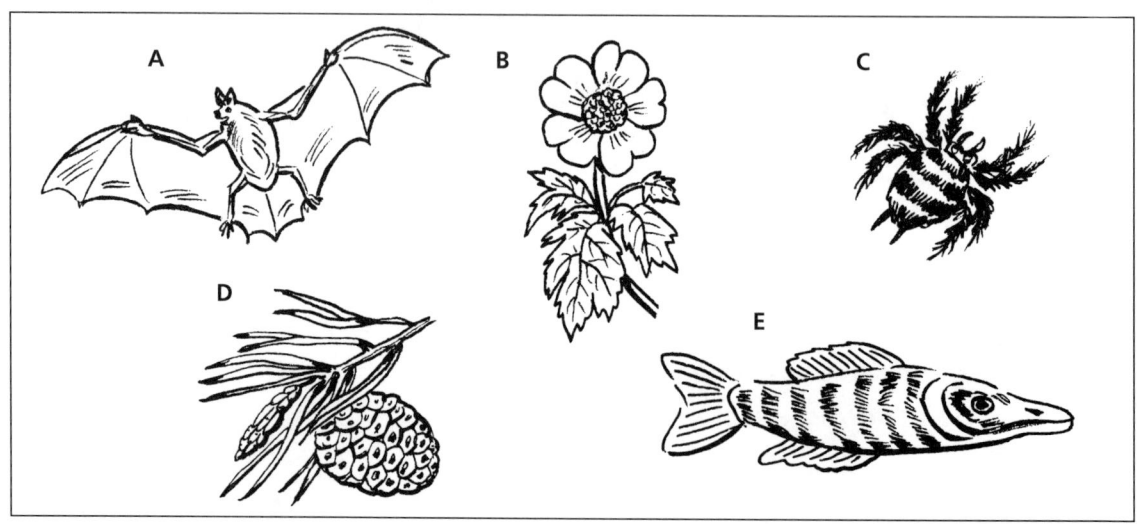

1 Is it a plant? .... Yes, go to Q2.
   .... No go to 3

2 Is it a flowering plant? .. Yes, buttercup.
   .. No, Scots pine.

3 Does it have legs? .... Yes, go to Q4.
   .... No, pike.

4 Does it have 8 legs? ...... Yes, tarantula.
   ...... No, pipistrelle.

Living things in their environment

Surviving in the environment

Living things need water, space, light, minerals, food and shelter. The size of each population in a habitat depends on how much of all these resources is available. When a population becomes too large for the resources in its habitat, it stops growing.

Living things also **compete** against each other for these resources. The size of a population of one species often depends on how well it competes against other populations for what it needs. Sometimes a newly introduced species thrives, e.g. grey squirrels have out-competed the native British red squirrel because they are bigger and more aggressive. In Australia, rabbits have become a real nuisance because they have no natural predator and are therefore breeding unchecked.

> If wheat is planted closely the farmer can increase the yield because more wheat can be fitted into the field. But if the plants are too close together they compete for space, water and light, and do not grow as well. This results in a reduced yield.

Adapting to survive

Each population is **adapted** to survive in its particular habitat. For example:

polar bear – very cold habitat	camel – an arid habitat	fish – water
• thick coat of fur to keep body heat in • large body means it loses less heat to the air.	• long thin legs • does not sweat very much • no layer of fat under the skin • hump of stored fats can be broken down to provide water.	• streamlined to move easily through the water • waterproof scales • fins for swimming • gills for 'breathing'.

Plants are also adapted to survive. For example, small plants on woodland floors flower very early before the leaves grow on trees and block the light from the Sun. Many plants also have to protect themselves against animals to survive. They use spines, stings or poisons to avoid being eaten.

Predator and prey relationships

Predators are animals which eat other animals (their **prey**). Predators are more likely to catch their prey if they:
- are **camouflaged** and difficult to see, like a polar bear in the snow
- have large teeth, claws, sting or poison to kill their 'food'
- have good senses – sight, hearing or smell – to find the 'food'.

Prey try to escape being caught by:
- camouflage that makes them hard to see, e.g. a stick insect
- colours which warn that they are unpleasant to eat, e.g. yellow and black wasps
- tasting horrible – predators soon learn which caterpillars are tasty.

Predators depend upon prey, so if the numbers of prey in a habitat go down, then some predators will starve and the number of predators will also go down.

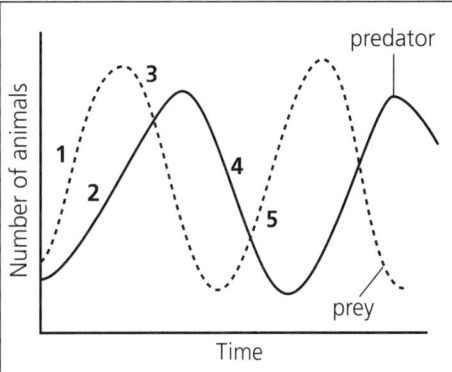

1 Prey has plenty of food, so breeds and increases in number.
2 More prey means more food for predators, so predators breed and their numbers increase.
3 More predators eating more prey means prey numbers decrease.
4 Fewer prey, therefore some predators starve.
5 Fewer predators, therefore not so many prey eaten and prey numbers start to increase again.

Life Processes and Living Things

Food chains

Feeding relationships

Green plants make their own food (glucose and starches) using energy from the Sun. They are called **producers** because they convert the light energy from the Sun into chemical energy (food), which is stored in organic compounds such as glucose and starch. Other living things are called **consumers** because they have to get their food by eating (consuming) green plants or other animals.

All animals rely on plants, even if they do not eat them directly. Animals may eat other animals but there is always an animal which eats only plants (a **herbivore**) at the start of the line. Animals which eat only meat are called **carnivores**. Animals which eat plants and meat are called **omnivores**.

Feeding relationships can be drawn as a **food chain**. Some of the energy captured from light by plants is passed down the food chain as plants and animals are eaten. The Sun is the source of energy for *all* food chains.

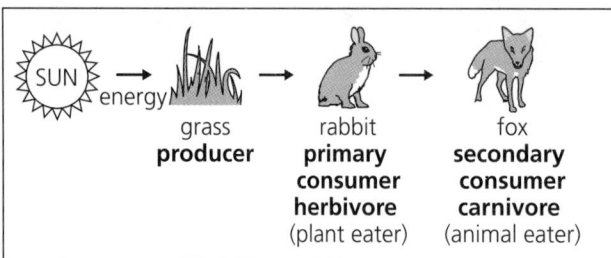

> **Hint**
> The arrow *must* point towards the animal that is eating, because it shows the direction the energy is moving in.
>
> grass → rabbit   means the rabbit eats the grass
>
> grass ← rabbit   would mean that the grass eats the rabbit!

Each feeding level is called a **trophic level**. The first trophic level contains the producers, the second trophic level the herbivores or primary consumers, and subsequent trophic levels contain all the carnivores. Because most living things eat more than one type of food, a food chain is usually changed into a **food web** in which all the feeding relationships are shown.

Pyramid of numbers

Another way of showing feeding relationships is as a **pyramid of numbers**. Here, each trophic level is represented by a block. The size of the block represents the number of individuals.

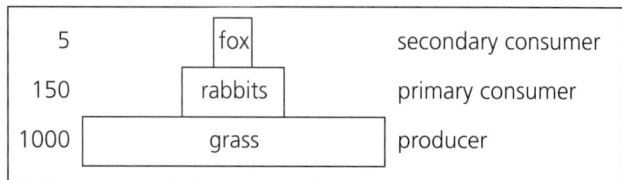

??? Now do this

1   On a moorland the main plant is heather, which is the food for lots of animals, including rabbits, grouse, bees and deer. There are also several fox families and a pair of eagles, which survive by hunting the grouse and rabbits.
   a Name **one** moorland producer, **one** primary consumer and **one** predator.
   b Draw **two** food chains using some of the living things mentioned in the passage.
   c Draw pyramids of numbers based on your food chains.

Living things in their environment

But it does not always work, for example:

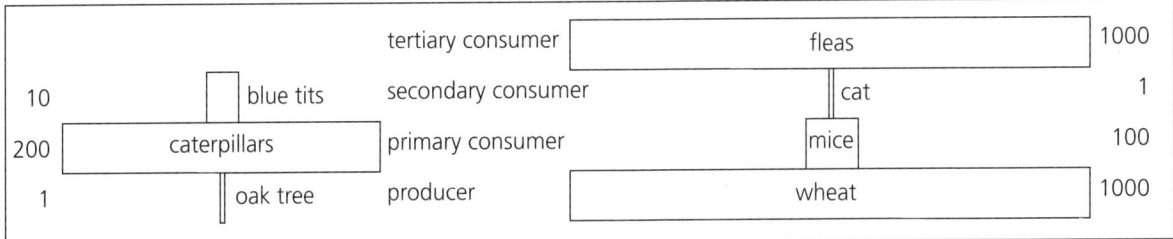

Don't be put off – always put the producer at the bottom and arrange the other feeding levels above it, keeping to the order in which they appear in a food chain.

Pyramid of biomass

A more accurate way of representing feeding relationships is to produce a **pyramid of biomass**. Here the size of the block represents the mass of the animals and plants feeding at that level, rather than the number. Samples of the plants and animals are heated in an oven to remove their water content and then their dry mass is recorded. The dry mass is used to construct the pyramid. A pyramid of biomass for the oak tree example is shown.

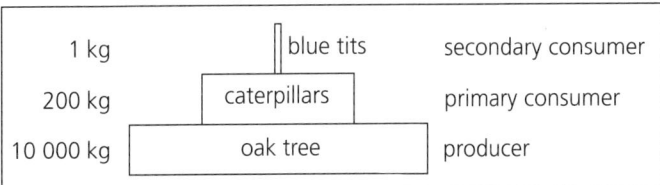

As you move along a food chain, energy is lost from each trophic level. Some is lost as heat energy, some as waste materials (excretion), and some through death. This can be shown pictorially:

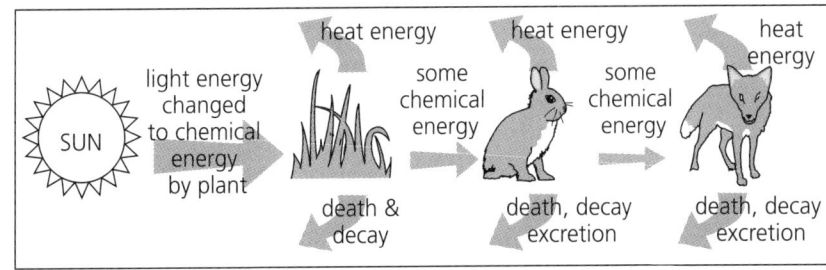

Therefore there is less energy available at each step of the food chain. This is why a pyramid of biomass gets progressively smaller as it moves along the food chain.

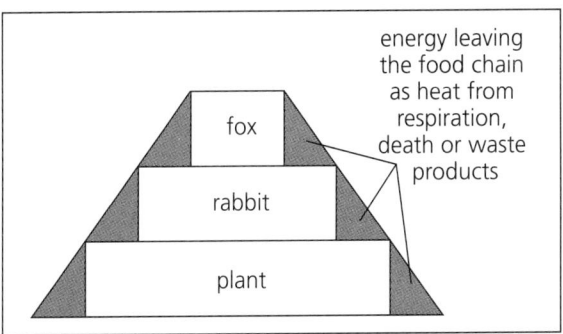

An area of land can produce more plant food, and therefore feed more people, than if the same area is used to produce meat.

 **Now do this**

2. In what form does energy enter the environment?

3. What is the difference between a food chain and a food web?

4. Explain why a pyramid of biomass is a more accurate representation of an ecosystem than a pyramid of numbers.

5. Explain why most food chains are restricted to only four trophic levels.

Cycling and decay

What happens to all the dead bodies and waste produced by organisms in a food chain? In every ecosystem there are living things called **decomposers** which feed on dead plants and animals and their waste materials.

Some **bacteria** and **fungi** are decomposers. They make dead things **decay** so that the useful substances these things contain can be used again by other living things. One of these useful substances is carbon, which is part of all living things because it is present in all proteins, carbohydrates and fats. Decomposers return carbon to the atmosphere as carbon dioxide, and plants remove it from the atmosphere to convert it into carbohydrates during photosynthesis. Therefore a cycle is produced.

Decomposers are living things and therefore have the same needs as other living things. They need:
- food – the material they are going to decompose
- moisture
- oxygen
- warm temperatures.

The carbon cycle

In the carbon cycle:
- soil bacteria and fungi release carbon dioxide into the air as they respire; they also return minerals to the soil
- plants and animals release carbon dioxide into the air as they respire
- carbon dioxide is used by plants for photosynthesis
- energy in some decomposing materials becomes trapped as fossil fuels, e.g. coal, oil
- burning fossil fuels releases carbon dioxide
- burning all organic materials, including wood, paper and animal tissues, releases carbon dioxide.

Now do this

1. Name **two** groups of living organisms which can act as decomposers.
2. Explain why decomposers are so important within an ecosystem.

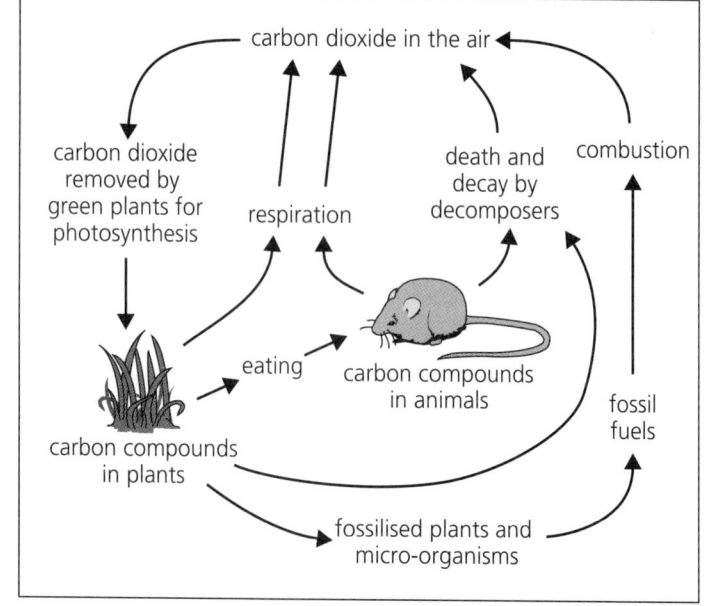

Now do this

3. Describe **three** ways in which human activities are in danger of upsetting the carbon cycle.
4. State the main way in which carbon dioxide is removed from the atmosphere.

Living things in their environment

The nitrogen cycle

In addition to carbon, nitrogen is vital to living things. It is needed to make proteins, which animals and plants need to grow. Although the atmosphere contains a large amount of nitrogen, atmospheric nitrogen must be changed into soluble nitrates and nitrites before it can be used by most living things.

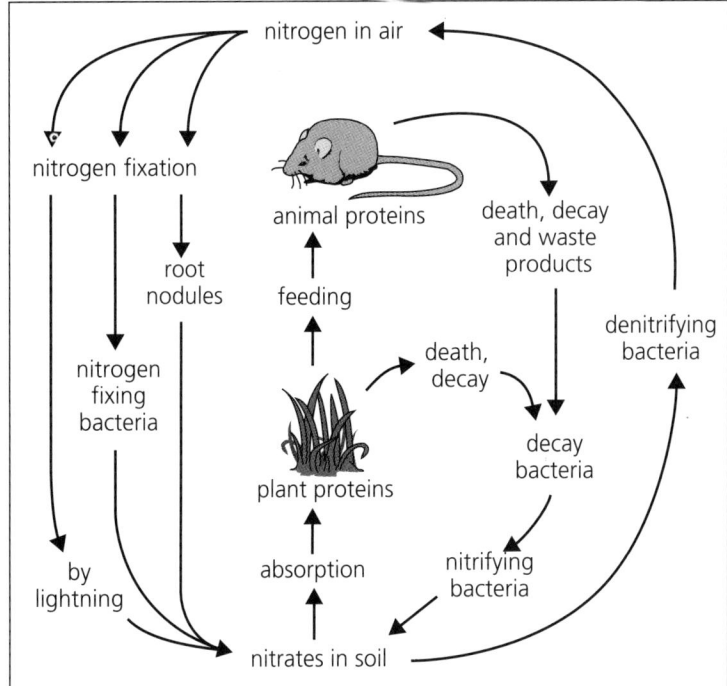

Carbohydrates contain carbon, hydrogen and oxygen, proteins contain carbon, hydrogen, oxygen and nitrogen, therefore all of these are recycled in ecosystems.

The nitrogen cycle at work

- Nitrogen-fixing bacteria convert atmospheric nitrogen into amino acids and proteins. Some of these bacteria are free living in the soil and others live in the root nodules of leguminous plants, e.g. clover, beans, peas.
- Lightning converts atmospheric nitrogen into nitrates.
- Plant roots absorb nitrates from the soil and convert them into amino acids and proteins.
- Decay bacteria convert proteins and urea into ammonia.
- Nitrifying bacteria add nitrates to the soil by converting ammonia into nitrates.
- Farmers artificially boost the nitrate content of soil by adding fertilisers.
- Farmers can also boost the nitrate content of soil by ploughing plant remains, especially leguminous plant remains, back into the soil so they can decay.

 **Now do this**

5   The nitrogen cycle involves nitrogen-fixing bacteria, denitrifying bacteria and nitrifying bacteria. Explain the **three** different roles they have in the cycle.

6   Explain why traditional farming techniques include crop rotation, in which every five years a field is planted with beans and, instead of cropping the beans, the farmer ploughs them back into the soil.

The human influence on the environment

The human population is growing rapidly, all the time producing more mouths to feed. More land is required for food production. Some areas of land which are not suitable for plant crops are used to graze sheep or deer, but the rest is increasingly being used for intensive food production.

Intensive food production ensures that the chemical energy produced remains in the food, plant or animal, for us to eat, rather than being lost as energy to:
- competing plants (weeds)
- pests
- heat – farm animals kept indoors do no use up as much energy in keeping warm. Therefore intensive food production improves the efficiency of energy transfer.

Farmers can produce more food if they use:
- **herbicides** to kill weeds which otherwise compete with their crop
- **pesticides** to kill pests which otherwise might eat their crop
- **fertilisers** to provide extra nitrates and minerals for the crop to grow
- **intensive practices**, e.g. hedge removal to make larger fields
- **biological control** – non-chemical methods of pest control, e.g. using ladybirds to eat the aphids in greenhouses.

Intensive farming practices cause practical problems and ethical problems.

Damaging the food chain

Herbicides may kill plants which are an important part of a food chain. Animals which normally feed on them either die or find something else to eat, possibly the crop itself.

Pesticides may kill non-pest organisms either directly or through the food chain. The following is an example of this:

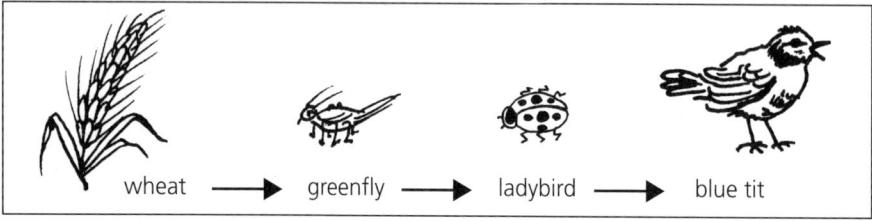

If the pesticide kills the ladybirds, then the blue tits may well starve, and the greenfly population will become enormous because there will be no ladybirds left to eat them.

Pollution

Fertilisers provide plants with the extra nitrates and minerals they need to enable them to grow big and strong. The fertilisers have to be soluble so that the plant can take them up through the roots. But this means that if too many are added to the crop, or if it rains hard after they have been added, there is a good chance they will be washed (**leached**) out of the soil and into nearby waterways.

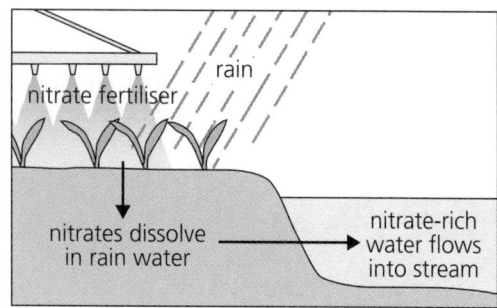

Living things in their environment

Fertilisers leaching into waterways cause **nitrate pollution**. This results in a waterway of dead and decomposing plants and animals beneath a layer of surface-growing plants (often algae). Lack of oxygen and/or light kills the rest of the living things in the waterway. This process is called **eutrophication**.

Destruction of habitats

Removing hedges destroys habitats. Many insects and birds which live in hedges act as predators of pest species. Without a home their numbers will decline. The farmer will then have more pests to control.

Treatment of animals

Intensive farming of animals raises an ethical problem. Many animals are reared indoors where they can be fed and checked for disease regularly. However, a growing number of people do not like this form of farming. They claim that it is the wrong way to treat animals and are calling on farmers to go in for more **free-range farming** where animals are free to live outside in fields and outdoor pens.

Other problems

The human population continues to grow rapidly and threatens the planet with the following forms of pollution.
- Nitrate-rich sewage enters the waterways.
- More people means more household waste.
- Sulphur dioxide dissolves in rainwater to form **acid rain**, which kills plants and attacks some buildings.
- Carbon dioxide is a **greenhouse gas** and causes heat to be trapped in the atmosphere, leading to **global warming** and its possible consequences of:
  - ice caps melting
  - increased sea levels
  - loss of low-lying habitats.

It is the developed countries, including the UK, which have the smallest populations but the greatest impact on global pollution, because of their access to global resources – for example, fossil fuels.

Now do this

1. Describe **three** ways in which farmers can improve the yield of their crops.
2. Give **one** advantage and **one** disadvantage of using a pesticide.
3. Explain the process of eutrophication and its effects on waterways.

Remember that, although the animals are kept inside, the food they eat still has to be grown outside, and therefore a reasonably large area of land is still needed to support them.

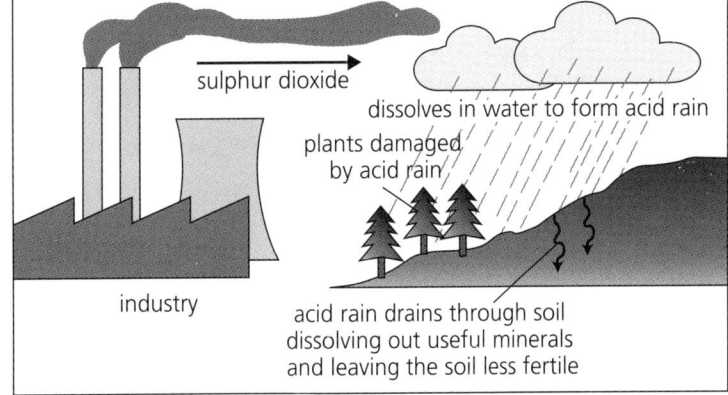

Formation of acid rain

Now do this

4. State **two** environmental problems associated with the increases in the human population, and suggest ways of overcoming them.

Fossil fuels and minerals are **finite** resources. Once they are gone, they are gone forever.

The working plant

The parts of a plant

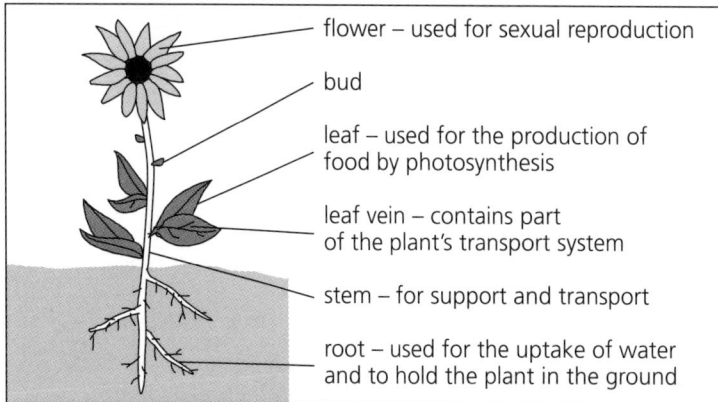

How do plants produce their food?

Plants **make** their own food by **photosynthesis**. To do this plants use light energy to join water and carbon dioxide, producing carbohydrates. (Photosynthesis comes from 'photo', meaning light, and 'synthesis', meaning to make.)

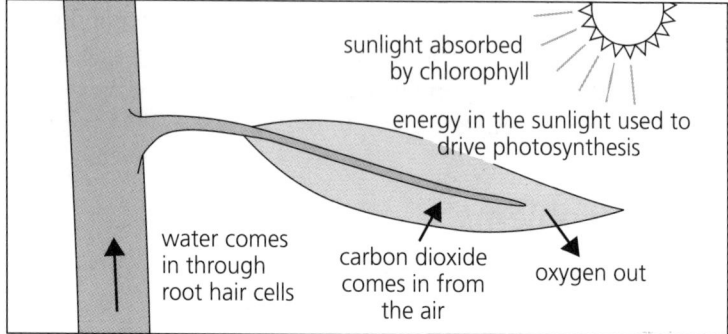

Photosynthesis can be written as an equation:

$$6CO_2 + 6H_2O \xrightarrow{\text{chlorophyll and light energy}} C_6H_{12}O_6 + 6O_2$$

carbon dioxide   water   →   glucose + oxygen

Carbon dioxide and water are needed for photosynthesis. They are called the **reactants**.

Glucose and oxygen are produced by photosynthesis. They are called the **products**.

What makes plants photosynthesise faster?

- The more carbon dioxide that is available, the faster the photosynthesis, because carbon dioxide is one of the reactants.
- The more light that is available, the faster the photosynthesis, because the energy of the light is used to drive the reaction. The colour of the light is also important. Most plants appear green because they reflect green light. This means green light is not absorbed to be used to drive photosynthesis. Red and blue light are absorbed, therefore these colours are the most important ones for photosynthesis.
- The higher the temperature, the faster photosynthesis will occur.

Now do this

1. Explain, with the help of an equation, how green plants make their food.
2. Explain where a plant gets the reactants for photosynthesis from.

Green plants do not eat, they photosynthesise.

Plant life processes

What happens if carbon dioxide, light and temperature are in short supply?

If any of these are in short supply they limit the amount of photosynthesis which can occur. Therefore they are called **limiting factors**.

On a hot, sunny day the temperature is usually high enough and there is plenty of light for photosynthesis to take place. In these conditions the rate of photosynthesis will depend on how much carbon dioxide there is. Carbon dioxide is then said to be the limiting factor.

Therefore a hot, sunny day will allow a plant to photosynthesise more quickly than a cold, dull day. Plants grow faster in the summer because they can produce more food by photosynthesis.

Where do plants make their food?

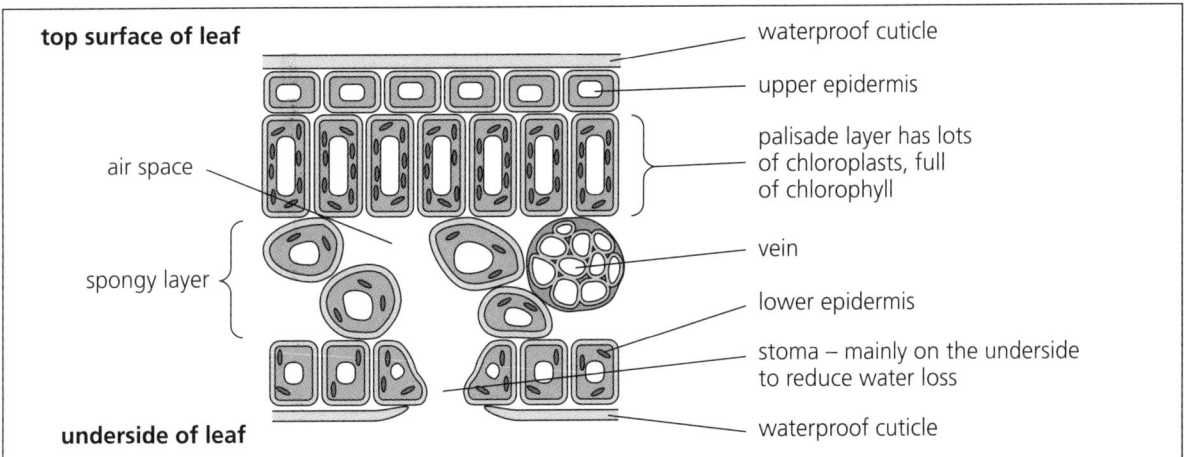

Plants make their food in their leaves because they are:
- **broad**, so they can catch as much sunlight as possible
- **thin**, so that light reaches all the cells easily
- **full of chlorophyll** to trap light energy
- supplied by a **good transport system (veins)**
- have **stomata** to allow gases (carbon dioxide and oxygen) in and out
- their internal surface area to volume ratio is very large.

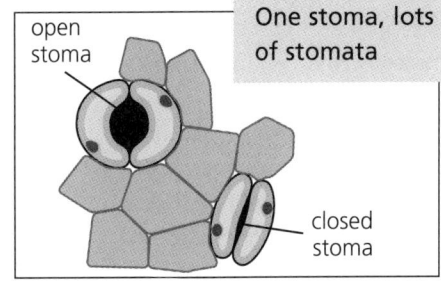

One stoma, lots of stomata

 ## Now do this

3 Give **three** ways in which leaves are adapted for photosynthesis.
4 Name **two** substances which pass out through stomata on a sunny day.
5 Do plants photosynthesise at night? Explain your answer.
6 Many offices have lovely pot plants that are illuminated by green lights. The lights make the leaves look attractive and healthy, but the plants do not grow very well. Explain why this happens.

Moving materials around the plant

Plants use glucose produced during photosynthesis to make all the materials they need to live and grow.

Glucose may be:
- moved around the plant
- changed into sucrose to be transported to the growing areas in the roots, shoots, flowers, fruits and buds
- changed into cellulose for new cell walls
- changed into proteins
- changed into large insoluble storage substances such as starch.
- used to release energy (respiration)

Now do this

1 Describe **three** uses of glucose in a plant.

Sucrose on the move

The **phloem** is part of the transport system of plants. It carries dissolved sucrose to other parts of the plant and is made of living cells. The movement of materials through the phloem is called **translocation**.

Moving materials in and out of cells

There are three ways of moving materials in and out of cells.
- **Diffusion**
  This is the movement of particles from an area where there are lots of particles (high concentration) to an area where there are very few particles (a low concentration). Substances with small particles, e.g. water, minerals, oxygen and carbon dioxide, pass across cell membranes by diffusion down a **concentration gradient**. It does not require energy and is therefore a **passive** process. It is a consequence of the random motion of the particles.

- **Active transport**
  This is the movement of particles from an area with low concentration to an area with high concentration. It uses energy because it is against the concentration gradient.
- **Osmosis**
  This is a special case of diffusion for water. Osmosis is the movement of water particles from an area of a high water concentration through a **partially permeable membrane**. Cell membranes are partially permeable because they allow some things to pass through, but not others.

Now do this

2 Why is a cell membrane considered to be partially permeable?

Plant life processes

Water on the move

Plants need water in their leaves for photosynthesis. Water enters the plant by osmosis through the **root hairs**, and travels up to the leaves in the second plant transport system, the **xylem**. The xylem forms long tubes throughout the plant. It is made up of dead cells with no cytoplasm (they look a bit like drinking straws).

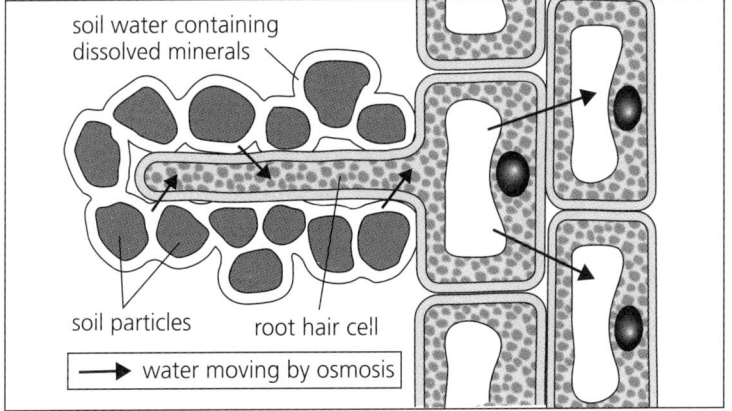

Root hair cells are good at taking up water because they are:
- long and thin, and therefore have a large surface area
- have thin walls to help water to pass through.

Root hair cells also take up minerals, e.g. nitrates, dissolved in the water. Depending on the concentration gradient, minerals are taken up by diffusion or active transport.

Once in the root hair cell the water and dissolved minerals move by diffusion across the root to the xylem.

Plant minerals

Nitrogen, phosphorus and potassium are the main minerals a plant requires, together with small amounts of magnesium, which is needed to make chlorophyll.

Plants will not grow so well, or as much, if there is not enough of any of these minerals. Fertilisers contain these important minerals.

Now do this

3   Explain why raw potato chips become shorter when left in concentrated sugar solutions, but become longer when left in dilute sugar solutions.

Nitrogen is used to make amino acids, proteins and DNA. Phosphorus is used to make DNA and cell membranes.

Monoculture involves growing single crops which are harvested without allowing many minerals to return to the soil. Fertilisers are used to replace these essential minerals. Crop rotation will also help because different crops have their own special mineral requirements.

Now do this

4   Name the **two** transport systems in plants, and state what each one is used for.
5   Suggest why plants which do not get enough magnesium look yellow and small.
6   Explain why farmers need to use fertilisers if they are going to grow the same crop, in the same field, every year.
7   Explain **two** functions of root hair cells.

Tracking the xylem and phloem

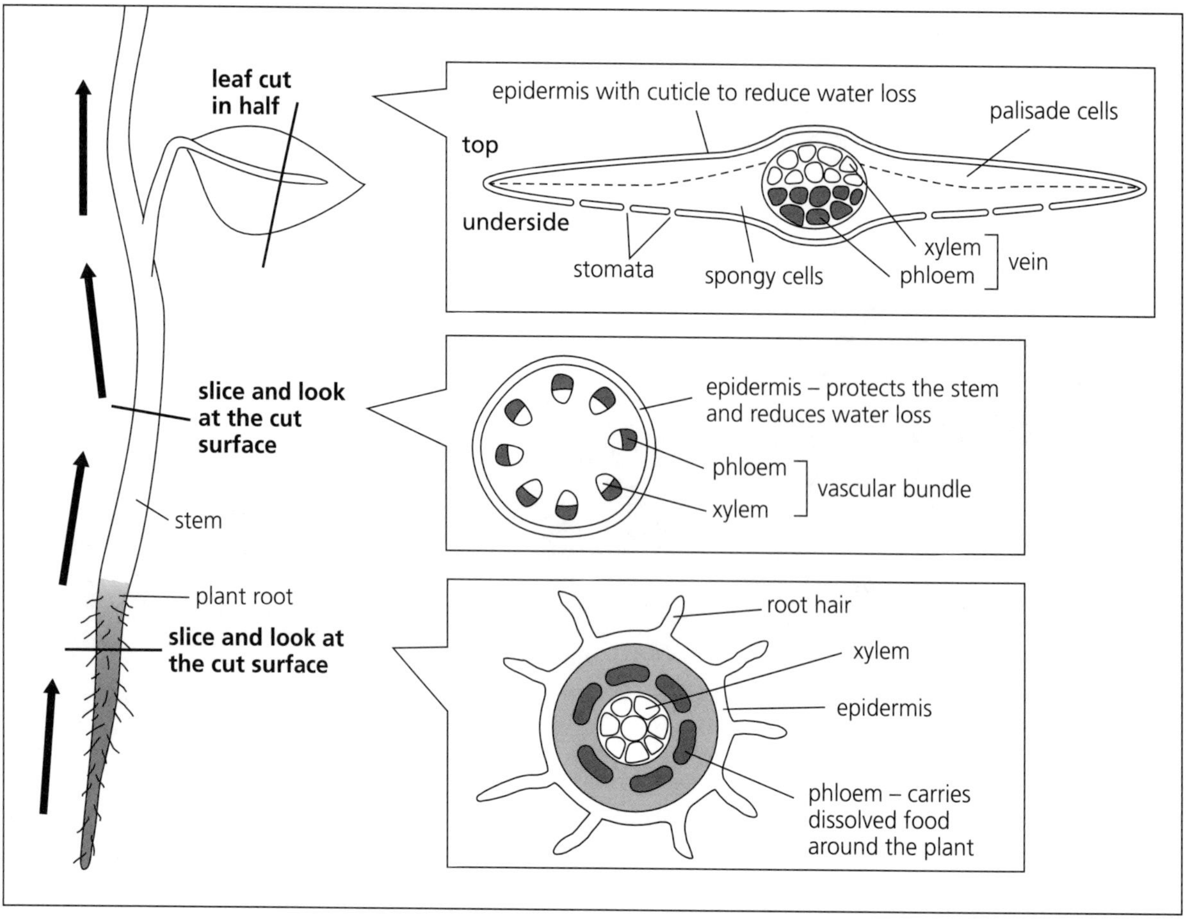

Going up!

The xylem transports water and dissolved minerals from the roots to the leaves. They are 'sucked' up the xylem by a process called **transpiration**.

Transpiration is the evaporation of water from inside the leaves to the surrounding air. The water vapour passes out of the leaves by diffusion.

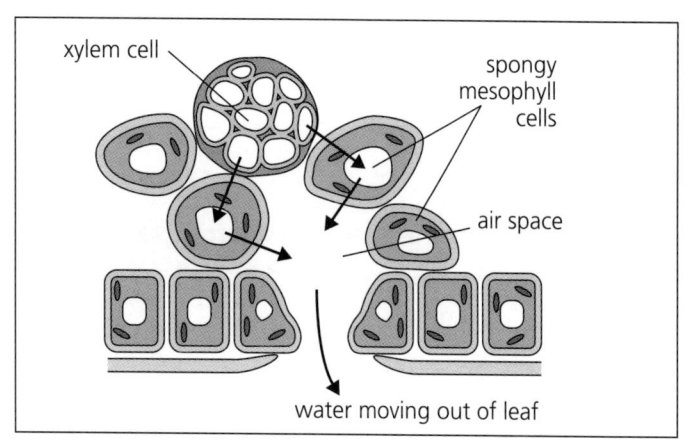

Transpiration provides water for:
- photosynthesis
- cooling the plant (it is the plant version of sweating)
- movement of minerals
- support.

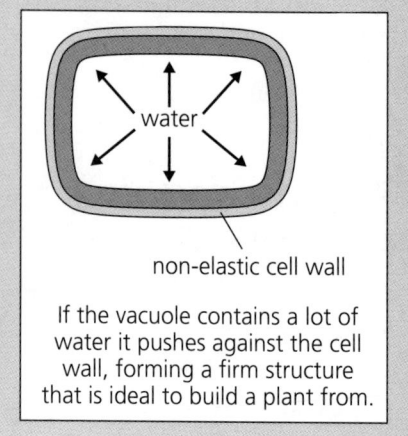

If the vacuole contains a lot of water it pushes against the cell wall, forming a firm structure that is ideal to build a plant from.

Plant life processes

This is what happens in transpiration:
- water diffuses from the xylem into the spongy mesophyll cells
- water evaporates into the air space
- water vapour diffuses out of the stomata
- water lost from the spongy mesophyll cells is replaced by more water from the xylem.

What affects the speed of transpiration?

Transpiration is increased by:
- more light, because water is used up as the plant photosynthesises more
- increased temperatures, because photosynthesis and evaporation increase with temperature
- increased air movement increases evaporation
- decreased humidity, because water evaporates more easily into dry air
- the state of the stomata.

Stomata

Stomata can open or close by changing the shape of their **guard cells**.

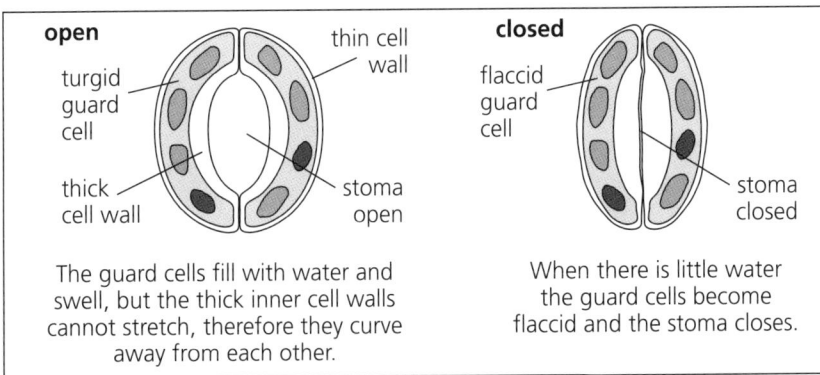
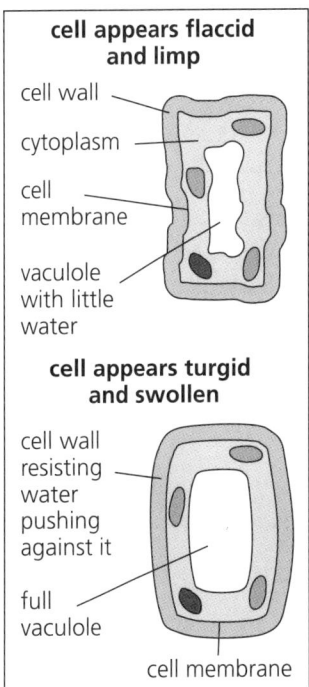

Stomata can open or close in response to what is going on outside the plant. They may close to prevent excessive water loss, but if they do, carbon dioxide cannot get in for photosynthesis. Stomata tend to be found mainly on the underside of leaves away from direct sunlight. Plant cells are able to survive some water loss by wilting, because the cell wall is too stiff to shrink too much.

 **Now do this**

1. What is a vascular bundle?
2. Stomata are mainly on the underside of a leaf. Suggest why this is advantageous to the plant.
3. Explain what is meant by transpiration.
4. Give **three** reasons why transpiration is so important for plants.
5. Suggest how:
   a. the carbon dioxide needed for photosynthesis can get into a leaf
   b. the oxygen produced during photosynthesis can leave the plant.

Respiration – releasing energy

Your body needs energy just to stay alive!

You use energy to:
- keep the heart pumping
- work your muscles for movement
- keep your body temperature constant
- grow and repair cells
- actively transport materials

and many, many other activities in the body.

Energy is released from glucose, when it reacts with oxygen in our cells. This is called **aerobic respiration**.

It happens in *all* of our cells *all* of the time.

> Plant cells also respire all the time to produce energy.

Aerobic respiration can be written as an equation.

$$C_6H_{12}O_6 + 6O_2 \rightarrow 6CO_2 + 6H_2O + \text{ENERGY}$$
$$\text{glucose} + \text{oxygen} \rightarrow \text{carbon dioxide} + \text{water} + \text{ENERGY}$$

Working your muscles requires energy. Therefore, the more you exercise the more energy you need.

This is how the body copes with the need for more energy:
- breathing rate increases to bring more oxygen into the body
- pulse rate increases to speed up blood flow around the body, delivering more oxygen and glucose to the respiring cells
- aerobic respiration in the muscle cells increases.

> Your body is like the engine in a car. The petrol is the 'food', and it is burnt in oxygen to release energy to run the car.

Running out of oxygen

During vigorous exercise the body cannot get enough oxygen. Therefore the cells respire **anaerobically**, i.e. without oxygen.

Anaerobic respiration can be written as a word equation:

$$\text{glucose} \rightarrow \text{lactic acid} + \text{some ENERGY}$$

Anaerobic respiration releases energy, but much less than aerobic respiration. This is because a lot of the energy remains locked up in the lactic acid.

The lactic acid produced is a mild poison and builds up to cause **muscle fatigue** and **cramp**.

To get rid of the lactic acid the body needs oxygen. Therefore the build up of lactic acid causes an **oxygen debt**. The more lactic acid there is, the more oxygen is needed to get rid of it. This is why we puff and pant after vigorous exercise – we are trying to pay back our oxygen debt!

Keeping a healthy body

Now do this

1. What is respiration?
2. Write a symbol equation for aerobic respiration.
3. Give **two** differences between aerobic and anaerobic respiration.
4. Where does respiration occur?
5. Give **two** ways in which the body changes to cope with increased exercise.
6. Explain how one of these changes helps the body when it is exercising actively.

Plants can respire anaerobically, but when they do they produce alcohol (ethanol) and carbon dioxide.

This reaction is also called **fermentation** and can be written as a word equation.

glucose → ethanol + carbon dioxide + some ENERGY

During fermentation aerobic respiration takes place first, until all the available oxygen is used up, and then anaerobic respiration takes place.

Fermentation is used in breadmaking and brewing. In breadmaking the carbon dioxide makes the bread light and airy. In brewing the useful product is the ethanol which gives the beers and wines their alcoholic content.

Keeping a balance

The rate at which oxygen is taken into the body is a measure of how fast the body is using it up. That is, it is a measure of the **metabolic rate** of the body.

Different foods contain different amounts of energy, therefore care must be taken that:

energy intake	energy used up

Otherwise there will be an increase or decrease in mass, meaning you will get fatter or thinner!

Now do this

7. Give a word equation for anaerobic respiration in humans.
8. Explain what is meant by oxygen debt.
9. Explain why anaerobic respiration and aerobic respiration do not release the same amount of energy.

Life Processes and Living Things

Homeostasis

Homeostasis literally means keeping conditions inside your body more or less constant, to enable your cells to work most efficiently.

What conditions need controlling?

In the human body the following conditions need controlling:
- blood glucose concentration
- blood water and salt concentration
- blood carbon dioxide level
- blood temperature
- waste products in the blood, such as urea
- the composition of body tissue fluid.

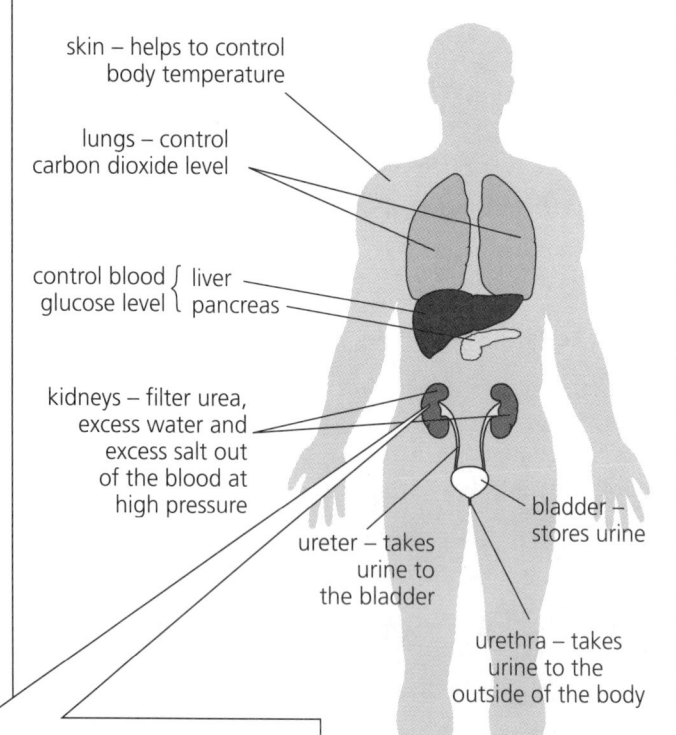

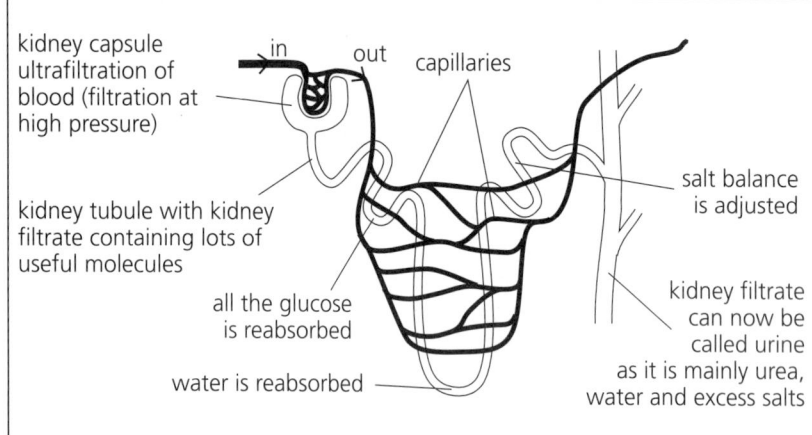

The water balance

If the balance of water in the body is upset we either dehydrate (dry out) or swell up with excess fluid.

food and drink (water in)	urine, sweat and breath (water out)

We cannot survive either extreme for long. The water content of the blood is monitored by the brain. If the water content of the blood is low, the brain causes the kidney to reabsorb more water. If the water content of the blood is high the brain causes the kidney to reabsorb less water, therefore more watery urine is produced and the water content of the body begins to return to normal.

The brain controls the water content of the blood by means of the hormone **ADH**. If the water content of the blood is low, the brain releases ADH, which makes the kidney reabsorb more water back into the blood. The water level returns to normal, so the brain stops releasing ADH. Therefore ADH prevents dehydration.

 **Now do this**

1. What does homeostasis mean?
2. Which **two** body organs are used to control blood glucose level?
3. What is passed out of the bladder down the urethra?
4. Suggest why high levels of carbon dioxide in the blood are harmful to the body.

Controlling body temperature

When our cells respire, some of the energy released is heat energy. We use this to keep us warm.

Think about what you do when you feel cold. You might stamp your feet or rub your hands together, or even shiver. All of these actions involve respiration, which releases energy, therefore heat energy is also released to warm you up. The liver has a lot of reactions going on all the time, therefore it releases a lot of heat energy. It is like the boiler in your central heating system.

If the core body temperature increases, it causes the blood temperature to increase. If the core body temperature goes above 37 °C cells in the brain notice and switch on **cooling mechanisms** (e.g. sweating) to reduce the temperature. If the blood temperature goes below 37 °C the brain switches on **warming mechanisms** (e.g. shivering).

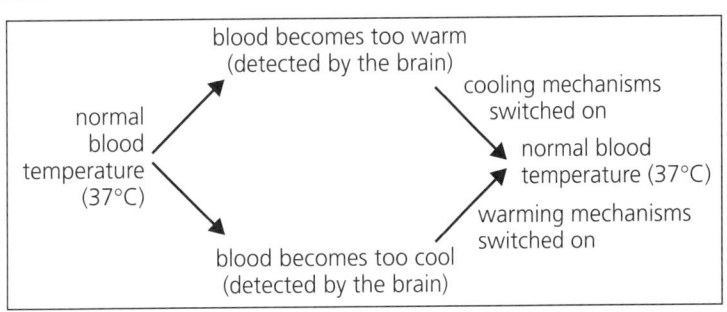

The mechanisms

Cooling mechanisms	Warming mechanisms
• Sweating – heat from the body is used to evaporate sweat from the skin surface. • Vasodilation – blood vessels near the skin surface open to allow blood to flow near to the surface of the body and lose heat by radiation to the air. • Behavioural – take some clothes off.	• Shivering – muscles make heat by respiration to warm us up. • Vasoconstriction – blood vessels running near the skin surface close, diverting the blood back to the warmer parts of the body. • Behavioural – put some extra clothes on.

Homeostasis is achieved by **negative feedback**. This means that:
1. a change is detected by the body, e.g. the blood carbon dioxide concentration increases
2. the body responds to the change, e.g. the brain brings about an increase in the breathing rate
3. the situation returns to normal, e.g. blood carbon dioxide concentration decreases back to normal
4. the body response stops, e.g. the breathing rate returns to normal.

Now do this

5. Explain why you produce less urine on a hot sunny day than on a cold day.
6. Which part of the body checks the temperature of the blood?
7. Explain how sweating helps to cool us down.

Defence against disease

Your body has to defend itself against microbes which are able to attack it and cause disease. The body has a number of ways of stopping microbes getting in.
- The eyes: tears contain a substance that destroys microbes.
- The nose and breathing passages are protected by mucus and cilia.
- The mouth leading to the digestive system: relies on the stomach acid to destroy microbes.
- The skin: provides a barrier to entry.

Fighting back

If the skin is damaged, blood forms a second line of defence by:
- forming a clot and scab to block entry to microbes
- allowing white blood cells to escape from blood vessels to attack any invading microbes.

> Another word for microbes and other foreign materials in your body is **antigens**.

There are two types of white blood cell.

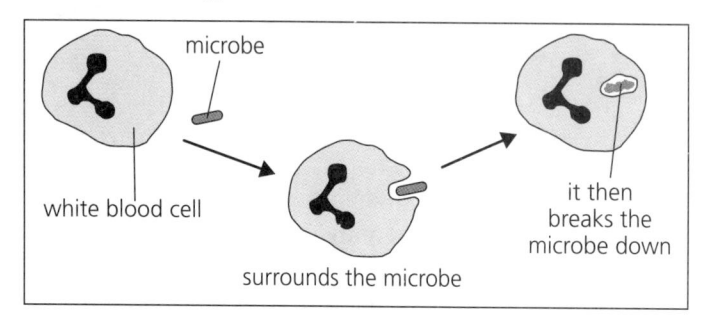

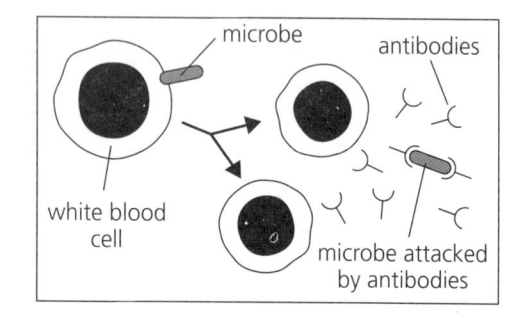

One type engulfs (eats) the microbes. The other type produces chemicals called **antibodies**, which attack the microbes and destroy them. The white blood cell makes contact with the microbe and identifies it. It then divides to produce a lot more white blood cells, all capable of releasing the right antibody. Each disease has its own antigens, therefore each one can be attacked by its own **specific antibodies**.

Immunity

Once your body has met a microbe and made antibodies against it, it does not forget. When you meet the same type of microbe again, your body is waiting. It quickly produces lots of antibodies, so you are unlikely to get the disease again. This is called **immunity**.

Unfortunately it does not work very well with colds and flu, because there are so many different strains of them. Antibodies to cold strain A will not give you immunity to any of the other cold strains!

Now do this

1. How are the eyes protected from microbe invasion?
2. If the skin is damaged, how does the body continue to protect itself?
3. What is an antibody?
4. Why is it important that white blood cells can escape from blood vessels?

> **Immunisation** is a means of giving the antigen without the disease. For example, a vaccine contains dead or inactive microbes which will enable your body to make antibodies against them without the risk of developing the disease. This is a way of protecting the population from serious diseases such as polio or smallpox.

Treatment

If you do become ill, you may need medicine to make you feel better. Medicines contain drugs. A **drug** is a substance that changes the way in which your body works.

When taken as painkillers or antibiotics drugs can be very useful. Unfortunately some drugs have side effects and some produce sensations which encourage people to misuse them.

Problems with drugs

Many drugs work either by speeding up brain activity or by slowing it down.

Stimulant – speeds up brain activity by increasing the activity of brain synapses.

Depressant – slows down brain activity by blocking some of the brain synapses.

Drug	Action	Negative effects
caffeine	stimulant	can cause sleeplessness
nicotine	anaesthetic	can stop cilia in the trachea beating, leading to a build up of mucus and a smokers' cough bacteria thrive in the mucus, causing lung infections
alcohol	depressant	may slow down brain activity to the point of passing out, reduces ability to make judgements prolonged use may result in damage to the brain it poisons the liver, leading to liver damage
solvents	depressants	may slow down brain activity so much that the brain stops

Some drugs are **addictive**, meaning that they produce a dependence in the person taking the drug. The person then has to keep taking the drug.

Analgesics – painkillers which depress brain activity.

Some drugs produce **withdrawal symptoms** if the user stops, or is prevented from, taking the drug. These vary in severity from a headache if you are deprived of coffee for the day, to sickness, blinding headaches and an inability to sleep, eat or do anything.

The body gets used to some drugs, which means that the drug user needs larger and larger doses to get the same effect. This is called **drug tolerance**.

Now do this

5 What is a drug?

6 Explain why smoking may make someone more likely to get lung infections.

7 What is the difference between a depressant and a stimulant? Give an example of each.

Reproduction

When plants and animals **reproduce** they make new plants and animals (offspring) like themselves. There are two main ways of reproducing.

Asexual reproduction takes place when one parent produces offspring which are identical to the parent. For example, spider plants and strawberries grow runners with new plants on them, potatoes produce tubers and tulips reproduce by forming bulbs.

In **sexual reproduction** two parents produce male and female sex cells called **gametes**. In animals, male gametes are called **sperm** and female gametes are called **eggs**. These join together at **fertilisation** to form a **zygote**. This develops into an embryo and then, in humans, into a baby. The result of sexual reproduction is offspring who are *not* identical to their parents but are similar to them. They inherit a mix of characteristics from their parents.

Passing on characteristics

The characteristics of every plant or animal are determined by **chromosomes** in the nucleus of their cells. Chromosomes are long molecules of the chemical **DNA**. Every chromosome carries thousands of **genes** and each gene controls some characteristic of the organism, e.g. eye colour or petal shape. These characteristics are passed on from parents to offspring during reproduction.

Mitosis

In asexual reproduction exact copies of the chromosomes are passed on. This is done by **mitosis**. The chromosomes in one cell are copied exactly and then one copy moves to each end of the cell. The cell divides into two, producing two genetically identical cells.

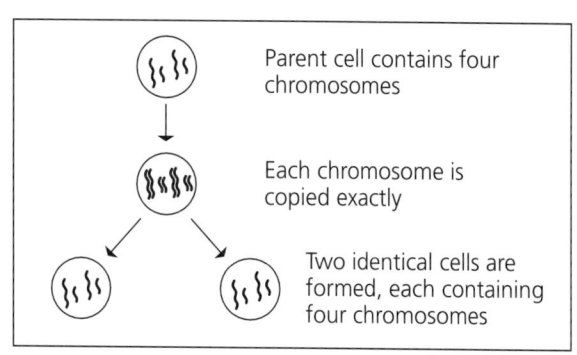

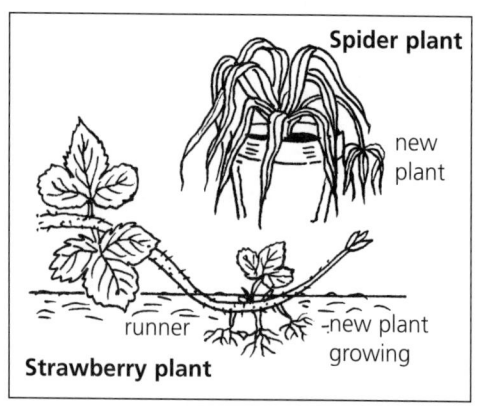

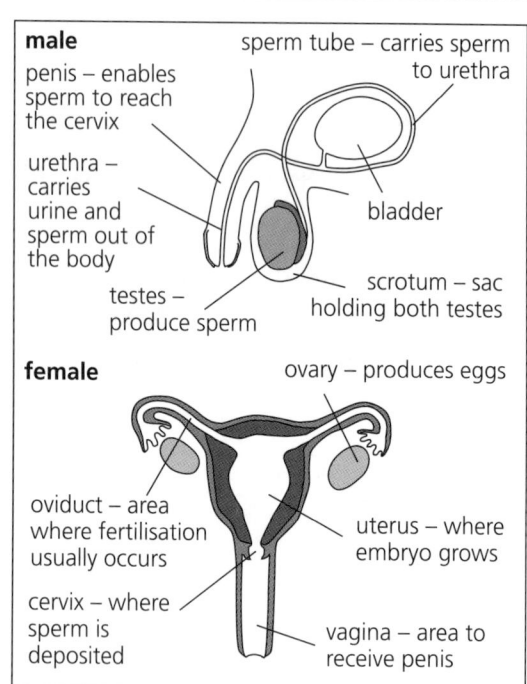

Parent cell contains four chromosomes

Each chromosome is copied exactly

Two identical cells are formed, each containing four chromosomes

Meiosis

In sexual reproduction, gametes have half the usual number of chromosomes. Gametes are produced in the sex organs of the parents by **meiosis**. When male and female gametes join together at fertilisation the zygote has a full set.

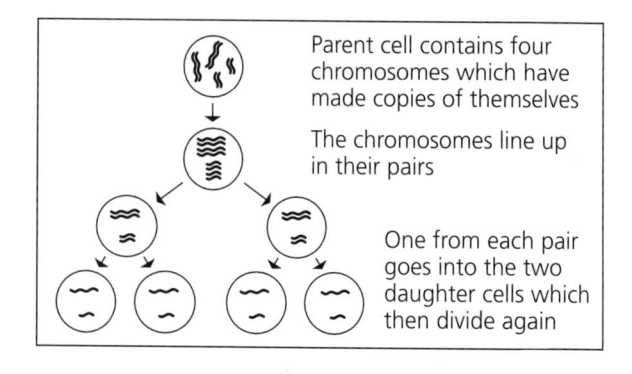

Parent cell contains four chromosomes which have made copies of themselves

The chromosomes line up in their pairs

One from each pair goes into the two daughter cells which then divide again

Inheritance and evolution

Most human cells have 46 chromosomes arranged in pairs. One of each pair came from your mother and the other from your father. Most of your characteristics depend on which of your parents' genes were carried by the gametes which formed you. So you may have similar characteristics to your parents, but in different combinations. These differences are called **variation**.

One pair of chromosomes determines your sex. There are two types of sex chromosome: the **X chromosome** and the **Y chromosome**. Female gametes, eggs, have X chromosomes. Male gametes, sperm, have either an X or a Y chromosome. If two gametes with X chromosomes fuse, the offspring is female (**XX**). If a gamete carrying an X and one carrying a Y fuse, the offspring is male (**XY**).

It is the male who determines the sex of the child

egg nucleus with X chromosome → sperm nucleus with Y chromosome
X + Y → fertilisation → XY
zygote will develop into a boy

egg nucleus with X chromosome → sperm nucleus with X chromosome
X + X → fertilisation → XX
zygote will develop into a girl

Now do this

1. When plants or animals grow, their cells increase in number by mitosis. Why does this growth use mitosis and not meiosis?

Mutations

Sometimes there are changes (or **mutations**) to the genetic code or the number of chromosomes. This has serious effects. For example, when a human egg has 24 instead of the normal 23 chromosomes the baby formed from the egg will have Down's syndrome.

Other changes can be caused by: chromosomes not being copied correctly in cells; exposure to radiation; exposure to certain chemicals.

Lookalikes

Sometimes two individuals do have an identical genetic make-up. Identical twins are formed from the same single fertilised egg, which divides after fertilisation. Non-identical twins are produced from two eggs released from the ovaries at the same time and fertilised separately.

Making use of mitosis

We can use mitosis to produce **clones**. A clone is an individual which is genetically identical to its parent, and cloning plants is big business. When we take **cuttings** of plants to grow we are producing clones. Commercially much smaller pieces of plant material are used. This is therefore called **micropropagation** or **tissue culture**.

A plant with the desired characteristics is divided into large numbers of small pieces of tissue. These are grown in a suitable growth medium using an **aseptic** technique, which prevents any microbes growing and spoiling the culture. When ready, the small plantlets are transferred to pots and sold.

Advantages of cloning	Disadvantages of cloning
All the desirable parental characteristics are transferred to the clones.	Any genetic weaknesses or defects will be passed on to all offspring.
A relatively quick and cheap way to obtain large numbers of offspring.	No genetic variation to overcome environmental change, e.g. a new disease could wipe out all the clones.

Now do this

2. Make a table comparing mitosis and meiosis.
3. Name **one** condition caused by a chromosome mutation.
4. What do you understand by the word clone?
5. What sort of cell division produces a clone?

Inheritance

Many genes have several different versions, called **alleles**. For example, there are blue and brown alleles for eye colour. If you inherit a blue one from each parent you will have blue eyes. But if you inherit one blue allele and one brown you do not have stripy eyes, you have brown eyes. Some alleles are stronger than others.

Strong alleles are called **dominant** and weak alleles are called **recessive**. We show a dominant allele by a capital letter and a recessive allele by a small letter.

The allele for brown eyes is dominant (**B**), the one for blue is recessive (**b**). If you inherit a **B** allele from one parent and a **b** allele from the other parent, you will have brown eyes because the brown allele is dominant. If you inherit a **b** allele from each parent you will have blue eyes.

The alleles you inherit are called your **genotype**. How you look because of these alleles is called your **phenotype**. A person with the phenotype of blue eyes can have only one genotype, **bb**. A person with the phenotype of brown eyes could have a genotype of **BB** or **Bb**.

> The first offspring of a cross are called the F_1 generation. The offspring produced when the F_1 generation is crossed are called the F_2 generation.

If you know the genotype of the parents you can work out what their offspring are likely to be.

For example, if one parent is **BB** for brown eyes and the other is **bb** for blue, we can work out the possible combinations of their alleles with a diagram like this:

genetic diagram for cross of two parents homozygous for brown and blue eyes

Gametes	B	B
b	Bb	Bb
b	Bb	Bb

all offspring have brown eyes

If one of these children has offspring with another **Bb** individual the combination of offspring would be this:

genetic diagram for cross of two parents heterozygous for brown eyes

Gametes	B	b
B	BB	bB
b	Bb	bb

three brown-eyed, one blue-eyed offspring

If both the alleles are the same, **BB** or **bb**, the individual is called **homozygous**. If the alleles are different, **Bb**, the individual is called **heterozygous**.

Some diseases are caused by faulty genes inherited from the parents. Examples are sickle-cell anaemia, cystic fibrosis, muscular dystrophy and haemophilia. Many of these are caused by recessive genes.

Inheritance of cystic fibrosis

Gametes	F	f
F	FF	fF
f	Ff	ff

Both parents are heterozygous Ff.
Cystic fibrosis is controlled by the recessive allele f.
A child with homozygous ff will suffer from cystic fibrosis.
A child with heterozygous Ff will be a carrier like its parents.
A child with homozygous FF will not have the abnormal allele at all.

Inheritance and evolution

Working out the probabilities

The way a characteristic is inherited can be studied by breeding two individuals and observing the characteristics in their offspring. This is called a **monohybrid cross** because it only follows the inheritance of one characteristic. We can make predictions about the probable outcome of a monohybrid cross.

The probability of two heterozygous brown-eyed parents producing a blue-eyed child is 1 in 4, or 25%. This means that when they have a child, there is a 25% chance that it will have blue eyes.

Now do this

1. Explain what ratio of offspring would be expected from a cross between a blue-eyed parent and a heterozygous brown-eyed parent.
2. Tongue rolling is an inherited characteristic. The 'tongue rolling' allele is dominant (**T**). What ratio of tongue rolling offspring would you expect from a heterozygous tongue rolling mother and a non-rolling father?

Sex linkage

Some inherited human disorders such as red-green colour blindness and haemophilia are caused by a recessive allele which appears only on the X chromosome. These are called **sex-linked** disorders.

A female can carry a recessive allele on one of her X chromosomes without being affected. However, if a male has the allele on his X chromosome there is no corresponding allele on the paired Y chromosome, so he will have the disorder. For example, a normal-sighted woman carrying one allele for colour blindness (**X^{c}X**) and her unaffected husband (**XY**) can have a colour blind son.

Gametes	X	X^c
X	XX	X^{c}X
Y	XY	X^{c}Y

X Normal X chromosome
X^c Chromosome with allele for colour blindness
Y Normal Y chromosome

Environmental variation

Some of your characteristics are also affected by your environment. For example, your genes may make you tall, but if you are well fed as a child you may be even taller. A child's weight at birth is partly determined by genes but partly by its mother's health and age. Very hot sun can make fair skin brown and brown hair fair. And you can change your hair colour and shape with chemicals any time you like!

Plants are also affected by their environment. For example, wind can affect the shape of a tree, and soil can affect the growth of crops.

Continuous variation is controlled largely by the environment. Examples are height, weight.

Discontinuous variation is controlled by the genes. Examples include eye colour, blood group.

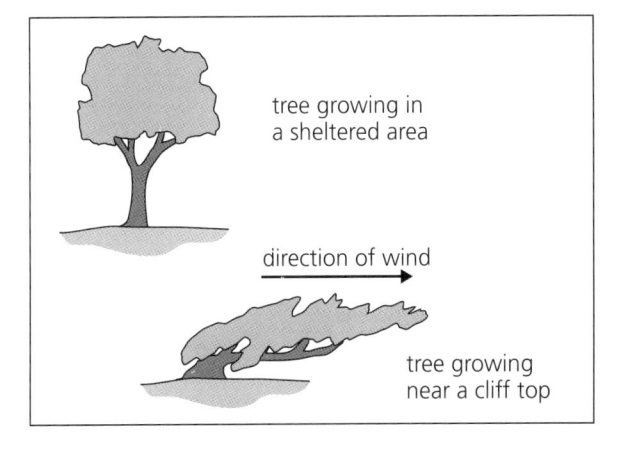

tree growing in a sheltered area

direction of wind →

tree growing near a cliff top

Now do this

3. Girls can be born colour blind, although this is rare. Draw a genetic diagram showing how a girl could inherit two recessive alleles for colour blindness.
4. Which of these characteristics can be affected by environment as well as genes: eye colour, weight, fingerprints, body shape?

Natural selection and evolution

Animals and plants have gradually developed (**evolved**) from much simpler forms over many millions of years. This process is called **evolution**.

We only know about evolution from the fossils that have been found. **Fossils** are the remains of dead organisms which have become preserved in rock.

Fossil formation

An organism dies by the water's edge.

The water level rises and the dead organism gradually becomes covered in silt.

The soft parts decay, but the hard bits (bone and cellulose) survive long enough to absorb minerals from the water.

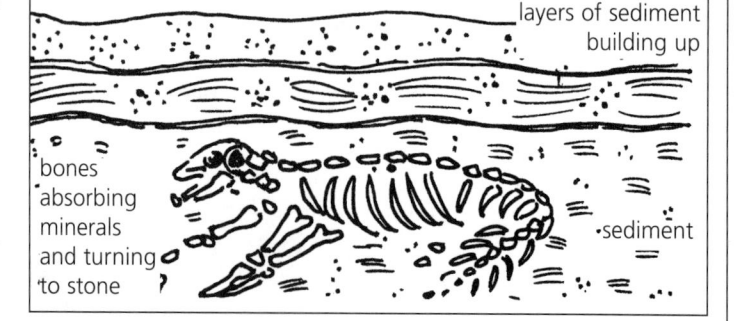

As layers of sediment build up on top of the fossil, it becomes embedded in a layer of sedimentary rock.

The fossil record

The fossil record shows that the variety of living things in the world today did not appear all at once many years ago. This happened very gradually over millions of years, with some things dying out while new ones evolved.

Dinosaurs existed until 65 million years ago, but we only know about them from fossils. Human beings are relative newcomers to the world, with our earliest ancestors making an appearance only 6 million years ago.

Inheritance and evolution

However, what we know about evolution from fossils is not the whole story. There are reasons for this:
- some body parts may not have fossilised
- fossilisation was a comparatively rare event
- we have not yet discovered all the fossils.

This means that what fossils show can be interpreted in different ways, according to the views at the time. It is possible to argue that dinosaurs and humans were created together, but we just have not found the fossil evidence yet!

Now do this
1. Suggest why fossils do not provide a complete record of evolution.

Natural selection

Charles Darwin explained evolution as the result of **natural selection**. This is the idea that those animals and plants best adapted to their surroundings (environment) will have the best chance of surviving and reproducing.

The genes of animals and plants determine how well they are adapted to their surroundings. These genes can then be passed on to the next generation. So, over a very long time a population can become better adapted to its surroundings. This happens because some alleles become more common and some (the less desirable ones) become less common.

Charles Darwin's theory was based on:
- the presence of natural variation within a population
- the inheritance of some of the variations
- the fact that all organisms potentially over-reproduce and yet population numbers tend to remain fairly constant over long periods of time
- the fact that the best adapted individuals are more likely to survive – this is **survival of the fittest**.
- the extinction of species unable to compete.

Natural selection in action!

1. Before the Industrial Revolution trees had pale bark, so the pale speckled peppered moth was camouflaged.

2. Chance mutation produced a black (melanic) version.

3. As the Industrial Revolution progressed, the landscape became coated with smoke and soot and the trees turned black.

4. By the start of the 20th century, 98% of the peppered moths were black. They were more numerous because they were better adapted to the environment and the pale ones were easier for the predators to spot.

At the time, Darwin's theory was greeted with hostility. This was because most people believed in the idea of creation, which was the belief that all living things had been created at the same time. Darwin's theory was difficult to understand because most people knew little or nothing about inheritance.

Now do this
2. Explain what is meant by the term natural selection.
3. Use the peppered moth as an example to explain what is meant by survival of the fittest.
4. Why have some species become extinct?

Artificial selection

We take advantage of variation when we selectively breed animals and plants. We pick individuals with the characteristics we want and breed them. Their best offspring are selected and bred. This is repeated over many generations.

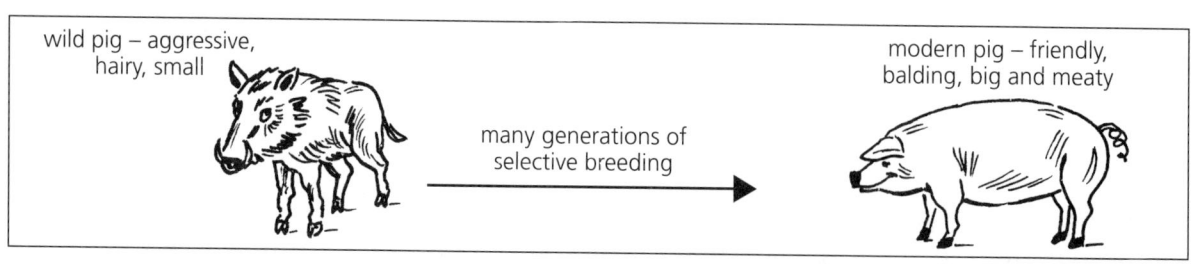

wild pig – aggressive, hairy, small

many generations of selective breeding

modern pig – friendly, balding, big and meaty

We selectively breed for many reasons. In animals we may want better yields of meat or milk, less aggression or a more attractive appearance. In plants we may want better yields of grain or fruit, better flavour or resistance to disease.

Now do this
1 a What characteristic would you want to breed into racehorses?
  b How would you do it?

Genetic engineering

Selective breeding takes a long time. It is unreliable because we cannot control exactly which genes are passed on, and is limited to living things within the same species. So, for example, you cannot breed a cow with a giraffe to produce a long-necked cow able to feed over hedges!

Genetic engineering gets round these problems by transferring genes directly from the cells of one living thing to the cells of another. The desired gene is first identified in an organism and then removed and isolated. It is replicated to make lots of copies and then inserted into the genetic material (the DNA) of the host organism.

For example, inserting the gene for human insulin into microbes has led to microbes capable of producing large amounts of human insulin for use in treating diabetes, which would otherwise be very difficult to produce.

Genetic engineering has a number of possible drawbacks. It is expensive to set up and develop. There are also worries about transferred genes finding their way into other species and about eating food which has been genetically engineered. Finally, there is a lot of concern about possibly engineering humans in the future for 'desirable' characteristics.

Now do this
2 Explain why selective breeding is still used a lot for animals nowadays, but not so much for plants.

3 Make a table showing the advantages and disadvantages of genetic engineering and selective breeding.

Inheritance and evolution

Making more DNA

One of the stages of genetic engineering involves producing lots of copies of DNA. When your cells divide, they also need to make copies of the DNA so that each new cell will contain the correct amount. This copying is called **replication**.

It is very important that the DNA is copied exactly so that the genetic information it carries is not changed in any way. DNA has a structure that makes it easy to copy exactly. DNA is a huge structure which is normally coiled up to occupy as small a space as possible. Once it is uncoiled, it looks like a step ladder.

The sides of the ladder are identical, but the rungs of the ladder are different. The rungs are made up of four chemicals called **bases**. They are referred to by the first letters of their chemical names. The four bases are A, T, G and C. They have different shapes and fit together as pairs.

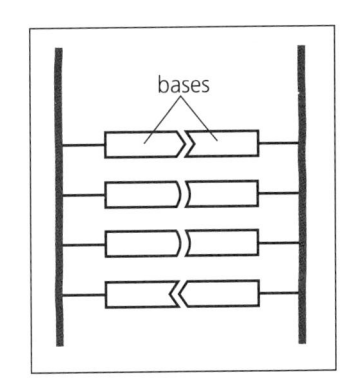

A has the correct shape to fit with T.
C has the correct shape to fit with G.

During replication the pairs of bases are separated by an enzyme. The rungs of the DNA ladder start to come apart.

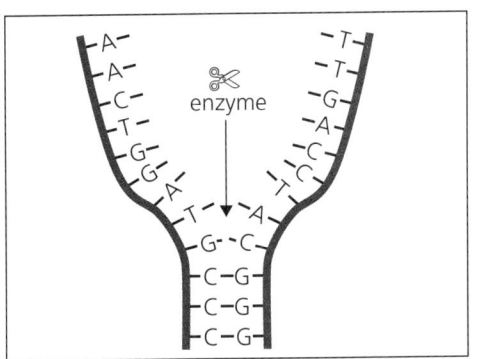

As the two sides separate, new bases move in to form two new strands.

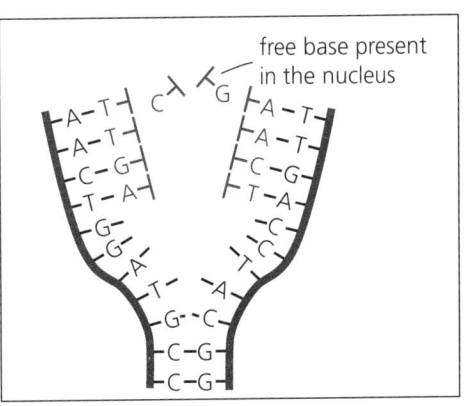

Look at the bases – they must still pair A to T; C to G. Therefore the two new strands will both end up identical to the original one.

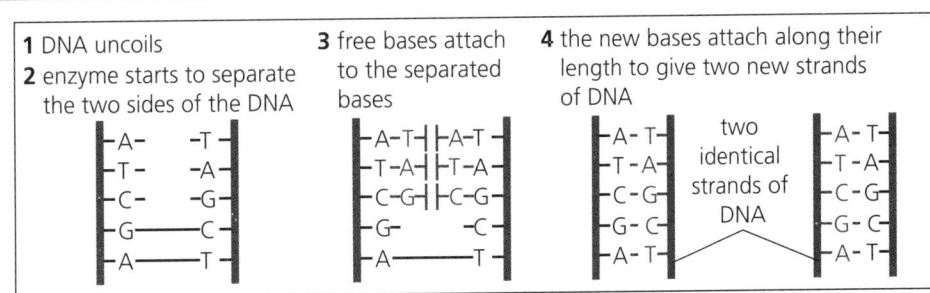

1 DNA uncoils
2 enzyme starts to separate the two sides of the DNA

3 free bases attach to the separated bases

4 the new bases attach along their length to give two new strands of DNA

two identical strands of DNA

Now do this

4 Give the symbols for the four bases which make up DNA. Show how they pair up.
5 Explain why newly formed DNA is said to contain half the original piece of DNA.
6 Why is it so important that DNA is replicated exactly?

Life Processes and Living Things

Concept map

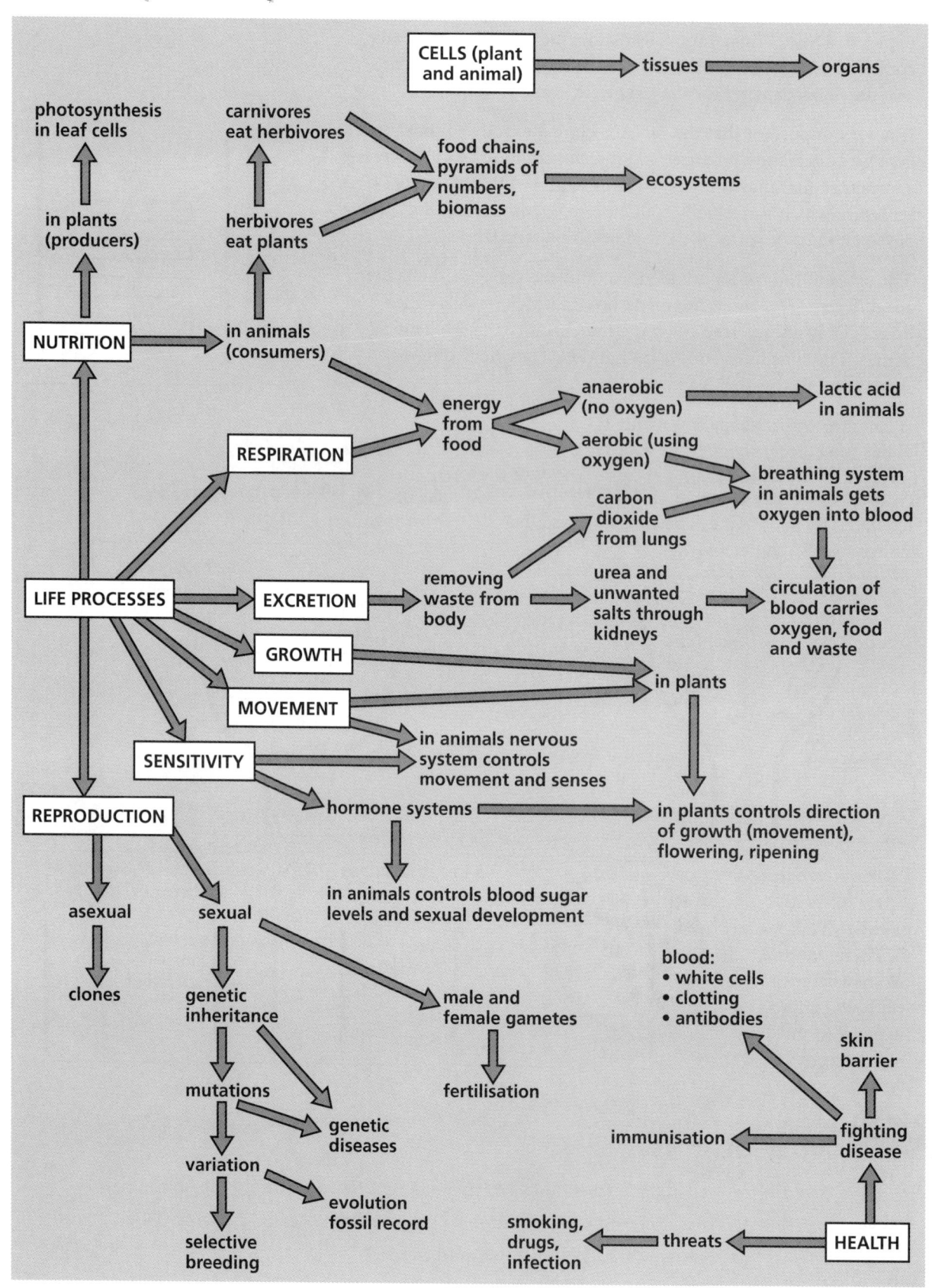

CELLS (plant and animal) → tissues → organs

NUTRITION
- in plants (producers) → photosynthesis in leaf cells
- in animals (consumers)
  - herbivores eat plants
  - carnivores eat herbivores
  → food chains, pyramids of numbers, biomass → ecosystems

LIFE PROCESSES

RESPIRATION → energy from food
- anaerobic (no oxygen) → lactic acid in animals
- aerobic (using oxygen)
  → carbon dioxide from lungs → breathing system in animals gets oxygen into blood → circulation of blood carries oxygen, food and waste

EXCRETION → removing waste from body → urea and unwanted salts through kidneys

GROWTH → in plants

MOVEMENT
- in animals nervous system controls movement and senses

SENSITIVITY → hormone systems
- in plants controls direction of growth (movement), flowering, ripening
- in animals controls blood sugar levels and sexual development

REPRODUCTION
- asexual → clones
- sexual
  - genetic inheritance → mutations → variation → selective breeding
  - → genetic diseases
  - → male and female gametes → fertilisation
  - variation → evolution fossil record

HEALTH → threats → smoking, drugs, infection
→ fighting disease
- skin barrier
- immunisation
- blood:
  - white cells
  - clotting
  - antibodies

Exam questions

1 The diagram shows a reflex arc.

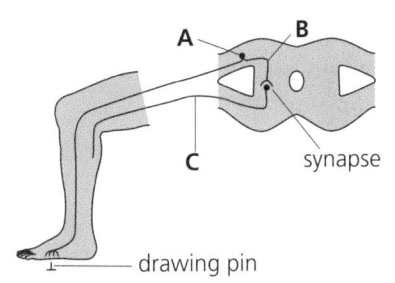

labels: A, B, C, synapse, drawing pin

a Which label shows the motor neurone? [1]
b i How do reflex actions help us to survive? [1]
 ii Give **two other** examples of reflex actions. [2]
c The diagram shows a synapse. Explain what happens to the nervous message when it reaches a synapse. [3]
[Total 7]

2 The diagram shows a section through an alveolus.

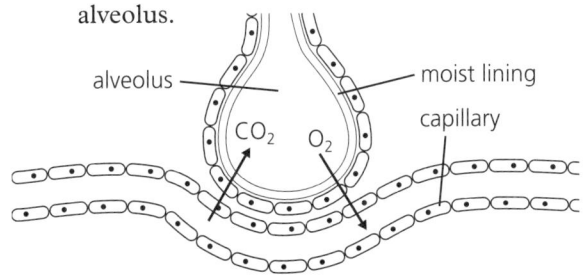

labels: alveolus, moist lining, capillary, CO_2, O_2

a An alveolus is adapted for efficient gaseous exchange. Explain **three** ways in which the alveolus is adapted for oxygen uptake. [3]
b Explain how gases are brought into the alveoli. [4]
[Total 7]

3 Five cylinders were cut from a piece of raw rhubarb. Each cylinder was 50 mm long and 5 mm in diameter. Each cylinder was placed in a sugar solution of different concentration. After 12 hours the length of each cylinder was measured again. The results are shown below.

Concentration of sugar solution (mol/dm³)	0	0.2	0.4	0.6	0.8
Length of cylinder after 12 h (mm)	53.3	52.0	48.2	46.1	44.9
Change in length (mm)	+3.3	+2.0	−1.8		−5.1

a Calculate the change in length for the cylinder in the 0.6 mol/dm³ sugar solution and complete the table. [1]
b Plot a graph to show the changes in length of the rhubarb cylinders in the different concentrations of sugar solution. [4]
c Use the graph to work out the concentration of sugar solution which would cause **no** change in the length of the cylinders. [1]
d Explain the process which causes the change in size of the rhubarb cylinders. [4]
[Total 10]

4 The table shows the volume of fluids entering and leaving the human digestive system during a 24 hour period.

Volume of fluid in litres	Area of digestive system
1.5	taken into the mouth
1.5	produced by salivary glands in the mouth
2.0	produced by stomach wall
3.0	produced by liver and pancreas
7.8	absorbed into the blood from the intestine
	egested from the body with the faeces

a Calculate the volume of fluid egested from the body with the faeces, and complete the table. [1]
b The fluid from the pancreas and liver contains water and other substances. One of these substances is bile.
 i What does bile do? [1]
 ii Explain how bile helps one of the other substances in the fluid to work. [2]
[Total 4]

Life Processes and Living Things

5 The polar bear is adapted to living in very cold, icy deserts. Look at the drawing.

a Suggest **three** ways in which the polar bear is adapted to survive in its environment. [3]

The polar bear is a mammal and is therefore able to maintain a constant body temperature. Humans are also mammals and maintain a constant body temperature.

b Explain **two** mechanisms our bodies could use if we started to get too cold. [2]

c How does our body detect changes to the core body temperature? [1]

d What is the advantage of being able to maintain a constant body temperature? [1]

[7 marks]

6 a The following equation for photosynthesis is not complete. Fill in the blanks.

$\quad\quad + 6H_2O \rightarrow C_6H_{12}O_6 +$ [2]

b Name the **two** other requirements for photosynthesis to occur. [2]

c Describe an experiment to show that the rate of photosynthesis in a water plant is affected by the wavelength of light. You may include a diagram in your answer. [5]

[9 marks]

7 The graph shows how oxygen demand and intake change during exercise.

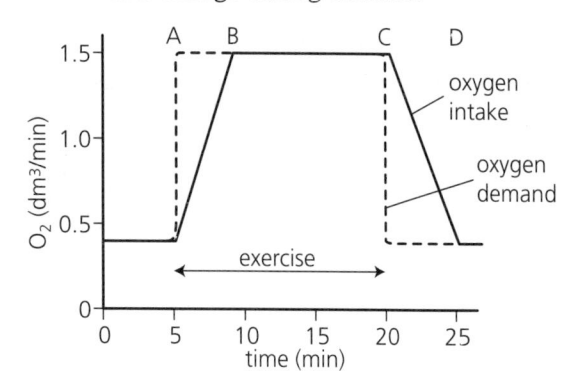

a Explain why oxygen demand starts to increase as soon as exercise starts. [2]

b During vigorous exercise it is quite normal for muscle cells to respire anaerobically.

  i Write a word equation for anaerobic respiration. [3]

  ii Anaerobic respiration leads to oxygen debt. Explain what this means. [3]

  iii Look at the graph. Which part of the graph shows the oxygen debt? [1]

[9 marks]

8 In America some farmers keep their pigs in indoor pens. The floors of these pens are metal slats which allow urine and waste to drop through into a reservoir. In some areas, nitrate-rich material from these reservoirs has seeped out into local waterways, causing widespread nitrate pollution. Explain fully what effect nitrate pollution can have on a waterway. [4]

[4 marks]

9 Look at the drawing. It shows a person frightened by a charging bull.

Adrenaline is released in the body of the person. It travels round the body in the bloodstream, preparing the body for action.

a Write down the name given to chemical messengers like adrenaline. [1]

b How does adrenaline prepare the body for action? Explain as fully as you can. [4]

[5 marks]

10 This question is about the plant hormone auxin. Auxin is produced in the tip of the shoot. Auxin causes shoots to grow towards the light.

a Write down the name of this response to light. [1]

b Suggest why this response is beneficial for plants. [2]

c Explain as fully as you can how auxin causes shoots to bend towards the light. [3]
[6 marks]

11 When a cell is preparing for cell division, the DNA strands start to unravel. Look at the diagram.

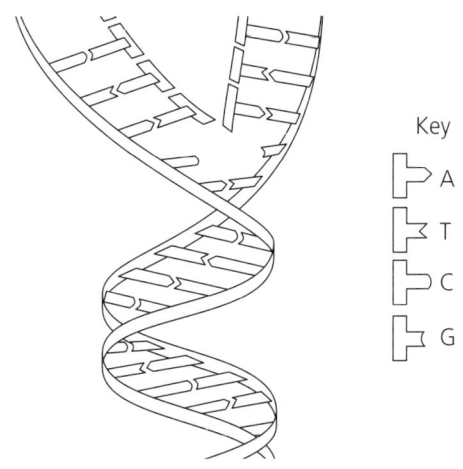

Key
⊢ A
⊢ T
⊢ C
⊢ G

a i Name the process shown in the diagram. [1]
ii Describe the process taking place in the diagram. [5]
b What is the importance of the order of the bases along a DNA strand? [1]
c What is meant by mutation? [1]
[8 marks]

12 Haemophilia is a sex-linked characteristic. People with haemophilia are unable to clot their blood properly. It is caused by a recessive allele.
a What do you understand by the term sex-linked characteristic? [1]
b What is a recessive allele? [2]
c Look at this family tree.

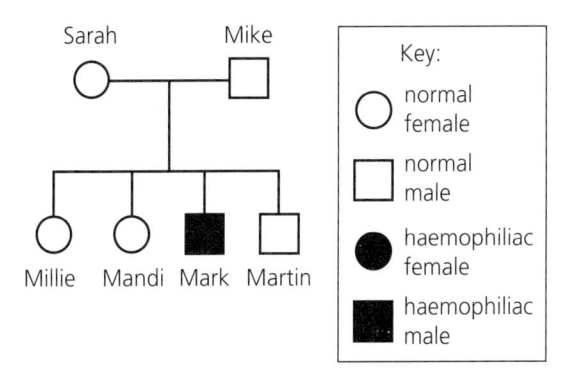

Sarah Mike

Millie Mandi Mark Martin

Key:
○ normal female
□ normal male
● haemophiliac female
■ haemophiliac male

i Explain who Mark inherited his haemophilia from. [2]

ii If Mark was able to have children, would he be able to pass his haemophilia on to his son? Explain your answer. [2]
iii Mark has a daughter who does not have haemophilia. What is the probability that his next child will be a girl? [1]
[8 marks]

13 The kidneys help the body to maintain conditions at a favourable level for cells to work efficiently.
a What is the name given to this type of control process? [1]
b List three conditions which the body needs to control. [3]
c Briefly explain how the kidney produces urine. [4]
d Explain the difference between the urine you would produce after a game of tennis on a hot summer day, and that which you would produce watching a rugby match on a cold winter day. [3]
[11 marks]

14 The figure shows a simplified nitrogen cycle.

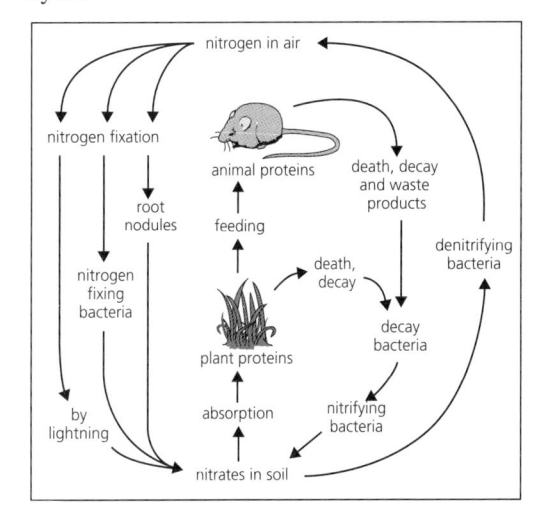

a Why do living things need nitrogen? [1]
b Explain why most living things cannot use the nitrogen in the air. [2]
c What does nitrogen fixation mean? [1]
d Give two ways in which farmers can increase the nitrogen content of their fields. [2]
e Explain the process of eutrophication and the problems it causes. [5]
[11 marks]

Life Processes and Living Things

15 This diagram shows some of the changes associated with the menstrual cycle. Look at the figure and use it to help you answer the questions.

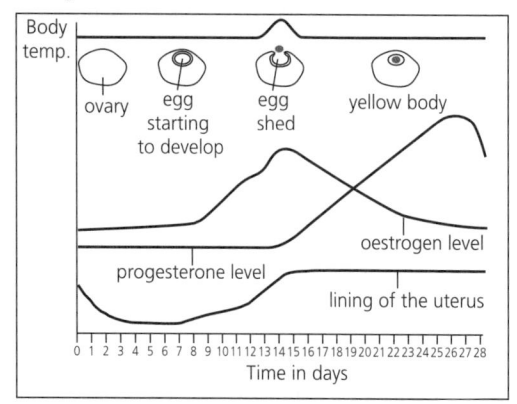

a What happens during days 1–7 of the cycle. [1]
b What is the main function of the hormone oestrogen? [1]
c On which day does ovulation occur? [1]
d If fertilisation occurs, explain what you would expect to happen to the progesterone level. [2]
e Some women use their body temperature as a form of birth control. Suggest one reason why this might not be very reliable. [1]

[6 marks]

16 The diagram shows some different types of cells.

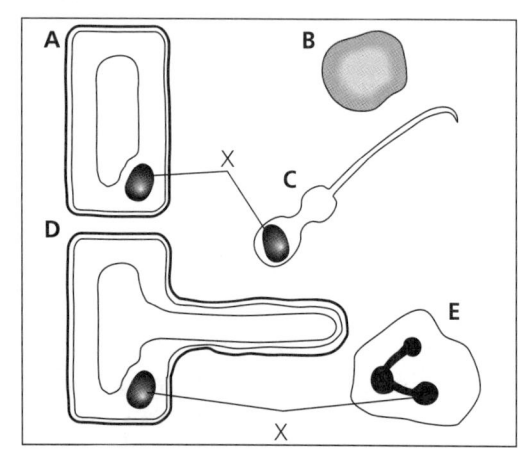

a What is the name of structure X, and what is its function? [2]
b Cell B does not contain structure X. Suggest a reason for this. [1]
c Cell C contains lots of mitochondria.
  i What is the function of mitochandria? [1]
  ii Why is it an advantage for this cell to contain lots of mitochondria? [1]
d Name one chemical which is made in cell A and is found in a high concentration in cell B. [1]
e Name one chemical which is taken up by cell D and transported to cell E. [1]
f Write down **two** of the cells which are plant cells, and give a reason for your choice. [3]

[10 marks]

17 The diagram shows a model gut set up to demonstrate digestion.

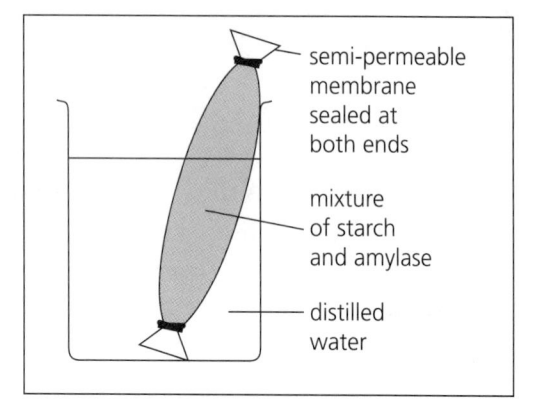

a Inside the model gut is the enzyme amylase. What do enzymes do in the digestive system? [2]

At the start of the experiment the model gut was filled with starch and amylase. After 30 min the distilled water was tested and found to contain glucose.

b Explain where the glucose has come from. [2]
c What does the distilled water represent in the model gut? [1]
d The distilled water does not contain any starch. Suggest a reason for this. [1]

A second model gut was set up with starch and amylase, but this time the amylase was boiled for 5 min before the experiment.

e What you would expect to find in the distilled water after 30 min and why? [3]
f Where in the body is amylase produced? [1]

[10 marks]

AT3

Materials and their Properties

Introducing chemistry	50
Earth and geological changes	58
Using the Earth's resources	66
Carbon chemistry	72
Using chemical equations	78
The Periodic Table	84
Concept map	90
Exam questions	91

Materials and their Properties

Atoms, elements, compounds and mixtures

Atoms, molecules and elements

The particles inside all chemicals are made from **atoms**. There are 104 different types of atom known. Each different type of atom is a different **element**. Some common elements are hydrogen, carbon, oxygen, sulphur, iron.

The particles inside a chemical might be single atoms on their own, or they might be made from groups of atoms. A small group of atoms combined together is called a **molecule**. Molecules can be made from atoms of one element, or from atoms of several different elements.

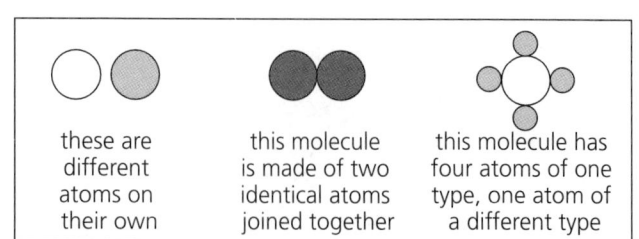

these are different atoms on their own

this molecule is made of two identical atoms joined together

this molecule has four atoms of one type, one atom of a different type

Enormous groups of atoms are called **giant structures** – you will come across these later.

Compounds and chemical bonds

Atoms of different elements can join together to make **compounds**. Compounds are always made from more than one element.

The atoms inside a compound are held to each other by **chemical bonds**.

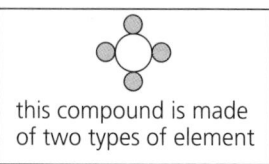

this compound is made of two types of element

Mixtures

Substances can be mixed together without them joining. They do not form compounds, they stay as mixtures. For example, air is a mixture of gases such as oxygen and nitrogen. Sea water is a mixture of water and salt – the salt is dissolved in the water, but it does not form a compound with the water. Substances in a mixture do not join, so they are easy to separate out.

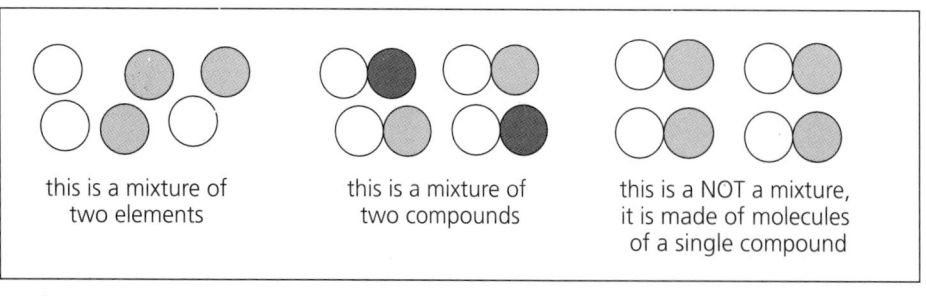

this is a mixture of two elements

this is a mixture of two compounds

this is a NOT a mixture, it is made of molecules of a single compound

Now do this

1. Which are compounds in the following list:
   hydrogen, hydrogen sulphide, oxygen, sugar, nitric acid, carbon?
2. Which are mixtures in the following list:
   salt and sand, sodium chloride, sugar, water, salty water?

Introducing chemistry

Separation techniques

Substances in a mixture are not joined together, so you can separate them out again using one of these methods.

Filtration

Use filtration to separate undissolved solid from a liquid. You could use this to get sand from a mixture of sand and salty water.

Evaporation/crystallisation

You can use this techique to get a solid from a solution. Gently heat the mixture so that the liquid evaporates into the air and the solid stays behind as crystals. You could you use this to get salt out of salty water.

Distillation

You can use distillation to get a pure liquid back out of a solution of a solid in a liquid. You heat the solution in a flask. The liquid boils and turns into a gas. The gas goes through a condenser, and the cold surfaces inside the condenser turn the gas back into a liquid – it **condenses**.

Fractional distillation

Solutions made of two liquids cannot be separated by normal distillation – both liquids will evaporate when you heat the solution. You will have to use a **fractionating column** instead. Crude oil is a mixture of liquids which is separated by fractional distillation.

Chromatography

You can use chromatography to see how many chemicals there are in a solution.

Put a drop of solution on a strip of filter paper and dip the end in water. As the water goes up the paper the chemicals separate and each moves a different distance up the paper.

You could use chromatography to see how many coloured dyes there are in black ink.

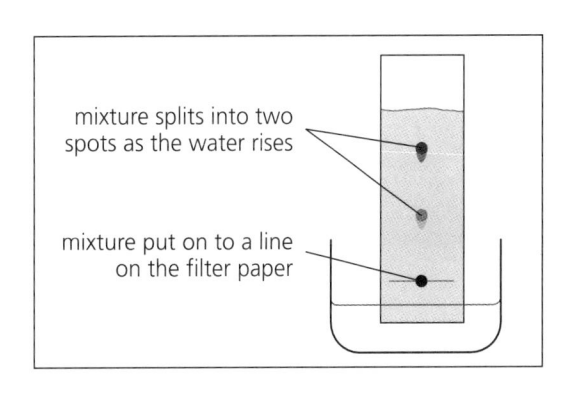

Now do this

3 Here are some separation problems. Some separations can be done by using just one of the techniques in the table. Others will need more than one method. Copy the table and tick the techniques that you need for each separation.

Separation problem	Technique		
	Dissolve	Filter	Evaporate
To get solid salt out of salty water (like the sea)			
To get sand from sand mixed with salty water			
To get solid salt from sand mixed with salty water			
To get solid salt from sand mixed with salt crystals			

Solids, liquids and gases

Everything is made of very small particles that are too small to see. The particles are always moving; the hotter they are the more they move. Particles are arranged in different ways in solids, liquids and gases.

Solids

The particles are close together. The particles stay in the same places, so solids keep their shape – even though the vibrations increase as the solid gets hotter. You can't move the particles any closer, so solids can't be compressed into a smaller space. The forces between the particles are strong.

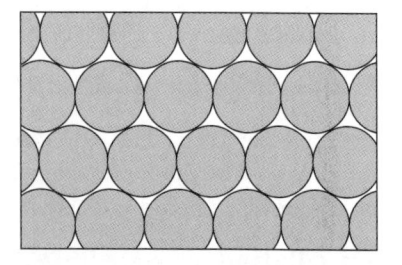

Liquids

Usually the particles are *slightly* further apart than in a solid. They can now move about, so liquids do not have a fixed shape. You still can't move the particles any closer so liquids can't be compressed into a smaller space. When a liquid gets hotter, the particles move faster.

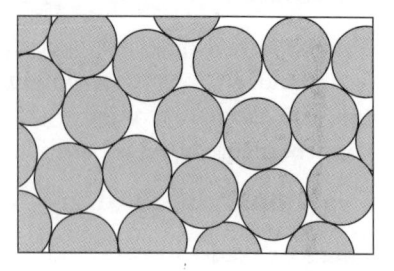

Gases

The particles are *very* far apart. This means that gases have no shape and it is easy to compress them into a small space. In gases the forces between the particles are very weak, so they don't stick together.

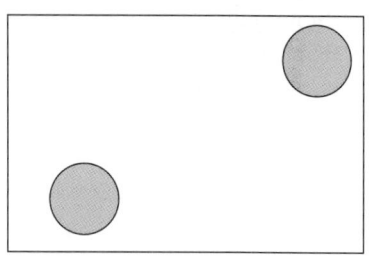

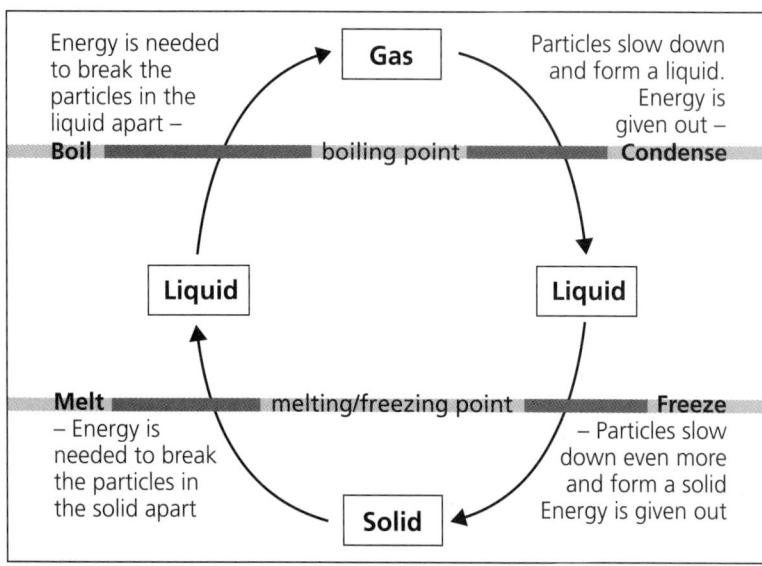

```
Energy is needed            Particles slow down
to break the      Gas       and form a liquid.
particles in the            Energy is
liquid apart –              given out –
Boil ========= boiling point ========= Condense

        Liquid              Liquid

Melt ========= melting/freezing point ========= Freeze
– Energy is                 – Particles slow
needed to break             down even more
the particles in            and form a solid
the solid apart   Solid     Energy is given out
```

Hint
Remember that in solids the particles move in a different way.

Remember to draw gas particles really far apart.

Now do this

1. Give **two** ways in which liquid particles are similar to gas particles.
2. Why are solids hard?

Linking particles together

Physical changes

water ⇌ steam

When water boils it changes from a liquid into steam. It is easy to change steam back into liquid water. The molecules inside the water move further apart when it boils but the molecules do not change: no new substance has been made. This is called a **physical change**. Dissolving is another physical change.

Dissolving things

Dissolving a solid in a liquid is a physical change; it is easy to get the solid and the liquid back apart. Sugar dissolves in water because the forces between the water and the sugar molecules are stronger than the weak forces that hold one sugar molecule to the next. Substances such as calcium carbonate will *not* dissolve because the forces holding the calcium carbonate particles together are stronger than the forces between the water and the calcium carbonate.

A substance that will dissolve is **soluble**. A substance that won't dissolve is **insoluble**. The liquid that it dissolves in is a **solvent**. The solvent with the substance dissolved in it is a **solution**. Water is a very useful solvent; lots of chemicals will dissolve in it.

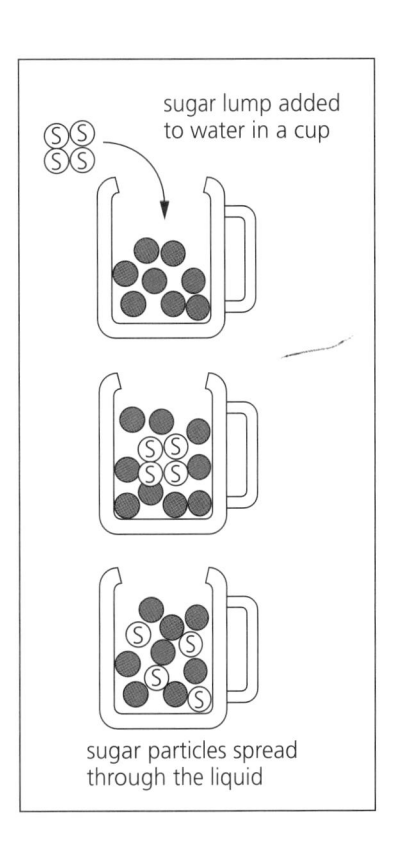

Chemical reactions

When sodium combines with chlorine, the two substances turn into sodium chloride – something totally new. This is a **chemical reaction**.

For changes like this to happen the bonds inside the chemicals must break up and new ones form. This isn't easy, so chemical reactions are very dificult to undo.

Most chemical reactions either need heating to make them start or give out heat as they happen – this is one sign that a chemical reaction is taking place.

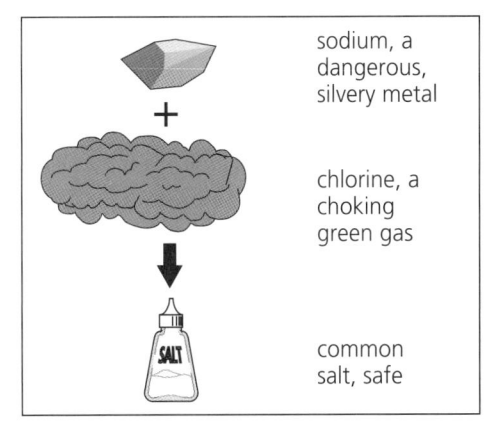

Now do this

3 When you put iron filings into copper sulphate solution, the solution gets warm, it changes colour, and it is difficult to get the iron filings and copper sulphate back again. What are the **two** clues that tell you that this is a chemical change?

4 Copy and complete the following sentences:

When steam is cooled it turns back into liquid water; we say that it has _____. If you put sugar into water the sugar will _____. Water behaves as a _____. The water and sugar make a _____.

Symbols, formulae and chemical equations

Symbols for the elements

- Elements have symbols of either one or two letters.
- If the symbol has one letter, that letter must be a capital.
- If the symbol has two letters, the first letter is a capital the second letter is a little letter, e.g. Fe.

Formulae for compounds

The formula for a compound tells us which elements are inside the compound. It also tells us how many atoms of each element are in the compound.

The formula of a hydrogen molecule is H_2.
It is made of two hydrogen atoms bonded together.

molecule diagram	formula
H—H	H_2

The formula of hydrogen chloride is HCl.
It is made of one atom of hydrogen and one atom of chlorine bonded together.

molecule diagram	formula
H—Cl	HCl

If the molecule of a compound contains different numbers of atoms inside it, write the numbers of each element in small letters after each symbol in the formula.

The formula of water is H_2O.
It has two atoms of hydrogen and one atom of oxygen bonded together. See how the '2' comes after the 'H' in H_2O.

molecule diagram	formula
H—O—H	H_2O

The formula $(NH_4)_2SO_4$ looks more complicated. It is made of two atoms of N, eight atoms of H, one atom of S and four atoms of O.

Now do this

1. Copy and complete this table for the following compounds:
   HCl, H_2O, CH_4, $AlCl_3$, H_2SO_4, $C_6H_{12}O_6$.

Formula	Number of atoms in the formula	Number of different elements

2. Write down the formula of the hydrogen sulphide molecule shown in this diagram: H—S—H

3. Write down the formula of ammonia shown in this diagram:
   H
    \\N—H
   H

4. Write down the formulae for the following metal compounds:
   magnesium chloride (Mg Cl Cl), iron oxide (Fe Fe O O O).
   (the chemical bonds are not shown)

Introducing chemistry

What is a chemical equation?

A chemical equation tells us what happens in a chemical reaction. The chemicals at the start are the **reactants**, and they change into the **products**.

Nothing is left over at the end.

sodium	+	chlorine	→	sodium chloride
reactant	+	reactant	→	product

In this reaction two chemicals have turned into one product chemical. All the atoms inside the two reactants are now inside the product chemical.

Balancing equations

All the atoms inside the reactant molecules end up inside the product molecules, so equations always have the same number of atoms on each side of the equation sign.

For example, hydrogen gas and chlorine gas will react with each other.

hydrogen + chlorine → hydrogen chloride

The symbol equation *might* look like this

$H_2 + Cl_2 \rightarrow HCl$ ✗

This means that there are two atoms of hydrogen and two of chlorine on the left, but only one of each on the right.

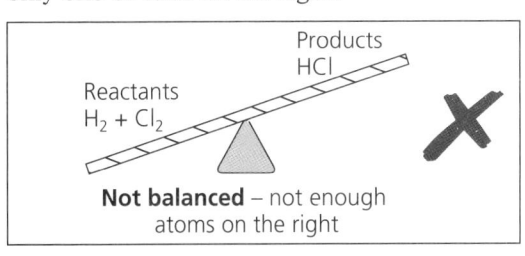

To balance this up we make sure that all the atoms of hydrogen and chlorine are used.

$H_2 + Cl_2 \rightarrow 2HCl$ ✓

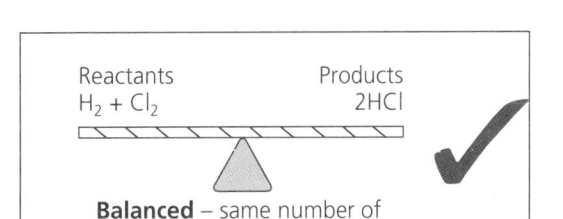

Reactants $H_2 + Cl_2$ — Products HCl
Not balanced – not enough atoms on the right ✗

Reactants $H_2 + Cl_2$ — Products 2HCl
Balanced – same number of atoms on each side ✓

Now do this

5. Copy each equation, then write down all the atoms of each element on **a** the reactant side **b** the product side. State whether the equation balances.
   $Mg + O_2 \rightarrow 2MgO$
   $CH_4 + 2O_2 \rightarrow CO_2 + 2H_2O$

6. Copy and complete these equations – there is a line for each missing number.
   $H_2 + Cl_2 \rightarrow \underline{\ \ }HCl$
   $Mg + \underline{\ \ }HCl \rightarrow MgCl_2 + H_2$
   $C_3H_8 + 5O_2 \rightarrow \underline{\ \ }CO_2 + \underline{\ \ }H_2O$
   $C_2H_4 + \underline{\ \ }O_2 \rightarrow 2CO_2 + 2H_2O$

Warning
You can only change the numbers *in front of* a formula. Never change any other numbers in the equation!

Rates of reactions

Chemical reactions happen at different speeds. You can see some of them around you. Rusting is a slow chemical reaction. Burning is a fast chemical reaction. Explosions are even faster! The speed of a reaction is called its **rate**.

Speeding up reactions

Reactions happen when reactant particles collide and turn into products. Most ways of speeding up reactions make the particles collide more often – there are more collisions per second; the frequency of the collisions increases. There are several ways of making a reaction go faster.

- Increase the **temperature**. Reactant particles move faster, so there are more collisions per second. They also hit each other harder because they have more energy, so there is more chance of each collision causing a reaction.

  Sodium thiosulphate solution ('thio') goes cloudy with dilute acid. If you warm the liquids the reaction will go faster.

- Increase the **concentration**. This only works with a solution! Increasing the concentration makes the particles closer together, so there are more collisions per second.

  'Thio' goes cloudy more quickly when it is more concentrated.

- If one of the reactants is a solid, you can break it down into smaller lumps. This increases the **surface area**, giving more places for reactions to happen. There will be more collisions per second.

  Large marble chips react slowly with acid. If you use smaller marble chips with acid the reaction will go faster.

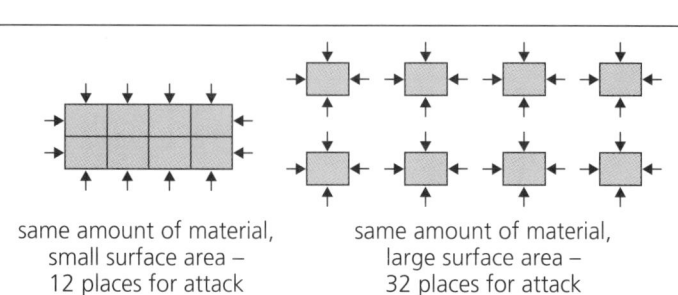

- Use a **catalyst**. Catalysts speed up a reaction. They are only needed in small amounts and are not used up by the reaction. Catalysts can be re-used. Different reactions need different catalysts to speed them up.

Hydrogen peroxide slowly breaks down into water and oxygen:

hydrogen peroxide	→	water	+	oxygen
$2H_2O_2$	→	$2H_2O$	+	O_2

To speed this up you can add manganese dioxide as a catalyst. All the manganese dioxide is left in the beaker at the end, and it can be used again.

> Energy is needed to break the bonds to allow the reaction to take place.
>
> The higher the temperature, the more particles that have enough energy to break bonds.

look down here (wear goggles!)
thio and acid go cloudy
mark on paper disappears

particles far apart, few collisions per second
particles close, many collisions per second

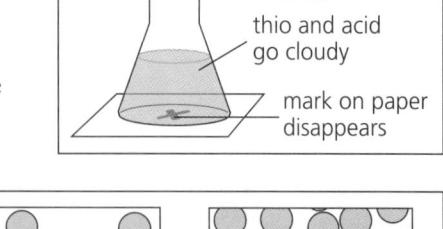

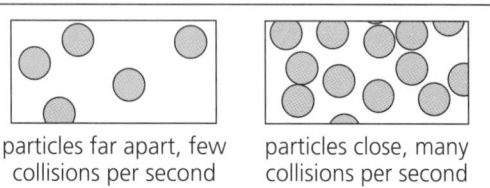

same amount of material, small surface area – 12 places for attack
same amount of material, large surface area – 32 places for attack

> **How does a catalyst work?**
> Reactant particles stick to the surface of the catalyst.
>
> The catalyst holds the particles close to each other and the right way round for them to react. Once they have reacted they break away from the catalyst, leaving spaces for more particles to stick to the catalyst and react.

Measuring the speed of a reaction

The easiest way to measure the speed of a reaction is to find out how fast one of the products is made.

For example, when marble chips react with acid you can measure the amount of carbon dioxide gas given off every minute. You can do this with a large syringe, or by catching the gas in a test tube.

Reactions always start fast, and then slow down as the reactant chemicals are used up.

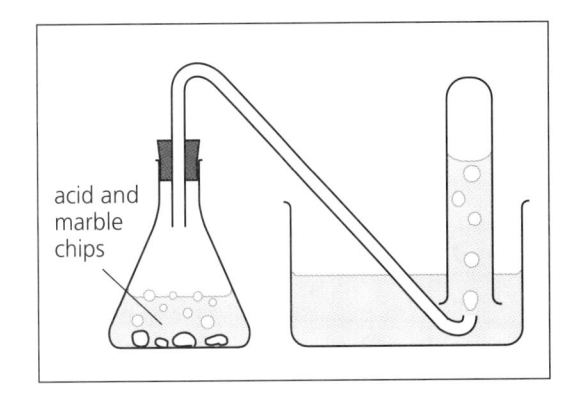

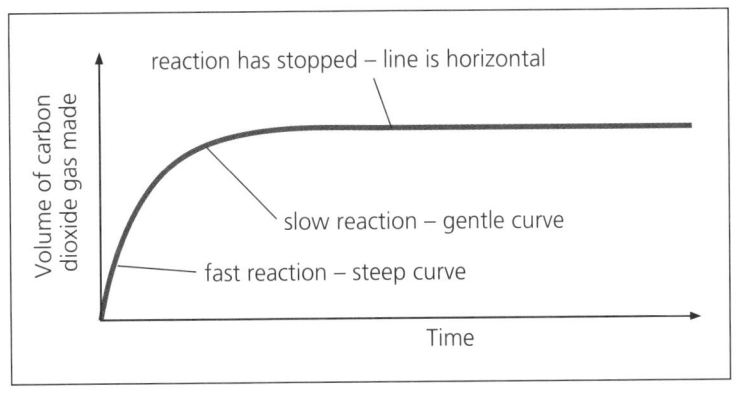

Reactions carry on until one of the reactants runs out.

Making more product?

Increasing the speed of a reaction will not make more product. It just means that the reaction finishes more quickly. The only way to make more product is to use more reactants.

Now do this

1. Give **three** ways of speeding up the reaction between an acid solution and a solid carbonate.
2. Which method will still work for a reaction between an acid solution and a carbonate solution?

   This graph shows the way the mass of marble chips changes during a reaction with acid.

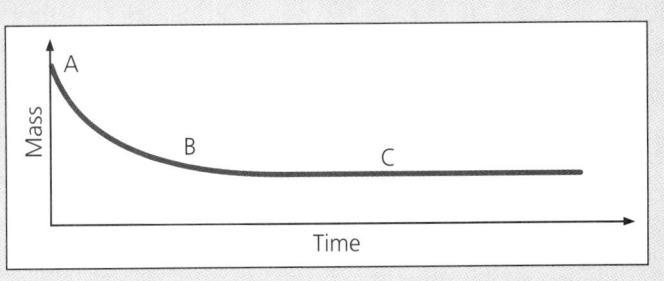

3. Which letter shows where the reaction is fastest? Explain why.
4. Which letter shows where the reaction has stopped?

Energy and reactions

Most chemical reactions transfer energy. The energy can be transferred in different ways – heat and light when something burns; sound when marble chips react with acid; electricity from the chemicals inside a battery.

Exothermic and endothermic reactions

Reactions which get hot are **exothermic**; they are giving out energy. The chemicals end up with less energy because they have given out heat.

Reactions which get colder are called **endothermic**; they take in energy from the surroundings. The chemicals end up with more energy because they turn heat from the surroundings into energy inside the chemicals.

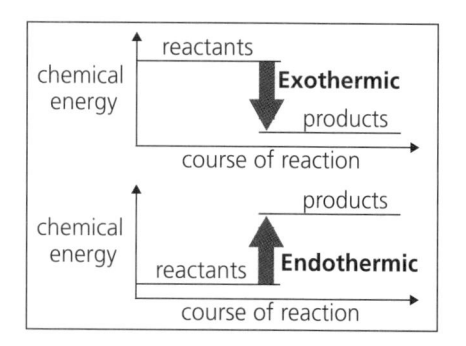

Bond making and breaking

When compounds react the first thing that they do is to split into their atoms. Then the atoms join together again to make different compounds. To pull the atoms away from each other the bonds have to be broken. When the atoms join back together, new bonds are made.

Energy has to be put *in* to *break* the bonds – this is an endothermic process.

Energy is given *out* when bonds are *made* – this is an exothermic process.

If more energy is taken in than given out, the whole reaction is endothermic.

If more energy is given out than is taken in, the whole reaction is exothermic.

Using bond energies to calculate the energy transfer in a reaction

$$CH_4 + 2Cl_2 \rightarrow C + 4HCl$$

Write out all the bonds in the equation. Calculate the energy needed to break all the bonds in the reactant molecules: calculate the energy released on making all the bonds in the products.

The energy transferred in this reaction is 2712 − 1728 = 984 kJ
The reaction took in more energy than it gave out, so it is endothermic.

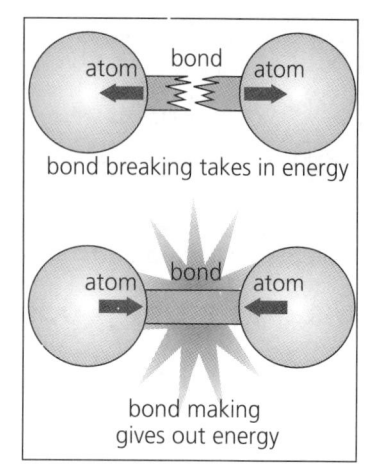

Bonds broken
4 × C—H = 1740
4 × Cl—Cl = 972
Total = 2712

Bonds made
4 × H—Cl = 1728
Total = 1728

Now do this

$$CH_4 + Cl_2 \rightarrow CH_3Cl + HCl$$

H—C(—H)(—H)—H + Cl—Cl → H—C(—H)(—H)—Cl + H—Cl

1 a Calculate the total energy needed to break all the bonds.

b Calculate the total energy given out when bonds are made.

Bond	C—H	C—Cl	Cl—Cl	H—Cl
Energy to break the bond (kJ mol^{-1})	435	346	243	432

Earth and geological changes

Now do this

2 a Calculate the total energy transfer for the reaction in question 1.
  b Was the reaction exothermic or endothermic?

3 Calculate the energy transferred by 2.5 g of fuel if it will raise the temperature of 400 g of water by 4.5°C. (The specific heat capacity of water is 4.2 J/g°C.)

Energy and the environment

Burning hydrocarbon fuels produce two gases that cause a lot of pollution. One is carbon dioxide, the other is sulphur dioxide. Carbon dioxide is a major cause of the greenhouse effect.

The greenhouse effect

Ultraviolet rays from the Sun go through the Earth's atmosphere and heat up the Earth's surface. The heated Earth gives off infra-red radiation, which leaves the Earth. Greenhouse gases in the atmosphere trap some of the infra-red radiation and stop its energy getting out. This means that the Earth gets warmer still.

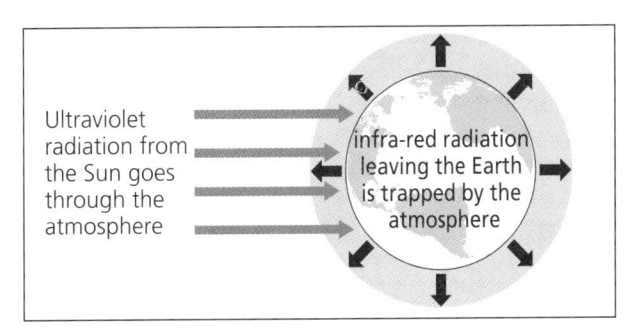

Ultraviolet radiation from the Sun goes through the atmosphere

infra-red radiation leaving the Earth is trapped by the atmosphere

The major greenhouse gas is carbon dioxide. Because we burn millions of tonnes of oil and coal every year carbon dioxide is being produced faster than it is being removed. This is slowly making the Earth warmer. Another greenhouse gas is methane, which is produced by farm animals and rotting vegetation.

Sulphur dioxide and acid rain

Fossil fuels such as coal and oil contain small amounts of sulphur. Sulphur turns into sulphur oxides when the fuel burns. These oxides dissolve in rain water to make several acids, including sulphuric acid. This makes acid rain. Acid rain can corrode buildings. It also changes the soil slightly, which harms animals and plants.

sulphur dioxide

acid rain

Now do this

4 Copy and complete the following sentences:
When carbon compounds burn, _____ gas is formed. This affects the temperature of the Earth, so it is called a _____ gas. It lets _____ radiation from the Sun through the atmosphere but it won't let _____ radiation from the Earth back out again. Fossil fuels also contain small quantities of sulphur. This produces _____ when it burns, which causes acid rain.

Air, oceans and the carbon cycle

Air is a mixture of gases

Oxygen is one of the two most important gases in air, but it does not make up a large amount of the air. The air is made of approximately
- 80% nitrogen – which does very little
- 20% oxygen – a most important gas
- small amounts of other gases, including
- 0.04% carbon dioxide – the other important gas, even though there is only a very small amount of it.

The atmosphere also contains large amounts of water vapour, but the amount changes with the weather.

The amounts of nitrogen and oxygen are approximately constant because they are being made at about the same rate as they are being used up. The amount of carbon dioxide is also approximately constant. We think that it is increasing *very* slowly, because it is being made slightly faster than it is being used up.

What happens to the carbon dioxide?

Carbon dioxide from the atmosphere is taken in by plants during photosynthesis. When the animals eat the plants, carbon goes from the plants to the animals. When plants and animals respire and when plants such as trees burn, carbon dioxide goes back into the atmosphere. If the animals or plants turn into fossil fuels, such as coal and oil, the fuel forms carbon dioxide when it burns. If the animals form rocks, such as chalk, their carbon is locked away in the rock.

Test for carbon dioxide
Carbon dioxide turns lime water milky.

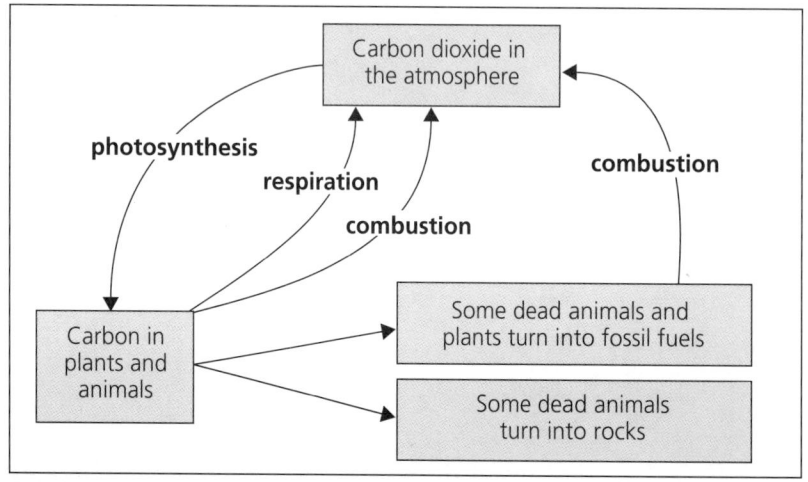

Now do this

1. What are the **two** main processes that put carbon dioxide into the atmosphere?
2. What is the main process that takes carbon dioxide out of the atmosphere?

Earth and geological changes

Where did the air come from?

Billions of years ago there was no oxygen in the Earth's atmosphere. Life did not exist. The atmosphere was formed by volcanoes, which were producing ammonia, methane, carbon dioxide and water.

Three billion years ago the first simple plant life appeared. The plants turned the carbon dioxide and water into food and oxygen – photosynthesis had started.

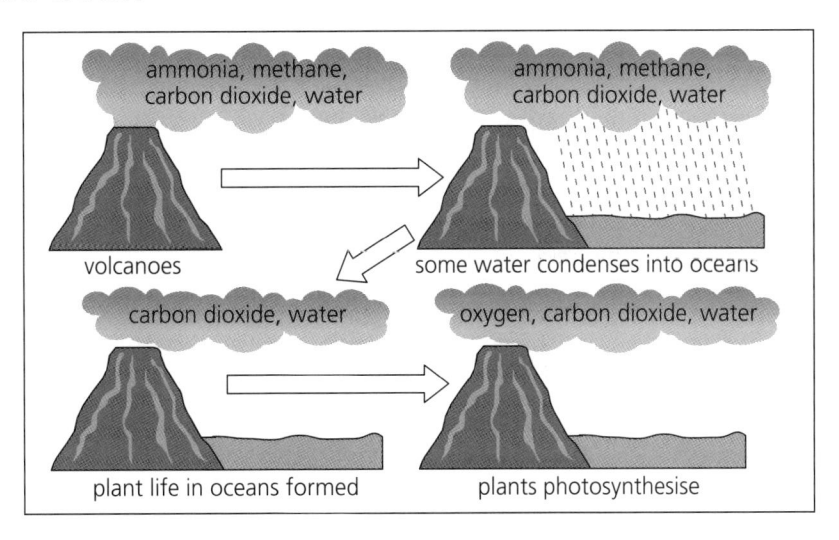

The amount of oxygen in the atmosphere increased, and the different types of living things increased, until the living things were using up the oxygen as fast as it was being made. This now keeps the amount of oxygen constant.

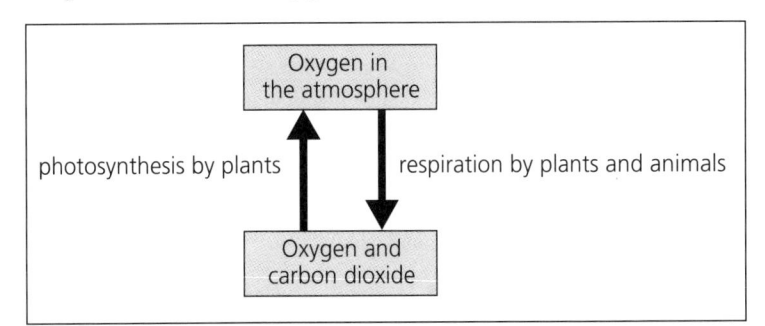

As first, all the oxygen produced by the plants reacted with iron in the rocks.

Once all the iron had reacted with oxygen, oxygen started going into the atmosphere.

Salts are being washed into the seas by rivers.

Salts are removed from the seas
- by chemical reaction to make sea-floor sediments
- by animals using the chemicals to make their shells.

In some very hot areas the seas evaporate and salts crystallise out to form salt deposits.

Where did the oceans come from?

When the Earth formed there was steam coming out of volcanoes. As the Earth cooled the steam condensed and turned into rain, which formed the oceans. The rain dissolved chemicals out of the rocks, so sea water contains a mixture of different salts dissolved in it.

Now do this

3 Copy and complete the following sentences:

The atmosphere is made of _____% nitrogen, _____% oxygen and _____% carbon dioxide. Plants produce _____ gas during photosynthesis; it is needed for respiration and things burn in it. Respiration is similar to burning because they both produce _____ gas. The amounts of carbon dioxide and oxygen in the atmosphere stay fairly constant because the rate of photosynthesis is balanced by _____ and _____.

The Earth's crust

What is the Earth made of?

The top layer of the Earth is a thin rocky **crust**.

The **mantle** is under the crust. It is made of very hot solid rock that can slowly move.

It can melt into **magma**.

In the middle of the Earth is the **core**. The Earth's core is even hotter and is liquid.

Plate tectonics

The shapes of the continents of Africa and South America fit together like a jigsaw. They have similar rocks and fossils on the coasts that face each other. This is because they were once joined together.

The thin rocky crust of the Earth is made up of large sections called **plates** which, because they have a lower density, float on top of the mantle. Heat from the core creates convection currents within the mantle. These currents move the plates slowly across the Earth's surface. Plates travel a few centimetres each year.

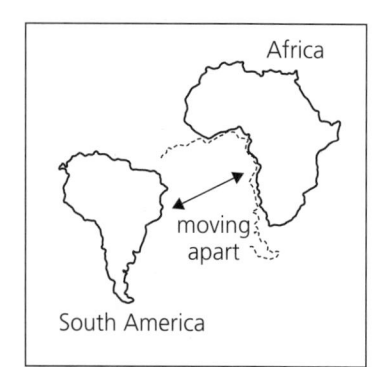

The plates may be moving away from each other, or into each other. The forces created where the plates move against each other are so strong that the edges of the plates are marked by earthquakes, volcanoes and mountain ranges.

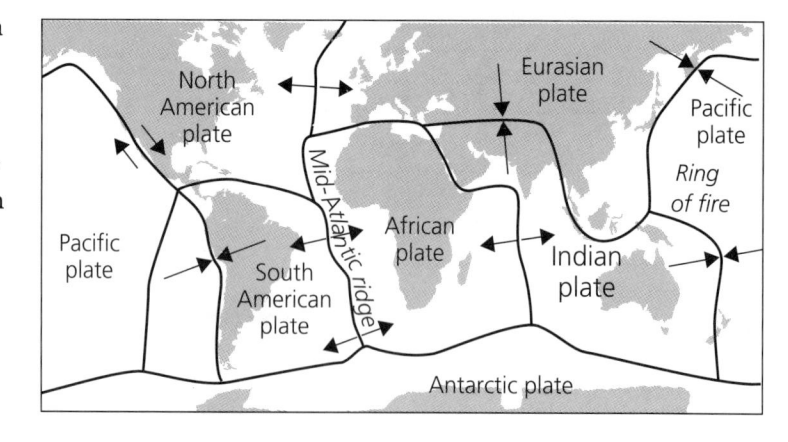

Now do this

The Pacific Plate is surrounded by a ring of volcanoes called 'The ring of fire'.

1. Find the volcanoes on the map.
2. How far are the volcanoes from the edges of the plates?
3. How far are the earthquake zones from the edges of the plates?

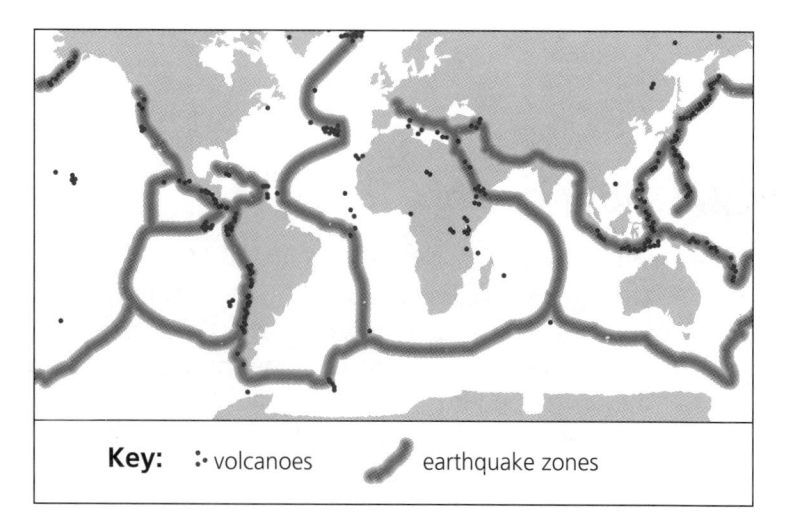

Key: ∴ volcanoes   earthquake zones

Earth and geological changes

What happens when plates move together?

When two plates collide, one plate is forced underneath the other; this is called **subduction**. As the plate is pushed down into the mantle the rock melts. This causes earthquakes and volcanoes. Rocks on the surface get pushed up into mountain ranges.

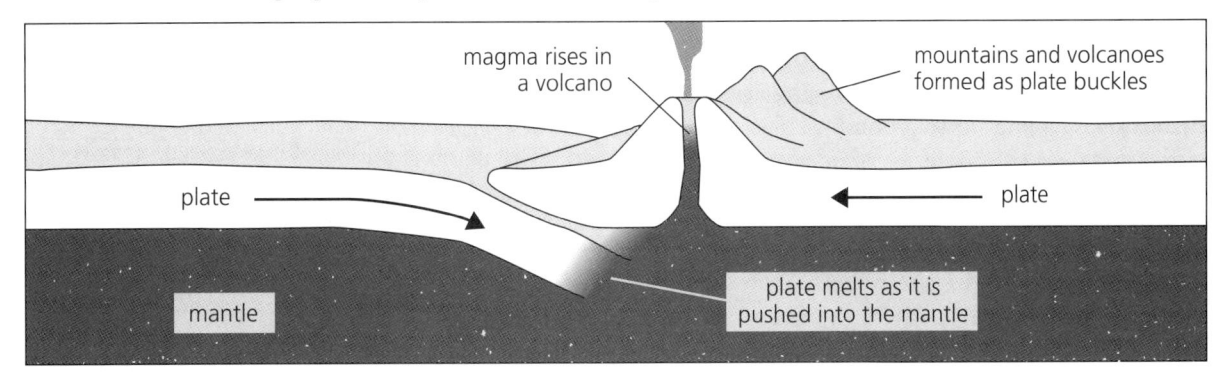

What happens when plates move apart?

The Atlantic Ocean is getting wider by at least a centimetre every year. This is because the plates under the ocean are moving apart, leaving a gap down the centre of the ocean floor. Magma flows into the gap, making a ridge of new igneous rocks. This is called **sea floor spreading**. There are earthquakes and sometimes volcanoes.

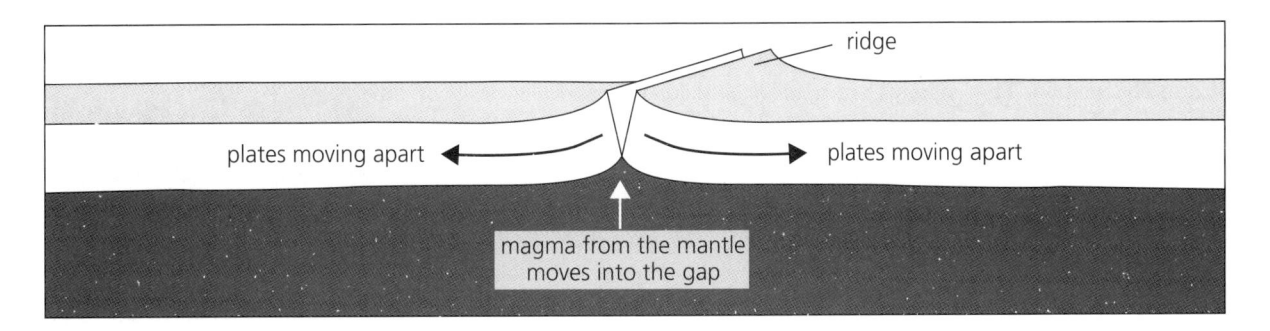

Scientists first realised that the sea floor was spreading when they found out that as you go further from the ridge the rocks get older.

Now do this

4 When two plates push into each other, one plate stays on the surface and the other plate disappears.
 a Where does this plate go?
 b What happens to the rocks of the plate that disappears?

5 What happens to the age of the rocks as you move away from a place where the sea floor is spreading?

If an oceanic plate collides with a continental plate, the oceanic plate goes underneath because it is more dense.

Rocks and the rock cycle

There are three types of rock – igneous, sedimentary and metamorphic.

Rock forms

Igneous rocks are made from magma which has cooled down and solidified. It usually forms interlocking crystals of different **minerals**. Cooling underground is slow. This produces a rock with large crystals, e.g. granite. Cooling at the surface is rapid. This produces a rock with small crystals, e.g. basalt.

Sedimentary rocks are small pieces of older rock, e.g. sand or mud, which settle and form sediments. The sharp edges of these pieces are usually worn away by the rivers which bring them down to the sea. As layers of sediment build up, the lowest sediments are compressed by the weight of the layers above them, which helps turn the lowest layers into solid rock. Often, chemicals soaking through the sediments will also cement the grains together into a solid.

Examples of sedimentary rock are: shale, which is made from mud; conglomerate, which is made from pebbles; sandstone, which is made from grains of sand. Sedimentary rocks can also be made from bits of animal or plant, e.g. limestone is made from seashells, and coal is made from prehistoric trees. Rock salt is made when seawater evaporates and leaves the salt behind.

Metamorphic rocks are rocks which have changed after they were originally formed. The changes are usually caused by high temperature or by pressure from other rocks. The final rock depends on what you start with and what happened to it. Marble and slate are metamorphic rocks. Both started as sedimentary rocks: marble as limestone and slate as shale.

What to look for

- Igneous – look for interlocking crystals, or glassy rock.
- Sedimentary – look for layers, bits of older rock grains and pebbles; some types may have fossils in them.
- Metamorphic – look for distorted grains, or distorted fossils.

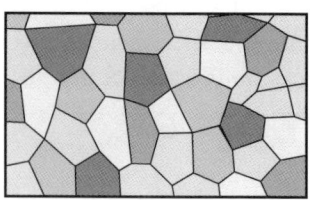

Igneous – slow cooling large interlocking crystals

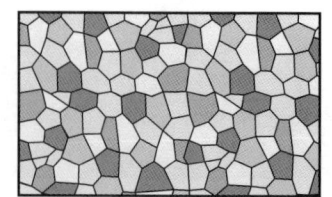

Igneous – rapid cooling small interlocking crystals

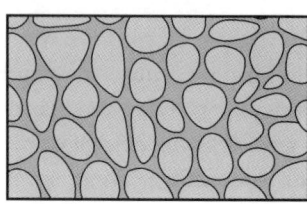

Sedimentary – rounded grains and fossils

Rocks which cool slowly deep underground are called **intrusive igneous rocks**. Granite is a typical intrusive igneous rock made from a high-viscosity magma which formed large crystals of mainly light-coloured minerals.

Rocks which cool rapidly near the surface are called **extrusive igneous rocks**. Basalt is a typical extrusive igneous rock made from a low-viscosity magma which formed small crystals of mainly dark-coloured minerals.

Slate, marble, schist and gneiss are examples of metamorphic rocks.

Now do this

1   Copy and complete the following sentences:
    Granite rock is made from magma which cools underground. This means that it will have _____ size crystals. It is a _____ type of rock. If rocks are then put under great pressure or temperature they will change to _____ rock.

Earth and geological changes

The rock cycle

Rocks on the surface of the Earth are continually being broken down into pieces. This is called **weathering**. One type of weathering happens when rocks get very hot, then very cold, as in a desert. This makes them expand and contract until they shatter. This is called **exfoliation**.

Another type of weathering happens when water gets into cracks in the rock and freezes. The water expands when it freezes and splits the rock. This is called **freeze-thaw**.

The pieces are then carried away by the wind or by streams and rivers. This is called **transportation**. The pieces hit each other as they move and their jagged edges are rounded off.

Eventually the pieces settle, are buried, and solidify into layers of **sedimentary rock**. Earth movements can then bring the rock back to the surface so that it is weathered all over again.

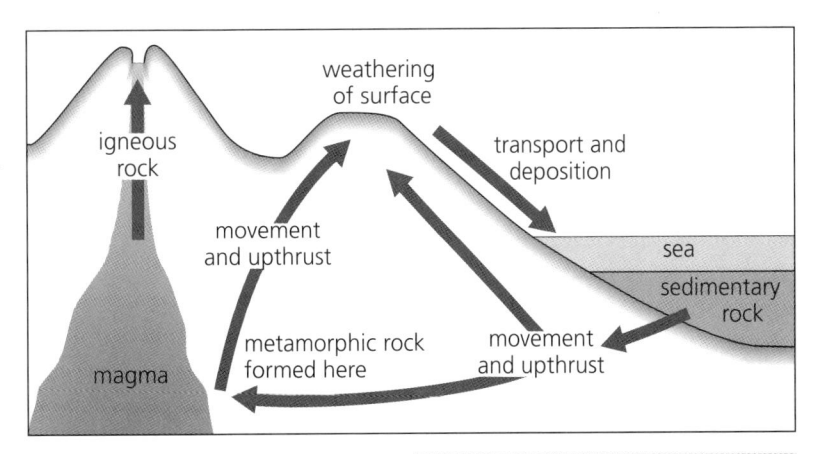

Earth movements can bring any of the three types of rock up to the surface, where they will be weathered and eventually form sedimentary rock.

The age of sedimentary rocks

Usually the oldest rocks form the bottom layer and the youngest rocks form the top layer.

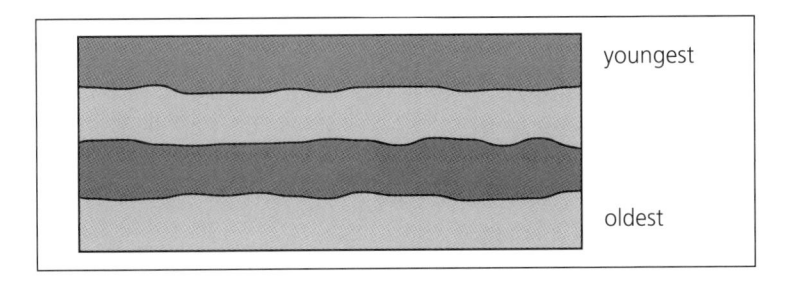

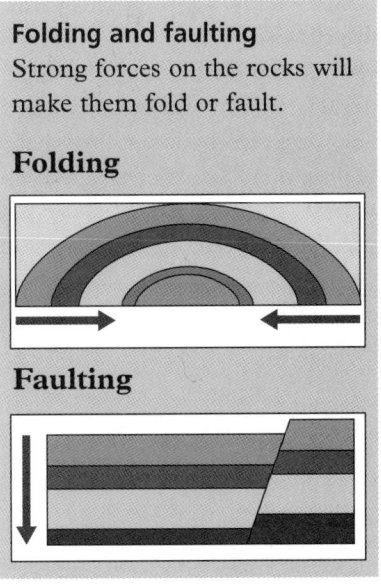

Folding and faulting

Strong forces on the rocks will make them fold or fault.

Folding

Faulting

Now do this

2   Copy and complete the following sentences:
    Rocks on the surface are slowly broken into small pieces. This is called _____. The pieces are carried to the sea where they settle and turn into _____ rock. If that rock is put under great pressure or temperature it will change into _____ rock. It can appear back on the Earth's surface because of _____.

Rock products – oil

The rocks of the Earth's crust are very useful to us, for example rock formations contain oil and gas.

Oil and natural gas

When microscopic sea creatures die, some of them settle to the sea bed and are covered in sediment, which eventually turns to rock. The solid sediments keep out air, and the pressure and temperature (90–120°C) of the layers of rock forms oil from the dead creatures. The oil soaks up through the rocks until it reaches a layer that it can't soak through (**non-permeable rock**). If that layer of non-permeable rock is the right shape (an oil trap), the oil will stay in the rocks just under the layer.

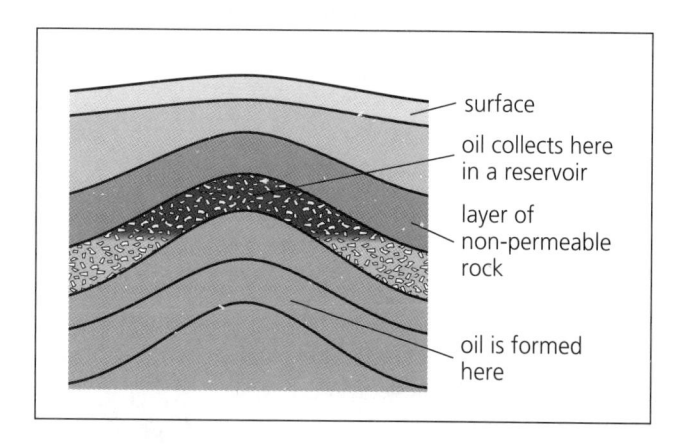

Separating oil products

Crude oil is a mixture of liquids which boil at different temperatures. These liquids can be separated by **fractional distillation**. The crude oil is boiled and the mixture of vapours sent up the fractionating column. The column gets cooler nearer the top. As each vapour reaches the part of the column that is just below its own boiling point, that vapour will condense. The highest boiling point liquids condense low down the column where it is hottest, and the lowest boiling point liquids rise up to the cooler part. The column has an exit point for each liquid.

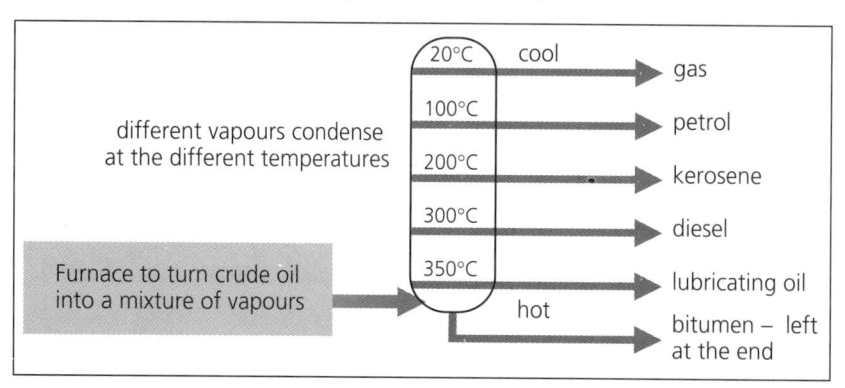

The boiling points of larger molecules are higher because they have more weak forces between them. It takes a higher temperature to overcome these forces and boil the liquid.

Now do this

1 What are the boiling points of diesel, petrol and kerosene?

2 Why does petrol leave the fractionating column higher up than kerosene?

3 Why does diesel have a higher boiling point than petrol?

Burning oil

Crude oil is mainly made of **hydrocarbons**. These are molecules made of hydrogen and carbon only. They have different numbers of carbon atoms inside their molecules.

One group of hydrocarbons is called the **alkanes**. Here are the first five alkanes.

methane, CH_4	ethane, C_2H_6	propane, C_3H_8	butane, C_4H_{10}	pentane, C_5H_{12}

Some hydrocarbons are used to make other substances such as plastics, but most are burned as a fuel because they transfer a lot of energy.
- Methane is natural gas – used for heating, cooking and in Bunsen burners.
- Propane and butane are used for heating and for camping gas stoves.
- Paraffin is used for heating and for lamps.
- Petrol and diesel are used as fuels for transport.

What happens in burning

When something reacts with oxygen to make an oxide we say that it has been **oxidised**. This is an **oxidation** reaction.

When a hydrocarbon burns with plenty of oxygen
- the hydrogen atoms form water
- the carbon atoms form carbon dioxide.

The reaction for methane burning in a gas cooker is:

$$CH_4 + 2O_2 \rightarrow CO_2 + 2H_2O$$
methane + oxygen → carbon dioxide + water

Beware If there is not enough oxygen in the room, the hydrogen part of the methane molecule reacts as normal but the carbon forms carbon monoxide instead of carbon dioxide. Carbon monoxide is poisonous and will kill you. Gas cookers and some gas fires are only safe if the room is well ventilated.

$$CH_4 + 1\tfrac{1}{2}O_2 \rightarrow CO + 2H_2O$$
methane + oxygen → carbon monoxide + water

A better way of writing this is

$$2CH_4 + 3O_2 \rightarrow 2CO + 4H_2O$$

If the oxygen levels drop further, the hydrogen atoms in the methane still react to make water but the carbon stops burning. It forms soot.

$$CH_4 + O_2 \rightarrow C + 2H_2O$$

Now do this

4. Propane is a hydrocarbon. Write a word equation to show what happens when propane burns in oxygen.

5. Propane has the formula C_3H_8. Write a balanced symbol equation to show what happens when propane burns in oxygen.

6. Pentane has the formula C_5H_{12}. Write a balanced symbol equation to show what happens when pentane burns in oxygen.

Rock products – metal ores

We can dig some rocks out of the ground and use them straight away to make useful substances, such as pottery from clay, cement from limestone (calcium carbonate), glass from sand (silicon oxide), and chlorine from salt (sodium chloride).

Minerals and ores

Most rocks can't be used straight away. The useful part of the rock, the **mineral**, is usually mixed in with other bits of rock that we don't want. This combination of mineral and other rock is called an **ore**. Sometimes the mineral is the metal element itself, such as gold, but usually the mineral is a metal combined with other elements such as oxygen or sulphur. For example, iron oxide is the mineral in some types of iron ore.

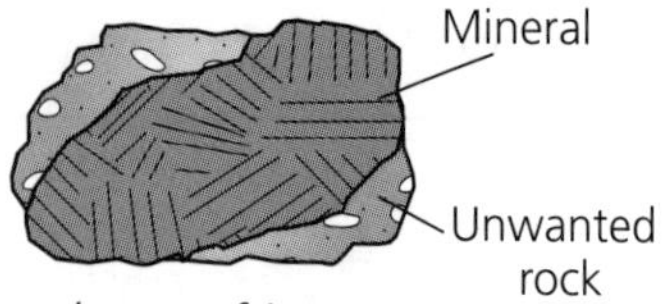

a lump of iron ore

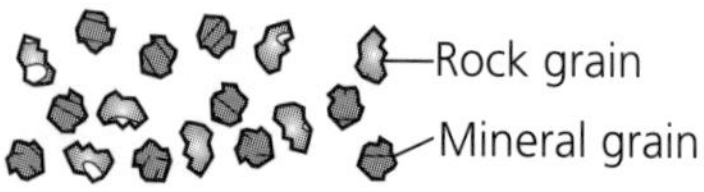

mineral grains from the ore

Reducing the ore

Once the ore has been extracted, we have to get the oxygen away from the metal. Removal of oxygen is called **reduction**. If a metal is not very reactive it is easy to **reduce** the oxide. Reactive metals form bonds with oxygen that are hard to break, so it is difficult to reduce them.

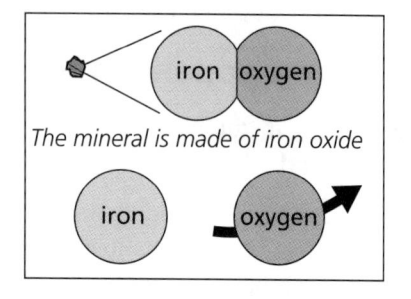

Sodium, calcium, magnesium and zinc are all very reactive. They will all bond tightly with oxygen from the air, they all give off hydrogen with water and with acids. Sodium and calcium are so reactive that it is too dangerous to put them with acids!

Less reactive metals such as copper and silver don't react with water or acids, so copper is used to make water pipes and silver is used for jewellery.

The mineral is made of iron oxide

Metals reacting with other compounds

Aluminium is more reactive than iron, so it can steal oxygen out of iron oxide. It reduces iron oxide.

aluminium + iron oxide → aluminium oxide + iron

Carbon is more reactive than iron and zinc, so carbon will take oxygen out of iron oxide and also out of zinc oxide, it reduces iron oxide and zinc oxide.

Zinc is more reactive than copper, so it can steal the sulphate out of copper sulphate solution and leave the copper behind. This is called **displacement**.

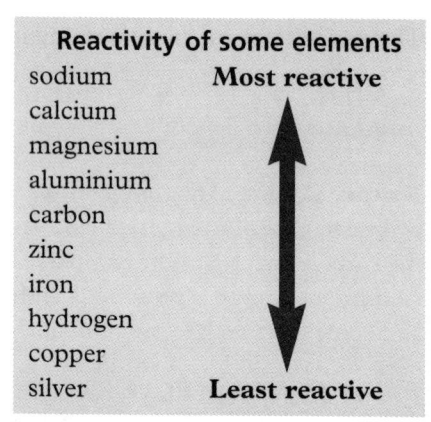

Reactivity of some elements

sodium — **Most reactive**
calcium
magnesium
aluminium
carbon
zinc
iron
hydrogen
copper
silver — **Least reactive**

zinc	+	copper sulphate	→	zinc sulphate	+	copper
grey metal		blue solution		colourless solution		red metal

Now do this

1. Copy and complete the following equation:
   zinc + copper oxide →
   _____ + _____

2. Which of these will hydrogen react with? iron oxide, copper oxide, silver oxide. What will be formed in the cases that do react?

Using the Earth's resources

Carbon as a reducing agent

Carbon is a very useful substance for taking oxygen away from (reducing) metal oxides. It is more reactive than iron and copper, which we have to extract in very large quantities. This means that carbon can take iron out of iron ore. Carbon also has the advantage of being fairly cheap.

Extracting iron

Iron is extracted from iron ore using carbon in a blast furnace. The carbon is converted into carbon monoxide inside the blast furnace, and it is the carbon monoxide which actually does the reduction.

Iron ore and coke are put in through the top of the furnace and air is pumped in through the holes at the side. So much heat is given out in this reaction that the iron melts and collects at the bottom of the furnace. Limestone is used to react with impurities in the iron ore and turn them into liquid slag. The slag floats on top of the iron and is drained out of the furnace before the liquid iron is run out.

Carbon and oxygen form carbon monoxide:

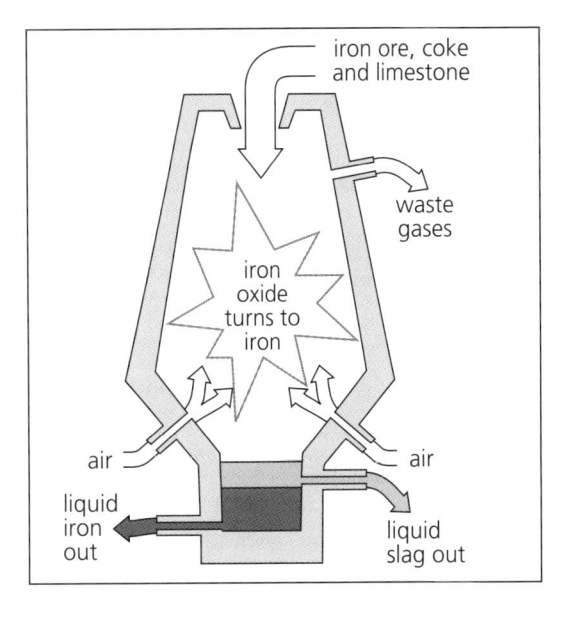

$$2C + O_2 \rightarrow 2CO$$
carbon + oxygen → carbon monoxide

Carbon monoxide reduces the iron oxide:

$$3CO + Fe_2O_3 \rightarrow 2Fe + 3CO_2$$
carbon monoxide + iron oxide → iron + carbon dioxide

Now do this

3 Metal C will take the oxygen from the oxide of metal A.
Metal B will take the oxygen from the oxide of metal D.
Metal A will take the oxygen from the oxide of metal B.
Put the metals in order of reactivity, starting with the most reactive.

4 aluminium + iron oxide → aluminium oxide + iron
Which substance has been reduced?
Which substance has been oxidised?

5 What do we call the reaction that takes oxygen away from something?

6 Carbon will take oxygen from copper oxide. Write a word equation for this.

7 a Which would you expect to corrode in air more quickly, iron or zinc?
   b Explain why.

Ions and electrolysis

Atoms are neutral. An atom can become electrically charged, but as soon as this happens it is called an **ion**. Atoms turn into ions by gaining electrons or by losing electrons.

> If an atom **gains electrons** it becomes a **negative ion**.
> If an atom **gives away electrons** it becomes a **positive ion**.

A chlorine atom gains one electron, forming a chloride ion	Cl →	Cl⁻
An oxygen atom gains two electrons, forming an oxide ion	O →	O⁻⁻
A sodium atom gives away one electron, forming a sodium ion	Na →	Na⁺
A calcium atom gives away two electrons, forming a calcium ion	Ca →	Ca⁺⁺

Ionic compounds and electric current – electrolysis

Ionic compounds do not conduct electricity when they are solid but they will conduct electricity if they are melted or dissolved. Ionic solids don't conduct electricity because the particles in a solid are held in one place. In liquids the ions can move, so they can carry the charge through the liquid. Ionic liquids are called **electrolytes**.

Ions are attracted by the oppositely charged electrode. The **cathode** is negative; it attracts positive ions. When the positive ions reach the cathode they pick up electrons from the cathode and turn into neutral atoms.

The **anode** is positive; it attracts negative ions. When negative ions reach the anode they usually give their extra electrons to the anode and turn into neutral atoms.

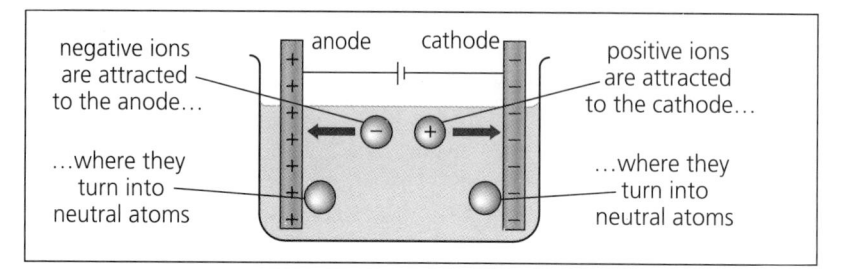

negative ions are attracted to the anode... ...where they turn into neutral atoms

positive ions are attracted to the cathode... ...where they turn into neutral atoms

Now do this

1. Metals give away electrons. What sort of charges do their ions have?
2. Some non-metals can gain electrons. What sort of charges do their ions have?
3. Magnesium atoms lose two electrons. Write the symbol for a magnesium ion.
4. Solid sodium chloride is ionic. Why doesn't it conduct electricity?
5. Which electrode will metals go towards during electrolysis?

Using the Earth's resources

Using electrolysis to extract aluminium

Aluminium ore contains aluminium oxide. Aluminium is very reactive (it bonds tightly to oxygen), so carbon isn't reactive enough to take the oxygen away from the oxide. Instead we melt the aluminium oxide and then electrolyse it. Aluminium oxide melts at a high temperature, so we add a substance called cryolite which lowers the melting point and saves energy.

The sides and the bottom of the tank are lined with carbon. The carbon lining is connected to an electricity supply to make the cathode. The anodes are also made of carbon. They are lowered into the molten mixture of aluminium oxide and cryolite.

Aluminium ions are positive, so they are attracted to the negative cathode and are neutralised. Molten aluminium collects at the bottom of the tank. Oxygen is formed at the carbon anodes and then reacts with the anodes to make carbon dioxide.

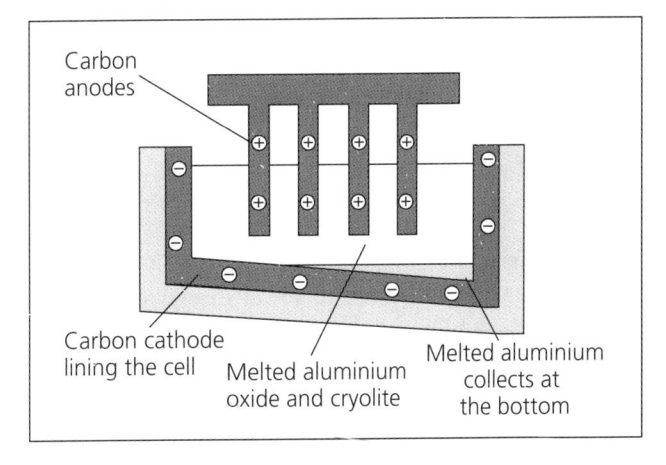

At the cathode
$Al^{+++} + 3e^- \rightarrow Al$

At the anode
$O^{--} \rightarrow O_2 + 2e^-$

Using electrolysis to purify or extract copper

The anode is the impure copper. The cathode is a pure copper plate. During electrolysis the copper dissolves from the impure anode and plates onto the cathode. The pure copper cathode becomes thicker as more copper plates onto it.

At the cathode
$Cu^{++} + 2e^- \rightarrow Cu$

At the anode
$Cu \rightarrow Cu^{++} + 2e^-$

Copper is sometimes extracted from boulders by this method. The impure copper boulder is the anode, a pure copper rod is the cathode.

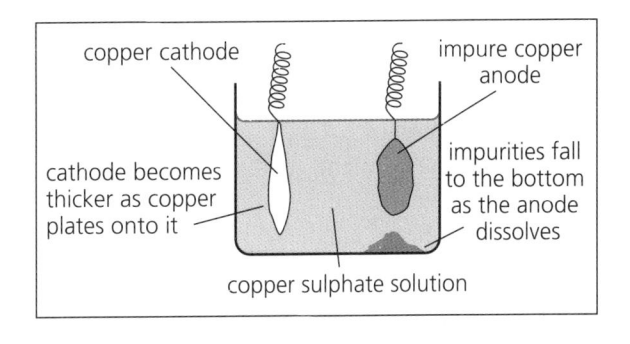

Now do this

6 What is the charge on
   a an anode?
   b a cathode?

7 Which electrode does aluminium collect at when aluminium oxide is electrolysed?

8 Which electrode does copper collect at when it is purified by electrolysis?

Bonding

Ionic bonding

Ions with opposite charges will hold each other together. This is **ionic bonding**.

We can use 'dot and cross' diagrams to show how these ions are made – this one is for sodium chloride, salt.

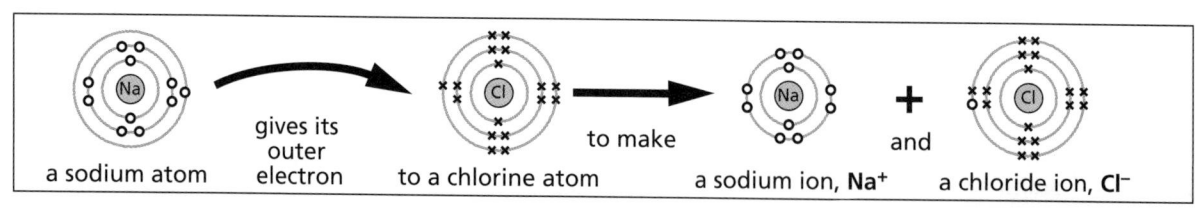

a sodium atom — gives its outer electron — to a chlorine atom — to make — a sodium ion, **Na⁺** — and — a chloride ion, **Cl⁻**

Ionic bonds are very strong forces. Substances with ionic bonds form enormous groups called **ionic giant structures**. Giant structures have high melting and boiling points because all the strong forces holding the particles together are dificult to overcome. Salt has a giant structure.

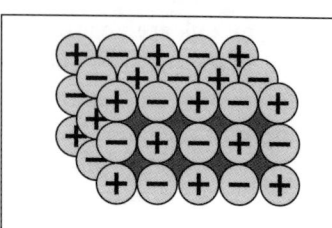

Covalent bonding

When non-metals react with each other they don't form ions, they share electrons instead. This is **covalent bonding**, and it is just as strong as ionic bonding.

The hydrogen molecule, H_2, has a single covalent bond. The outer shell of each hydrogen atom needs two electrons to make it stable.

hydrogen atoms have one electron in their outer shells → after bonding each outer shell is in contact with two electrons — or H—H

The chlorine molecule, Cl_2, also has a single covalent bond. The outer shell of each chlorine atom needs eight electrons to make it stable.

chlorine atoms have seven electrons in their outer shells → after bonding each outer shell is in contact with eight electrons — or Cl—Cl

The oxygen molecule, O_2, has a double covalent bond. The outer shell of each oxygen atom needs eight electrons to make it stable.

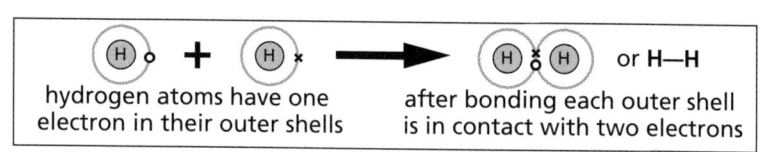

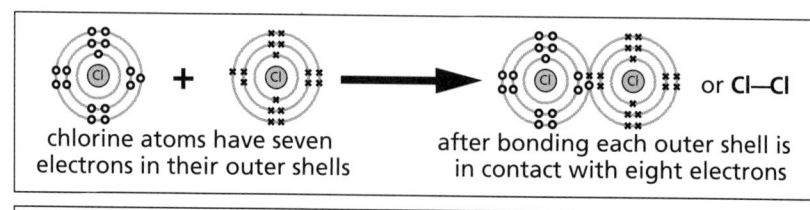

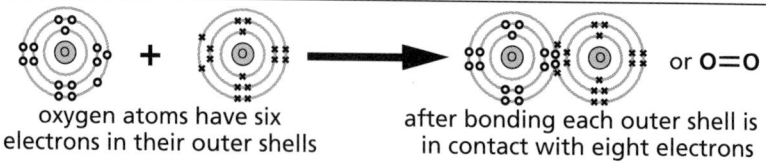

oxygen atoms have six electrons in their outer shells → after bonding each outer shell is in contact with eight electrons — or O=O

Now do this

1 Draw 'dot and cross' diagrams for the bonds in the following molecules:

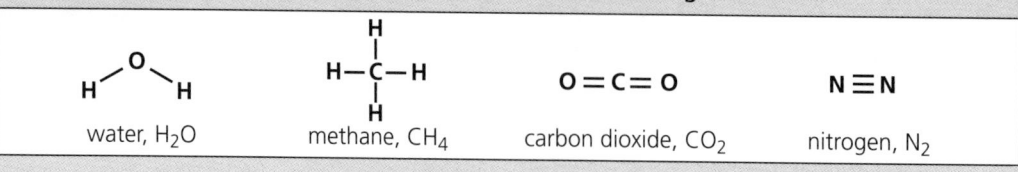

water, H_2O — methane, CH_4 — carbon dioxide, CO_2 — nitrogen, N_2

Carbon chemistry

Molecules and giants

Covalent compounds can form giant structures or they can form small molecules.

Covalent molecules

Molecules have strong covalent bonds inside them, but only very weak forces holding one molecule to another. The weak forces between molecules make it easy to separate molecules from each other; in other words they have low melting and boiling points.

Covalent giant structures

Sometimes all the atoms inside a structure are held together with covalent bonds, there are no weak forces. This makes a **covalent giant structure**. As the covalent bond is just as strong as the ionic bond, the structure will have very high melting and boiling points.

Carbon is special because it is an element that has three different forms; diamond, graphite and Buckminster Fullerene. Diamond and graphite are both covalent giant structures.

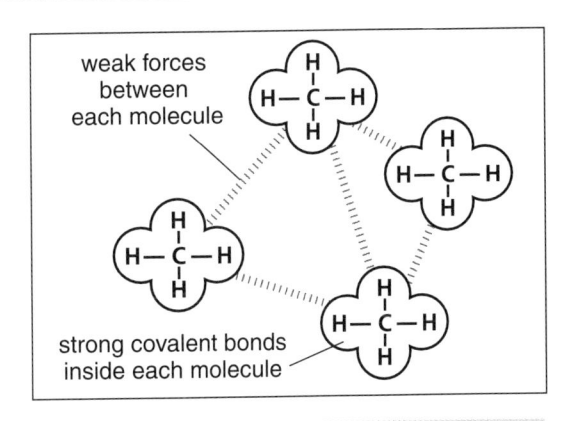

Metal elements are held together by a third type of strong force, **metallic bonding**. The metal atoms form ions in a sea of electrons which holds the whole structure together.

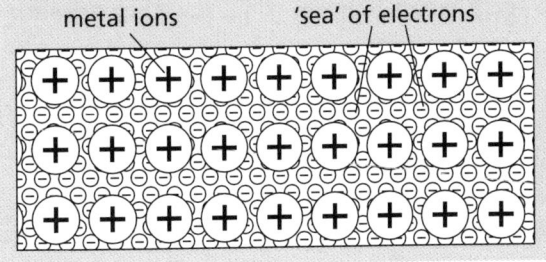

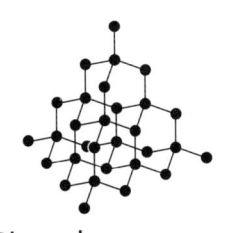

Diamond
covalent giant structure
hard
does not conduct electricity

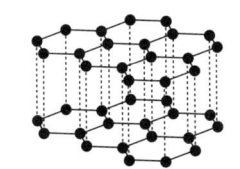

Graphite
covalent giant structure
soft
conducts electricity
weak forces *between* the layers allow the layers to slide

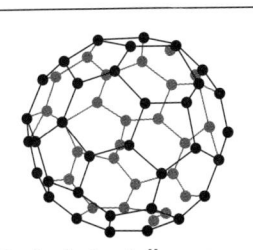

Buckminster Fullerene
Carbon atoms joined to make a microscopic football. This was only discovered in 1983

Covalent giant structure
- strong forces between molecules
- high melting/ boiling points

Ionic giant structure
- strong forces between molecules
- high melting/boiling points
- solid won't conduct electricity, liquid will

Molecular structure
- weak forces between molecules
- low melting/boiling points
- doesn't conduct electricity

Now do this

2. A solid melts at 100°C. What type of structure has it got?
3. A solid melts at 1000°C. What sort of structure has it got?
4. What sort of forces hold the atoms together inside a molecule of hydrogen?
5. What sort of forces hold one molecule of hydrogen to another molecule of hydrogen?

Alkanes, alkenes and plastics

There are millions of carbon compounds. Some of them are very similar, so we put them into groups. The two groups that you need to know are the **alkanes** and the **alkenes**. Both groups are made of carbon and hydrogen only, so they are both hydrocarbons.

Alkanes

The first alkanes in the group are:

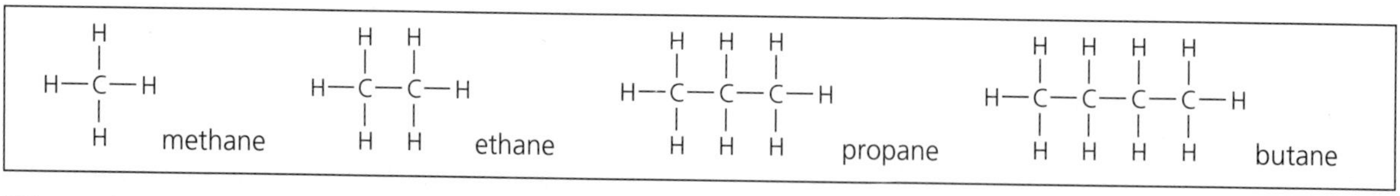

methane, ethane, propane, butane

The carbon atoms in the alkane molecules are linked by single covalent bonds only, so we say that they are **saturated**.

As the alkane molecule gets bigger, there are more weak forces between the molecules. The melting points and boiling points of the alkanes increase as they get bigger.

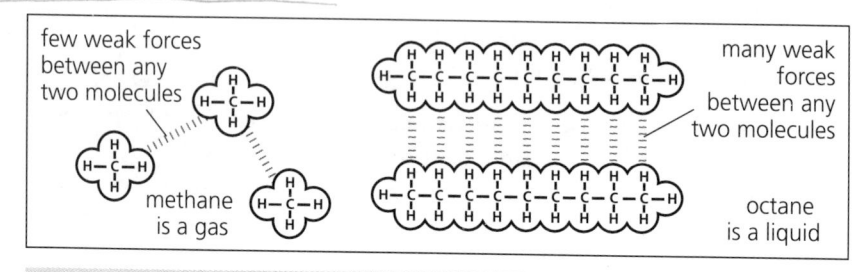

The alkanes all burn well with a clean blue flame.

$$CH_4 + 2O_2 \rightarrow CO_2 + 2H_2O$$

Larger alkane molecules are 'cracked' into smaller alkanes and into alkenes using a catalyst, high temperatures and high pressure. Cracking also produces hydrogen, which is used in the Haber Process.

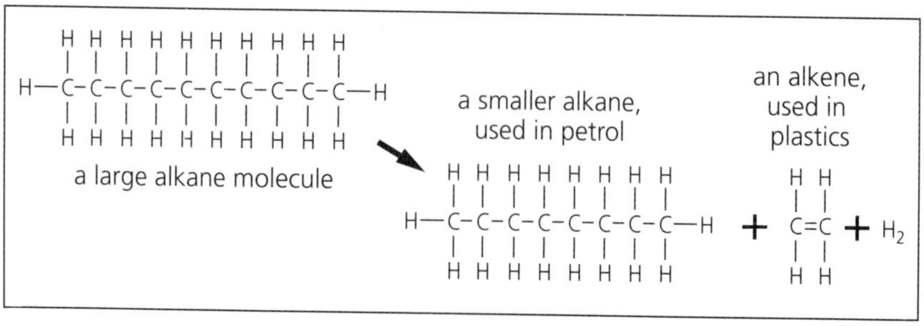

Alkenes

The simplest alkene is ethene, C_2H_4. Its structure is H₂C=CH₂.

It has a double bond between the carbon atoms so we say that it is **unsaturated**. Alkenes are often used to make plastics.

Plastics

Plastics are made of small molecules which are joined together into long chains. The small molecules are called **monomers**, the large molecule is a **polymer**. Polymerisation often needs high pressures and a catalyst.

Now do this

1. How many C—C bonds are present in ethane?
2. How many C—H bonds are present in ethane?
3. Draw a dot and cross diagram to show the covalent bonds inside an ethane molecule.
4. Why is octane a liquid at room temperature?

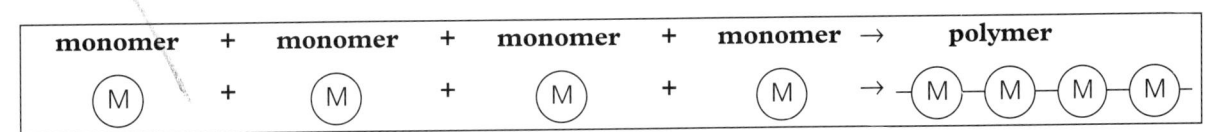

Carbon chemistry

monomer + monomer + monomer + monomer → polymer

Alkenes make excellent monomers. The double bond allows the alkene molecules to add on to each other to make the chains – this is **addition polymerisation**. Ethene is the monomer used to make poly(ethene), or polythene.

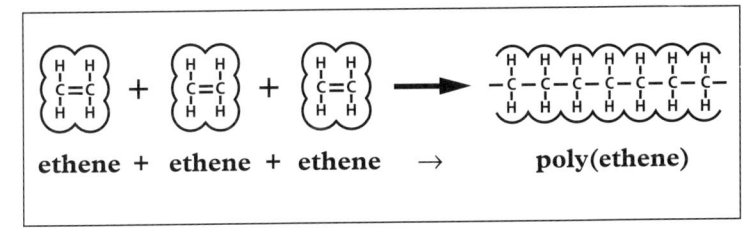

ethene + ethene + ethene → poly(ethene)

Different alkene monomers make different types of plastic which do different jobs. Polythene is cheap and flexible, so it is used to make polythene bags. Vinyl chloride is the monomer used to make poly(vinyl chloride), PVC.

vinyl chloride + vinyl chloride + vinyl chloride → poly(vinyl chloride) (PVC)

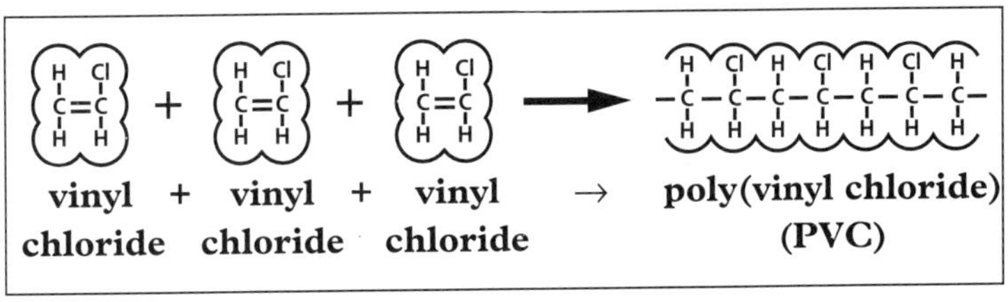

PVC is not as cheap as polythene but it lasts better outdoors, so it is used for drainpipes and window frames as well as clothing and vinyl records.

Some plastics bend easily, especially when warmed. The weak forces between their molecules allow the molecules to slide past each other. These are called **thermosoftening plastics**. Other plastics will not bend; they have strong 'cross-links' between their molecules which hold the molecules together. These are the **thermosetting plastics**. Forces between molecules are **intermolecular forces**. Forces inside the molecules – the bonds which hold it together – are **intramolecular forces**.

One problem with plastics is that when they are thrown away they are not attacked by decomposers in the soil, so they do not rot like most rubbish. Plastics are **non-biodegradable**. Some modern plastics have now been produced which will rot when they are thrown away, so these are **biodegradable**.

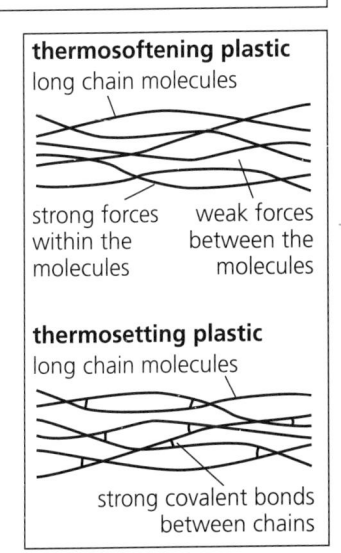

thermosoftening plastic
long chain molecules

strong forces within the molecules — weak forces between the molecules

thermosetting plastic
long chain molecules

strong covalent bonds between chains

- Vegetable oils are unsaturated; they have C=C bonds.
- Fats are saturated; they have only C-C single bonds.
- Margarine makers use hydrogen to turn vegetable oils into fats. The hydrogen changes the double bonds to single bonds; it saturates the oils. If there are some C=C bonds left, the margarine is polyunsaturated.

Unsaturated hydrocarbons have a C=C bond. They turn orange/brown bromine water colourless.

Saturated hydrocarbons have no C=C bond. They do not affect bromine water.

Now do this

5 Propene is $\begin{smallmatrix} H & CH_3 \\ C=C \\ H & H \end{smallmatrix}$. Show three links of a poly(propene) molecule.

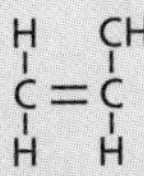

6 'Orlon' is a plastic used to make clothes. Part of an Orlon molecule looks like this:

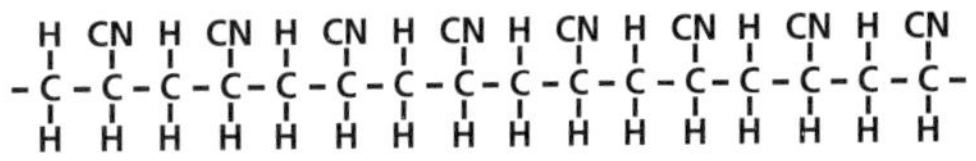

Draw a monomer of Orlon.

Enzymes and biotechnology

Catalysts are important in a wide range of industrial processes. In some important industries the catalysts used are **enzymes**. Enzymes are biological catalysts; they are produced inside living things.

Like other catalysts, specific enzymes are needed for specific reactions. Apples go brown when you cut them open because an enzyme speeds up the reaction of the apple with the air.

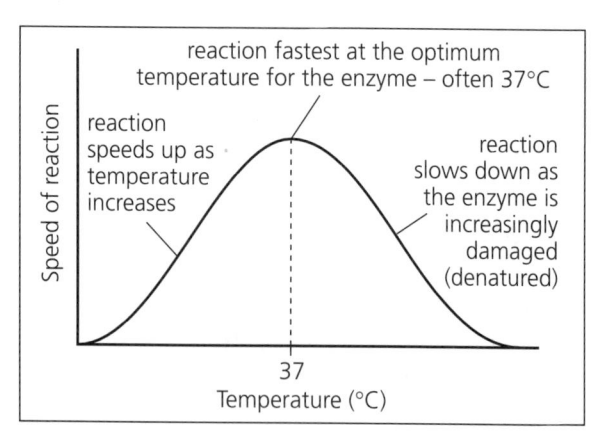

Unlike other catalysts, enzymes have a very delicate structure; they are quickly damaged by temperatures that are too high for them. All reactions go faster as they get hotter, but if an enzyme is involved the reaction will only get faster up to a certain temperature, then it will slow down or stop due to damage to the enzyme. As the temperature increases, all the molecules move about more and more. The molecules also vibrate, and the vibrations inside the enzyme molecules become so great that the delicate structure is damaged. We say that the enzyme has been **denatured**.

Using enzymes

Enzymes are important in the baking, brewing and dairy industries. Yeast is used in both baking and brewing because the yeast cells contain enzymes which convert sugar into carbon dioxide and alcohol during **fermentation**.

sugar → alcohol + carbon dioxide

Brewers use yeast for the alcohol, bakers use it for the carbon dioxide. In each case the yeast needs sugar, moisture and warm conditions to work.

Baking

Sugar and yeast are added to bread dough so that the enzymes in the yeast can produce bubbles of carbon dioxide. When it is cooked the dough solidifies round the bubbles, giving bread an open texture. The high temperature of the cooking kills the yeast and drives off the carbon dioxide and the alcohol.

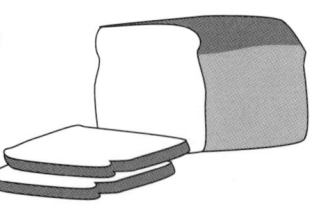

Brewing

Yeast is added to grape juice to make wine, and to barley grains to make beer. The enzymes in the yeast convert sugars from the grapes and barley into alcohol during fermentation. The carbon dioxide bubbles out of the liquid.

Carbon chemistry

Dairy industry

The enzyme rennin makes milk clot and form cheese, and enzymes in bacteria are used to convert milk to yoghurt.

Controlling enzymes in the kitchen

Some enzymes are a problem because they speed up the decay of fresh food. These enzymes might be part of the food itself, or might be from microbes on the food. They can be controlled by

- **cooking** – this destroys the enzyme and stops the food decaying. The food must be covered once it is cooked, otherwise microbes from the air will fall onto the food and fresh enzymes will start it decaying again
- **refrigeration** – this does not destroy the enzymes, but the low temperature slows down any reactions, so it keeps food fresh for a short time
- **freezing** – this does not destroy the enzymes, but it stops any reactions so it is a good way of keeping food fresh for a long time. Freezing stops the reaction in two ways. First, any reaction will slow down a lot because the temperature is so low. Secondly, any water turns into ice. This means that dissolved chemicals can no longer move through the liquid – they are trapped in a fixed position and cannot collide with the other chemicals to react.

Now do this

1. What happens to the speed of a reaction involving an enzyme:
   a if you start to heat it up?
   b if you heat it further?
2. What happens to the enzyme in **1a**?
3. When yeast ferments it converts sugar into two chemicals. What are they?
4. Apples go brown when you cut them open because of a reaction which is speeded up by an enzyme.
   a What does the apple react with when it goes brown?
   b Lemon juice stops the apple going brown – suggest why.
   c Cooked apples don't go brown – why?
   d Apples cut under water go brown more slowly – suggest why.

Acids and pH

Natural acids are all around us. Acids in orange juice and vinegar give a sharp taste; acids in nettles and bee stings hurt us; acids in our stomach help digest our food. Acidity is caused by the presence of hydrogen ions, H^+.

How acidic is it?

The pH scale tells us how strongly acidic something is. The lower the number, the greater the hydrogen ion concentration.

			NEUTRAL		
very acidic		slightly acidic	↓	slightly alkaline	very alkaline
0 1 2	3	4 5 6	7	8 9 10	11 12 13 14

Acids from the lab such as hydrochloric acid or sulphuric acid have a pH of about 1. Lemon juice and vinegar are much less acidic, with a pH of around 4. Sodium hydroxide is at the other end, with a pH of about 14, but baking soda is around pH 8.

Bases, alkalis and neutralisation

Anything that reacts with an acid is called a **base**. A base which will dissolve in water (such as sodium hydroxide) is an **alkali**. Metal oxides and hydroxides are usually bases and alkalis. Non-metal oxides are usually acidic.

Acids contain hydrogen ions, H^+; alkalis contain hydroxide ions, OH^-.

When an acid and a base react they **neutralise** each other. The hydrogen ions react with hydroxide ions to form water.

$$H^+(aq) + OH^-(aq) \rightarrow H_2O(l)$$

If you add acid to a beaker of alkali the pH of the liquid in the beaker will start at a high number and drop to pH 7 once the acid and alkali have neutralised each other. If you add too much acid you will go too far. The pH will go below 7.

When acids react with alkalis they produce a **salt** and water. The salt is the substance left over after the hydrogen ions have reacted with the hydroxide ions.

acid	+	alkali	—	salt	+	water
HCl	+	NaOH	→	NaCl	+	H_2O
hydrochloric acid		sodium hydroxide		sodium chloride		water

Acids always form salts when they react.

Salts made by neutralising acid with ammonia are used as fertilisers.

Acids and metals

If a metal reacts with an acid, the metal is behaving as a base. The hydrogen ions from the acid are converted to hydrogen gas and a salt is left behind.

acid	+	metal	→	salt	+	hydrogen
H_2SO_4	+	Mg	→	$MgSO_4$	+	H_2
sulphuric acid		magnesium		magnesium sulphate		hydrogen

Not all metals react with acids. Metals such as copper and silver are not reactive enough to be attacked by acids.

Acid + metal carbonate

Adding an acid to carbonates produces a salt, carbon dioxide gas and water. The bubbles of carbon dioxide are given off, the carbonate dissolves and forms a salt with the acid.

Marble chips are made of calcium carbonate. You may have done this reaction in the laboratory:

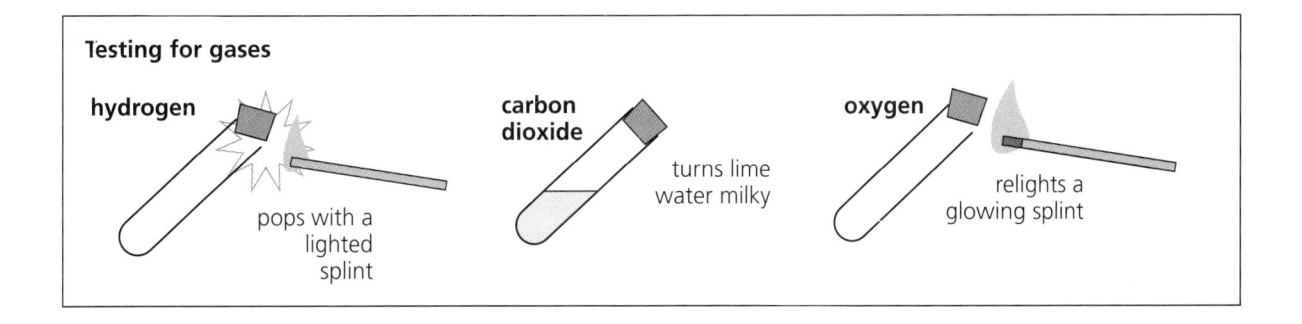

2HCl	+	$CaCO_3$	→	$CaCl_2$	+	H_2O	+	CO_2
acid	+	carbonate	→	salt	+	water	+	carbon dioxide

Testing for gases

- **hydrogen** — pops with a lighted splint
- **carbon dioxide** — turns lime water milky
- **oxygen** — relights a glowing splint

Now do this

1. If the acidity of something increases, does the pH rise, fall or stay constant?
2. Bee stings are acidic. Choose the best substance to neutralise a bee sting from those described under the pH scale.
3. Name the salt produced when sulphuric acid reacts with iron.
4. Magnesium reacts with hydrochloric acid (HCl).
   a Name the two products.
   b Write a balanced equation for the reaction.

Reversible reactions and ammonia

Some chemical reactions will go in both directions. If you put acid with pH indicator, the indicator will turn red. If you now add alkali the indicator changes to blue. Add acid again, and it goes back to red.

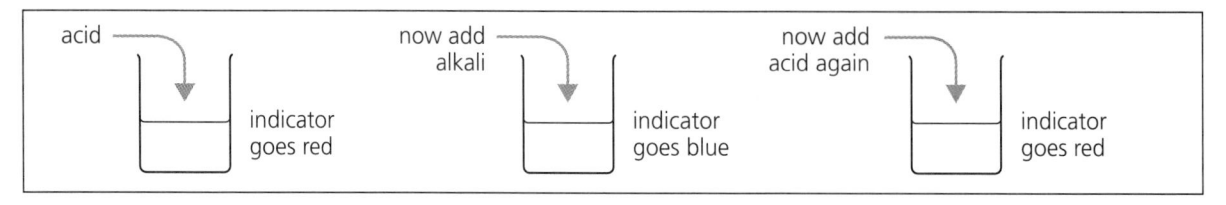

acid → indicator goes red   now add alkali → indicator goes blue   now add acid again → indicator goes red

You can do this as many times as you want. The reaction will go in either direction just as easily.

Usually it is very difficult to make a reaction go backwards, but in this case it is very easy. We call this type of reaction a **reversible reaction**.

Ammonia is made by a reversible reaction

Millions of tons of ammonia are produced every year so that we can make fertiliser. The method of making ammonia is called the **Haber Process** after the man who discovered it. Ammonia is made by the reversible reaction between nitrogen and hydrogen.

When nitrogen and hydrogen meet they start to react to form ammonia. The ammonia immediately starts to turn back to nitrogen and hydrogen. The reaction goes in both directions at the same time.

Eventually the forward reaction is going at the same speed as the backward reaction. From this point onwards there will not be any change in the amount of chemicals; they have reached **equilibrium**. The symbol for an equilibrium reaction is ⇌.

this is a 'forward reaction'
$$N_2 + 3H_2 \rightarrow 2NH_3$$
$$N_2 + 3H_2 \leftarrow 2NH_3$$
this is a 'backward reaction'

$$N_2 + 3H_2 \rightleftharpoons 2NH_3$$
nitrogen + hydrogen ⇌ ammonia

The Haber Process

Hydrogen is made by cracking hydrocarbons from crude oil and nitrogen is taken from the air. High pressure pushes the balance point of the equilibrium further to the right, so that more ammonia is made. Low temperature also pushes the equilibrium to the right, but a high temperature makes the reaction go faster, so we use an in-between temperature as a compromise.

Ammonia is removed as fast as it is made to stop it reacting back into nitrogen and hydrogen. A catalyst of iron, a transition metal, speeds up the reaction. Catalysts in equilibrium reactions speed up both the forward and the backward reactions, so the reactions get to their balance point more quickly.

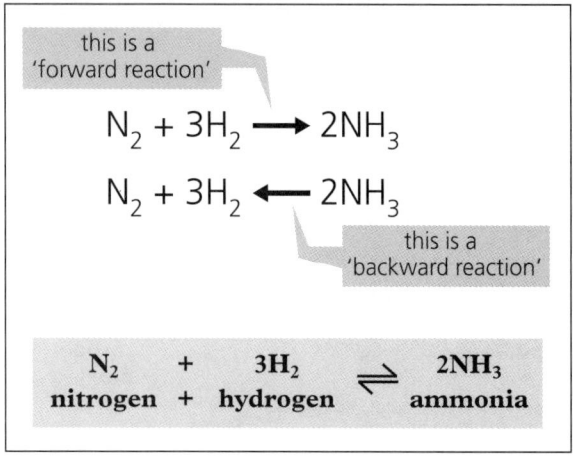

Now do this

1. What is a reversible reaction?
2. What is produced if you put an iron catalyst with ammonia?

Using chemical equations

Ammonia and fertilisers

One of the most important uses of ammonia is in making nitrogen-containing fertilisers. The nitrogen enables plants to grow faster and bigger, so farmers can get a bigger yield of crop from each field. The fertiliser needs to be in a soluble form, so that once it has dissolved in the water in the soil the plants can take the nitrogen compounds in through their roots.

Ammonia (NH_3) is a suitable compound but when it dissolves in water it forms alkaline ammonium hydroxide, which damages plants. The ammonium hydroxide can be neutralised with acid to make an ammonium salt. Sulphuric acid will make ammonium sulphate.

acid	+	alkali	→	salt	+	water
H_2SO_4	+	$2NH_4OH$	→	$(NH_4)_2SO_4$	+	H_2O
sulphuric acid	+	ammonium hydroxide	→	ammonium sulphate	+	water

Nitric acid (which is made from ammonia by another process) makes ammonium nitrate.

HNO_3	+	NH_4OH	→	NH_4NO_3	+	H_2O
nitric acid	+	ammonium hydroxide	→	ammonium nitrate	+	water

Ammonium sulphate and ammonium nitrate are common fertilisers. Nitric acid also contains nitrogen, so ammonium nitrate gives the plants a 'double dose'.

Pollution, fertilisers and eutrophication

Sometimes rain water runs off farmer's fields into lakes and ponds, carrying fertilisers with it. The lakes and ponds are polluted because the fertiliser increases the growth of microscopic plants at the surface. This layer of green plants cuts off the light to the rest of the pond, so the plants at the bottom die. The microbes, which rot the dead plants, use up the oxygen in the water, so everything else then dies. This is called **eutrophication**.

In some areas of the country the amount of fertiliser draining into the rivers is causing too high a level of nitrates in the drinking water, which could be dangerous to babies.

Now do this

3. Which fertiliser is made if you react ammonium hydroxide (NH_4OH) with sulphuric acid (H_2SO_4)?
4. Write a balanced chemical equation for this reaction.
5. What causes eutrophication?

Chemical calculations

How much do we need?

If you want to carry out a chemical reaction without wasting any of the chemicals you need to know precisely how much of each reactant to use. To measure out chemical reactions we weigh them. We weigh out atoms in 'pre-packed' quantities called moles. Moles of different elements weigh different amounts. The mass of a mole of atoms of an element is its **relative atomic mass** in grams.

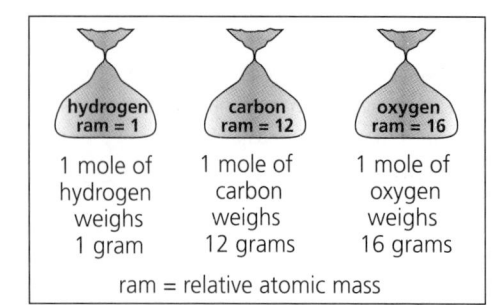

hydrogen ram = 1	carbon ram = 12	oxygen ram = 16
1 mole of hydrogen weighs 1 gram	1 mole of carbon weighs 12 grams	1 mole of oxygen weighs 16 grams

ram = relative atomic mass

For example, the equation for iron reacting with sulphur is

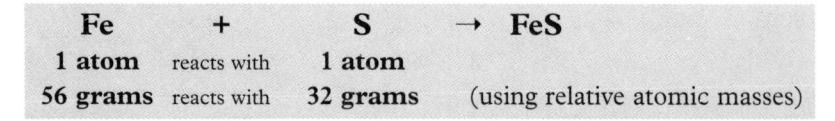

Fe   +   S   →   FeS
1 atom   reacts with   1 atom
56 grams reacts with 32 grams   (using relative atomic masses)

Now do this

1 You have 2 g of hydrogen.
  a You want the same number of atoms of carbon. How much do you weigh out?
  b You want twice as many atoms of oxygen. How much do you weigh out?

Formula masses

When we weigh out substances made of more than one atom, we have to add up the masses of all the atoms inside the formula. This is called the **formula mass**. It is the mass of one mole of the molecule.

A hydrogen molecule is H_2	The formula mass for H_2 is	1 + 1	= 2
An oxygen molecule is O_2	The formula mass for O_2 is	16 + 16	= 32
A methane molecule is CH_4	The formula mass for CH_4 is	12 + 1 + 1 + 1 + 1	= 16
Sodium chloride is NaCl	The formula mass for NaCl is	23 + 35.5	= 58.5

Calculating amounts used in chemical reactions

When chemicals react, their atoms join together in different ways. All the atoms at the start of the reaction are still there at the end. In a reaction the atoms never disappear, new atoms never appear. For example,

$H_2 + Cl_2 \rightarrow 2HCl$

This means that the mass of the chemicals is the same at the end of the reaction.

The mass of H_2 and Cl_2 at the start = H + H + Cl + Cl
                                         = 1 + 1 + 35.5 + 35.5 = 73
The mass of 2HCl at the end = H + Cl + H + Cl
                            = 1 + 35.5 + 1 + 35.5 = 73

The total mass of all the reactants will equal the total mass of all the products.

Moles and formula masses
You can work out how many moles there are of a chemical if you know its formula mass and how many grams of the chemical you have:

$$\text{Number of moles} = \frac{\text{mass}}{\text{formula mass}}$$

Using chemical equations

Calculating yields and formulae

Sometimes the amount of product is less than expected. The starting chemicals don't always completely react, and it is hard to get all the product out of the reaction mixture. Small amounts always 'get lost' somewhere.

Here are some reasons for 'missing' product:
- loss in filtration
- loss in evaporation – for something that can evaporate
- loss in heating – for something that can evaporate
- loss in transferring liquids.

Percentage yields

The **percentage yield** is the amount of product actually collected compared to the amount that was expected.

$$\% \text{ yield} = \frac{\text{actual mass of product}}{\text{expected mass of product}} \times 100$$

If a reaction produced 46 g of product, but we expected to have 80 g, the % yield

$$= \frac{46 \times 100}{80}$$
$$= \frac{4600}{80}$$
$$= 57.5\%$$

Moles in solution

The molarity of a solution is the number of moles that are dissolved in one dm^3 of the solution.

A one **molar** solution contains one mole dissolved in one dm^3 of solution.

A three **molar** solution contains 3 moles per dm^3 of solution

Number of moles = molarity × volume (in dm^3)

Some relative atomic masses
hydrogen	H	= 1
lithium	Li	= 7
carbon	C	= 12
nitrogen	N	= 14
oxygen	O	= 16
sodium	Na	= 23
sulphur	S	= 32
chlorine	Cl	= 35.5
iron	Fe	= 56
copper	Cu	= 64

Now do this

2 A reaction produced 32 g of chemical. You expected it to produce 50 g of chemical. What is the percentage yield?

How to find a formula from reacting masses

To work out a formula you must know the mass of each element inside the substance. The sort of question you might have to answer is:
3.5 g of lithium reacts with 4 g of oxygen to make lithium oxide. What is the formula of lithium oxide?
(Relative atomic masses: Li = 7, O = 16)

These are the stages to go through.

Stage 1
Find out how many moles of each element you used.

3.5 g of lithium is made of $\frac{3.5}{7}$ = 0.5 moles of lithium

4 g of oxygen is made of $\frac{4}{16}$ = 0.25 moles of oxygen.

Stage 2
Find the ratio of the numbers of moles of the different elements – this is the formula.

0.5 moles of lithium atoms react with 0.25 moles of oxygen atoms.
2 mole of lithium atoms react with 1 mole of oxygen atoms.
The formula of lithium oxide is Li_2O.

Now do this

3 8 g of copper combine with 1 g of oxygen. What is the formula of the copper oxide?
(Relative atomic masses O = 16, Cu = 64)

4 4 g of copper combine with 1 g of oxygen. What is the formula of this copper oxide?

Atoms, isotopes and electron shells

An atom is made of a tiny positive nucleus surrounded by shells of electrons.

The nucleus is made of protons and neutrons. Protons have a positive charge. Neutrons are neutral. They are both heavy particles.

The electrons fit in shells around the nucleus. They have a negative charge and weigh almost nothing.

Atoms are neutral. Their negative and positive charges cancel out. This means that the number of electrons must be the same as the number of protons.

Name	Charge	Mass	Where found
proton	+1	1	inside the nucleus
neutron	0	1	inside the nucleus
electron	−1	0	outside the nucleus, in shells

The number of protons in an atom is called the **atomic number** or the **proton number**. It tells you what element you have. If an atom has one proton, the element is hydrogen, two protons means helium and so on.

The mass of an atom is made up of all the protons and neutrons, because both are heavy particles. Add the two numbers together to make the **mass number**. The electrons don't weigh enough to matter.

We write all this information in a standard way.

The number of neutrons is the mass number minus the proton number.

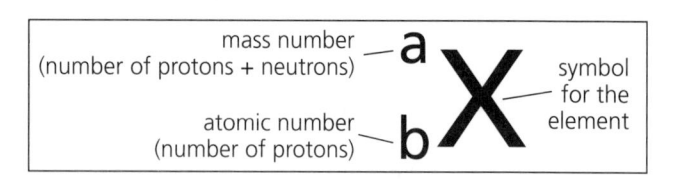

mass number (number of protons + neutrons) — a
atomic number (number of protons) — b
$^a_b X$ symbol for the element

Isotopes

Many elements have more than one mass number. These different forms of the same element are called **isotopes**.

$^{35}_{17}Cl$ has 17 protons, so it is chlorine. Work out how many neutrons it must have (mass number − proton number). You should have the answer 18 neutrons.

$^{37}_{17}Cl$ has 17 protons, so it is chlorine. Work out how many neutrons it must have (mass number − proton number). You should have the answer 20 neutrons.

The only difference between them is the number of neutrons in the nucleus. This makes one isotope heavier than the other, but otherwise it doesn't have much effect.

Now do this

1. What is the difference between $^{16}_8 O$ and $^{18}_8 O$?
2. How many protons are in $^{56}_{26}Fe$?
3. How many neutrons are in $^{56}_{26}Fe$?

The Periodic Table

How are the electrons arranged in an atom?

In a neutral atom the number of electrons outside the nucleus is the same as the number of protons inside the nucleus. Electrons are negative, protons are positive, and so the two sets of charges cancel out and the atom is neutral. Remember that the number of protons is the atomic number.

Electrons fit into shells around the nucleus. Two electrons fit into the first shell, then up to eight electrons fit into the next shell. Eight electrons is a stable number for all shells after the innermost shell.

Sodium has 11 electrons, so its electron arrangement is 2,8,1. This means that there are two electrons in the first shell, eight in the next and one in the outer shell.

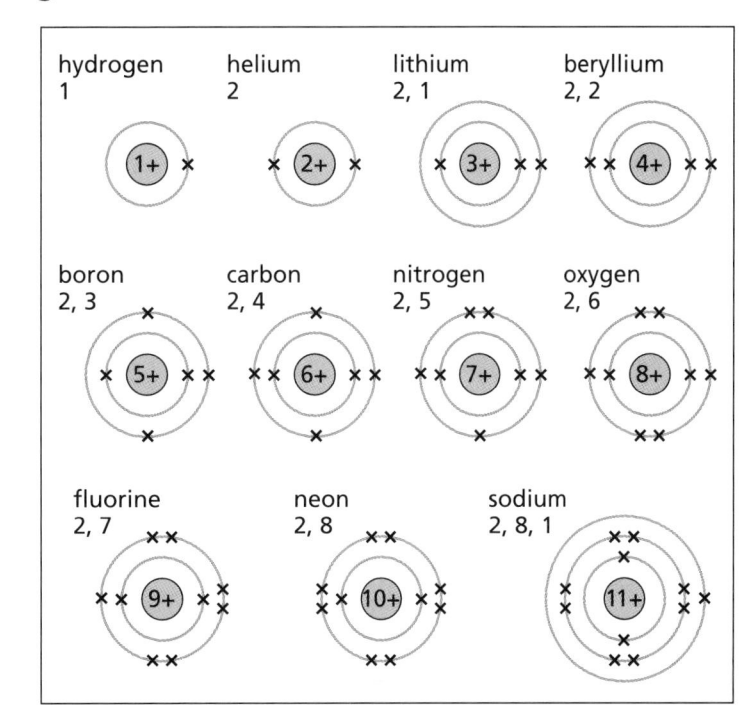

Ions

If the outer shell of an element is only a few electrons away from the eight, the element will form an ion. Electrons are gained or lost to end up with the eight. If more than two electrons have to move, the element usually won't form an ion. It shares electrons instead.

Elements whose atoms gain electrons to form ions

If there are 7 electrons in the outer shell, then gain one electron → X⁻ ion.

If there are 6 electrons in the outer shell, then gain two electrons → X²⁻ ion.

Elements whose atoms give away electrons to form ions

If there is 1 electron in the outer shell, then give away one electron → X⁺ ion.

If there are 2 electrons in the outer shell, then give away two electrons → X²⁺ ion.

Now do this

4 The atomic number of nitrogen is 7.
   a How many protons has it got?
   b How many electrons has it got?
   c How are the electrons arranged?

5 The atomic number of sodium is 11. What is its electron arrangement?

6 The atomic number of potassium is 19. What is its electron arrangement?

The Periodic Table

A Periodic Table is is a list of all the elements in order of their increasing proton numbers (atomic numbers). The order goes from left to right along each row, starting with the top row. A Periodic Table will be printed on the back of your examination paper.

Elements which are similar fit into vertical lines called **Groups**. The group numbers are written in Roman numerals, and are at the top of the table. They go from Group I to Group 0. Sometimes the last group on the right is called Group VIII. Hydrogen is the one element that is sometimes not put into a group.

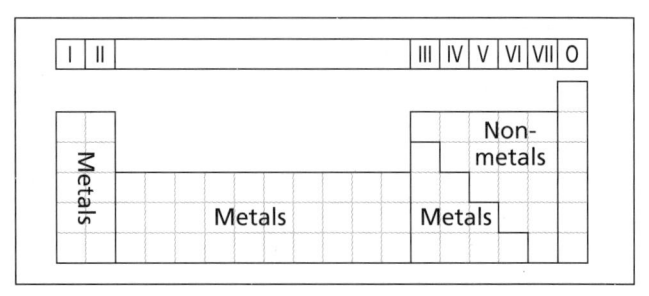

Do this. Find the proton number (atomic number) of sodium.

Metals and non-metals

There are two sorts of elements, metals and non-metals. The zig-zag line shows the boundary between them. Metals are on the left-hand side of the table, non-metals are on the right.

Metals will:
- react with oxygen to form oxides which are basic.

Most metals will also:
- react with water to form hydrogen and oxides or hydroxides
- react with acids to form hydrogen and a salt.

The most reactive metals are at the bottom left.

Non-metals often form acidic oxides. The most reactive non-metal is at the top of Group VII – it is fluorine.

Groups and electrons

The group number is the same as the number of electrons in the outer shell. These outer electrons are the most important electrons of an element, because that is where atoms touch, so the outer electrons dictate the chemical properties.

All the elements in a group have the same number of outer electrons. They are all similar, although there is a regular change in properties of the elements as you go down the group.

Eight electrons make a stable shell. Elements in groups which have only one or two electrons in the outer shell lose those electrons and form positive ions. Elements in groups which have six or seven electrons in the outer shell gain electrons and form negative ions.

Group number	I	II	III	IV	V	VI	VII	0
Outer electrons	1	2	3	4	5	6	7	8
Ion formed	M$^+$	M^{++}				X^{--}	X$^-$	

Now do this

1. Explain why elements in Group II form double positive ions.
2. Why don't Group 0 elements form ions?

Group I: The alkali metals

The Group I elements are called the **alkali metals**. You need to know about the first three: lithium, sodium and potassium.

Element	Symbol	Mass	Melting point (°C)
lithium	Li	7	180
sodium	Na	23	98
potassium	K	39	63
rubidium	Rb	85	39
caesium	Cs	133	29

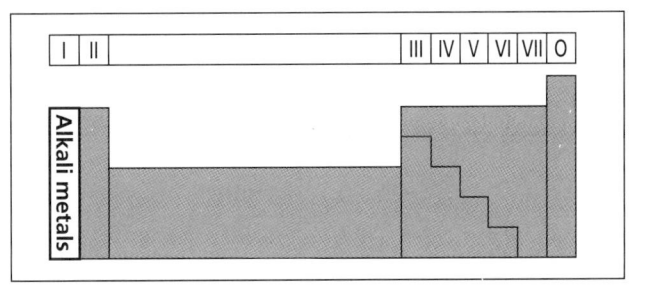

As these elements are in Group I they all have only one electron in the outer shell, and they lose that electron to form single positive ions. They are all very reactive, and get *more* reactive going down the group. The melting points and boiling points get lower going down the group.

The alkali metals are all very similar. Like all metals they are shiny and conduct electricity. Unlike most metals they have such low density that they will float on water. They are soft, and get softer as you go down the group.

Alkali metals all tarnish rapidly because they react with the oxygen in the air, so they are stored under oil to stop them reacting.

Reactions with water

All alkali metals float on water and react strongly to make alkaline solutions. They force hydrogen gas out of the water and make the metal hydroxide.

lithium	+	water	→	lithium hydroxide	+	hydrogen
2Li	+	2H$_2$O	→	2LiOH	+	H$_2$

The reaction with water gets more violent as you go down the group.
- Lithium reacts but does not melt because it is the least reactive.
- Sodium melts and moves about the surface of the water as it reacts.
- Potassium melts, moves about the surface and bursts into flame.

Testing for alkali metals

The metals and their compounds give coloured flames. You can use this to find out which metal is in a compound.
- Lithium burns with a red flame.
- Sodium burns with a yellow flame.
- Potassium burns with a lilac flame.

Alkali metal compounds

Alkali metal compounds melt at high temperatures. They dissolve in water and have colourless solutions.

Many of the compounds are very useful. Sodium chloride is salt, sodium hydrogen carbonate can neutralise acid in upset stomachs. Potassium nitrate is a fertiliser.

Use safety screens and goggles!

Sodium and potassium melt as soon as they are dropped in water. Lithium does not melt because it is the least reactive metal. Caesium is so reactive that it explodes when it touches water.

Now do this

3. Write a word equation for the reaction of sodium with water.
4. Write a balanced chemical equation for the reaction of sodium with water.

Sodium carbonate is used in soap powder and to make sodium hydroxide. Sodium hydroxide is used in making soap.

Sodium chloride is used to make chlorine and sodium hydroxide. There is more about chlorine in the next section.

Group VII: The halogens

The Group VII elements are called the **halogens**. You need to know about chlorine, bromine and iodine.

Element	Symbol	Relative atomic mass	Normal state	Colour
fluorine	F	19	gas	
chlorine	Cl	35.5	gas	green
bromine	Br	80	liquid	orange
iodine	I	127	solid	black

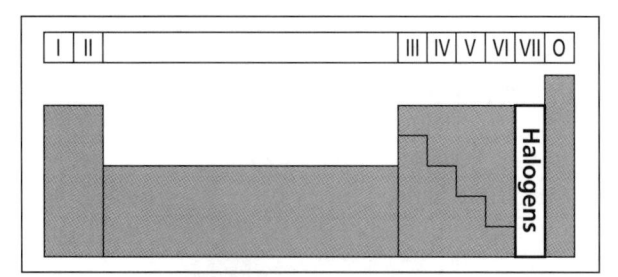

Halogens all have seven electrons in the outer shell, so they are very reactive and they all gain one electron to form a single negative ion. They get *less* reactive going down the group. Melting points and boiling points increase going down the group.

The halogens are all very similar non-metals. They are poisonous (bromine and chlorine should be handled only in a fume cupboard). They are acidic, they react with metals and their compounds usually dissolve in water.

Reactions with metals

The halogens react with lots of different metals. In each case they form a salt called a **halide**. Even less reactive metals, such as iron, will react vigorously with a halogen.

iron + bromine → iron bromide

Reactions with hydrogen

The halogens will all react with hydrogen. They form hydrogen chloride, HCl; hydrogen bromide, HBr; and hydrogen iodide, HI. These compounds are colourless gases which dissolve in water to give strongly acidic solutions. A solution of HCl in water is called hydrochloric acid.

What are the halogens used for?

Chlorine is used
- as a bleach to get rid of stains
- for killing bacteria in drinking water and in swimming pools
- for making plastics and insecticides
- to make hydrochloric acid. This has many uses including etching metals and making plastics.

Iodine is an antiseptic.

Bromine and iodine are used to make silver bromide and silver iodide. These chemicals turn black in sunlight, so they are used in photographic films.

Now do this

1. Write a word equation for the reaction between hydrogen and chlorine.
2. Sodium chloride has the formula NaCl. Write a balanced equation for the reaction between sodium and chlorine.

How can you tell which halogens are in a compound?

Dissolve the compound in water, then add silver nitrate solution.

Chlorine compounds give a white solid (precipitate).

Bromine compounds give a cream solid (precipitate).

Iodine compounds give a yellow solid (precipitate).

More reactive halogens will displace less reactive halogens from their compounds. Chlorine is more reactive than bromine. If you bubble chlorine through sodium bromide the chlorine will force the bromine out and take its place.

chlorine + sodium bromide →
bromine + sodium chloride

Bromine is more reactive than iodine.

bromine + sodium iodide →
iodine + sodium bromide

Group 0: The noble gases

The noble gases are helium, neon, argon, krypton, xenon and radon. They are colourless gases and have almost no reactions. This is because they all have a stable outer shell (usually eight electrons, except helium, which has two), so they don't form any bonds. As their atomic numbers increase down the group their boiling points and densities increase.

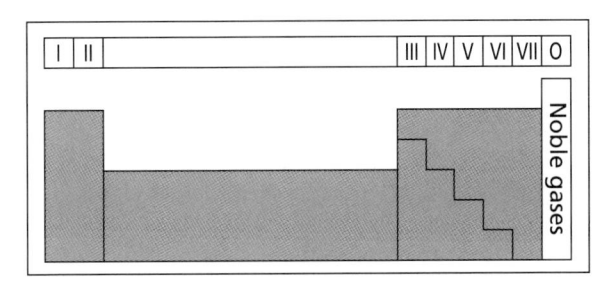

Uses of the noble gases

Helium is used to fill balloons because it is light and it will not burn. Neon, argon and krypton are used in different sorts of lights, especially coloured 'neon' lights, and in lasers. They are also used when an inert atmosphere is needed – as a replacement for air if you have a chemical which would react with air.

The transition metals

The **transition metals** contain common metals such as iron and copper, and also silver and gold.

They are all what we normally think of as metals – they conduct electricity and heat, they are are shiny, hard, strong, dense and have high melting points.

Transition metals and their compounds can make good catalysts, for example iron is the catalyst in the Haber Process for making ammonia.

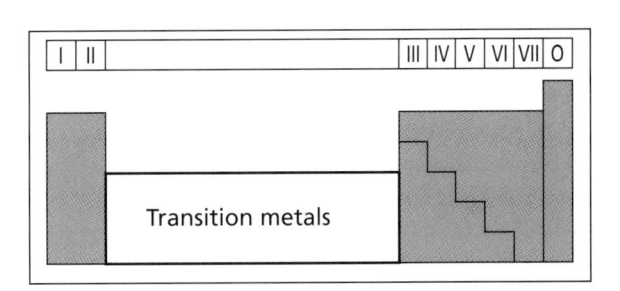

Compounds of the transition metals

Most of the transition metal compounds are coloured. The colour is due to the metal ion inside the compound, so the colour tells you which transition element is present. Often the metal will form more than one ion – iron will form Fe^{2+} ions (pale green compounds) and Fe^{3+} ions (rust red compounds). Copper forms the Cu^{2+} ion, which produces blue or green compounds.

Some transition metals that you should know

- **Iron**
  Produced in blast furnaces, small amounts of different elements are added to it to make different types of steel. It is used as a catalyst in the Haber Process.

- **Copper**
  One of the few metals which is coloured. Used in electric cables and also in water pipes because it is such a good conductor of electricity and heat.

- **Nickel**
  Usually mixed with other metals to make corrosion-resistant alloys. It also makes a good catalyst.

Materials and their Properties

Concept map

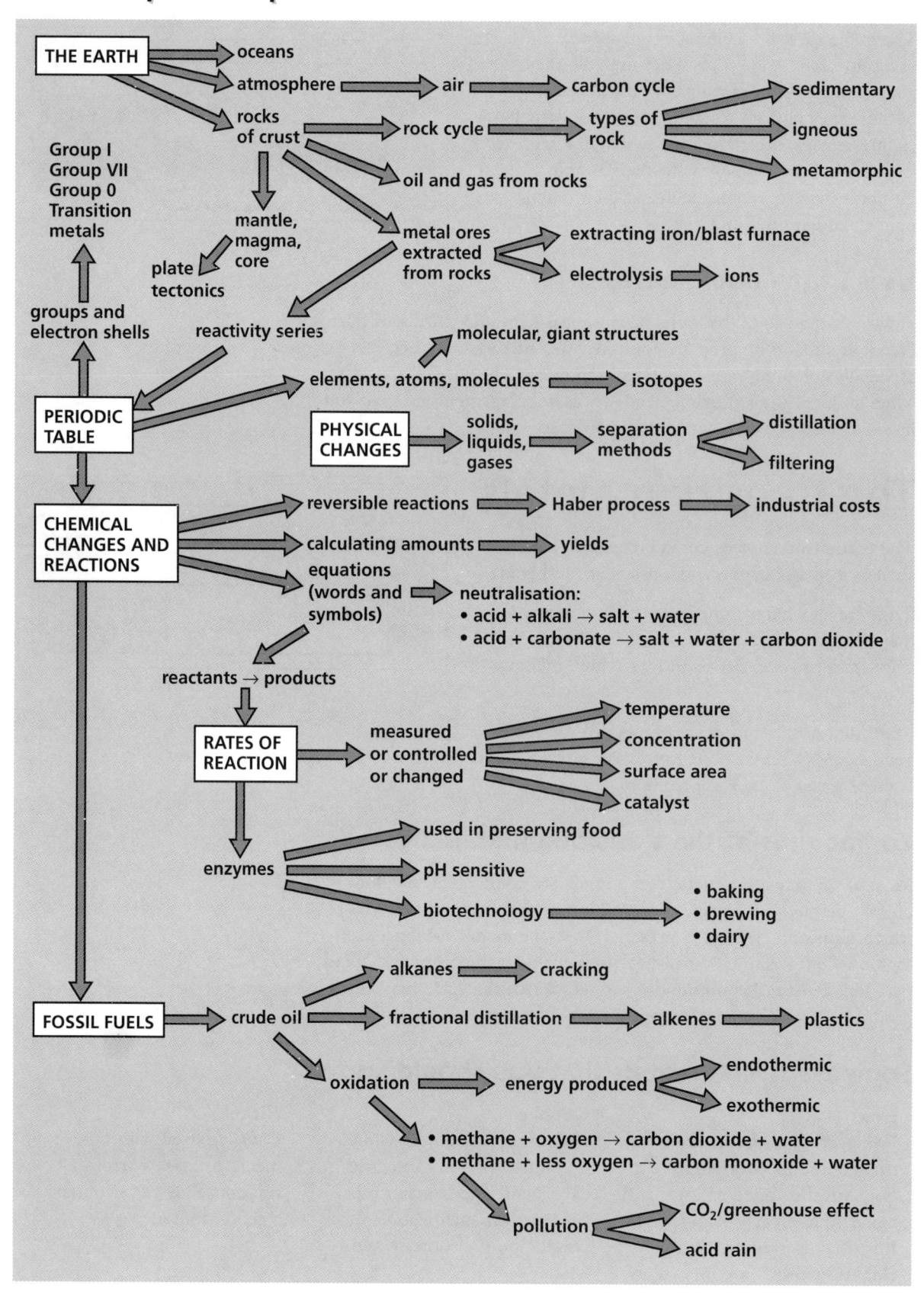

THE EARTH
- oceans
- atmosphere → air → carbon cycle
- rocks of crust → rock cycle → types of rock → sedimentary / igneous / metamorphic
- rocks of crust → oil and gas from rocks
- rocks of crust → mantle, magma, core → plate tectonics
- rocks of crust → metal ores extracted from rocks → extracting iron/blast furnace
- metal ores extracted from rocks → electrolysis → ions
- rocks of crust → reactivity series

Group I
Group VII
Group 0
Transition metals

groups and electron shells

PERIODIC TABLE → elements, atoms, molecules → isotopes
- → molecular, giant structures

PHYSICAL CHANGES → solids, liquids, gases → separation methods → distillation / filtering

CHEMICAL CHANGES AND REACTIONS
- reversible reactions → Haber process → industrial costs
- calculating amounts → yields
- equations (words and symbols) → neutralisation:
  - acid + alkali → salt + water
  - acid + carbonate → salt + water + carbon dioxide
- reactants → products

RATES OF REACTION → measured or controlled or changed
- temperature
- concentration
- surface area
- catalyst

enzymes
- used in preserving food
- pH sensitive
- biotechnology → baking / brewing / dairy

FOSSIL FUELS → crude oil
- alkanes → cracking
- fractional distillation → alkenes → plastics
- oxidation → energy produced → endothermic / exothermic
  - methane + oxygen → carbon dioxide + water
  - methane + less oxygen → carbon monoxide + water
- pollution → CO_2/greenhouse effect / acid rain

Exam questions

1 The syringe in the diagram has a blocked end, and is full of air.

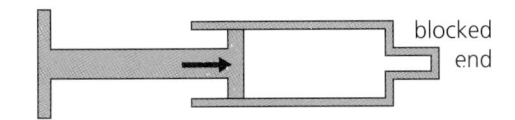

a Which of these diagrams could show the particles in air? [1]

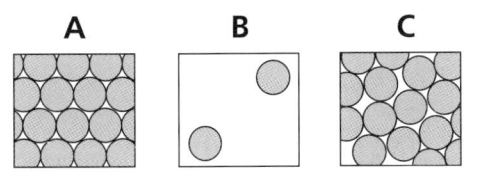

A   B   C

b i What will happen to the plunger when you push it? [1]

ii Use ideas about particles in gases to explain why. [2]

c i If the syringe is full of water, what will happen to the plunger when you push it? [1]

ii Use ideas about particles in liquids to explain why. [2]

d If you spill a liquid onto your skin it will cool you down. Use ideas about energy to explain why. [3]

[10 marks]

2 Calcium forms calcium oxide, CaO, when you heat it in air.

a Write a word equation for this reaction. [2]

b Write a balanced chemical equation for this reaction. [2]

[4 marks]

3 A student wanted to know if two green pens had the same type of ink inside them. She drew a line onto a filter paper and put ink spots from each pen onto the line. She then dipped the filter paper into water. After a few hours, this is what the paper looked like.

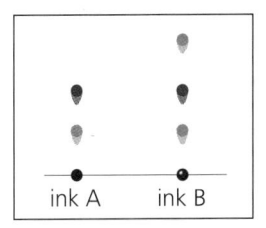

ink A   ink B

a What happened to the water? [1]

b Were the inks the same? Explain how you can tell. [1]

c i How many dyes were in ink A? [1]

ii How many dyes were in ink B? [1]

[4 marks]

4 Crude oil is a mixture of alkane molecules. We can separate these molecules by fractionation (fractional distillation).

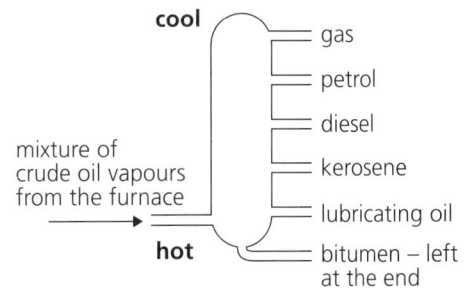

a Fractionation works because of an important difference between the different alkanes. How are they different? [1]

b Alkanes are made of carbon and hydrogen. When the alkanes such as methane, CH_4, burn they react with oxygen in the atmosphere.

i What do we call reactions where chemicals combine with oxygen? [1]

ii Name two chemicals that are made when methane is burned in a plentiful supply of air. [2]

iii Write a balanced equation for this reaction. [2]

iv Name two chemicals that are made when petrol is burned in a reduced supply of air. [2]

v Write a balanced equation for this reaction. [2]

[10 marks]

5 The energy of combustion of a fuel was found by using it to heat water in a beaker and measuring the temperature rise.

a What do we call reactions that give out heat? [1]

b In what units do we measure heat? [1]

c Scientists are worried that burning fuels will add to the greenhouse effect. Explain

Materials and their Properties

how the greenhouse effect could raise the temperature of the Earth. [3]

[5 marks]

6 A student wanted to see how fast magnesium reacts with hydrochloric acid. She used the same amount of acid and the same mass of magnesium for each experiment.

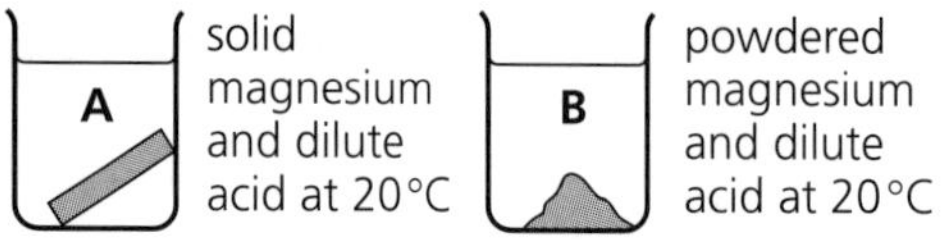

A: solid magnesium and dilute acid at 20°C
B: powdered magnesium and dilute acid at 20°C

a Use the idea of particles to explain why the reaction in beaker B was faster than A. [2]

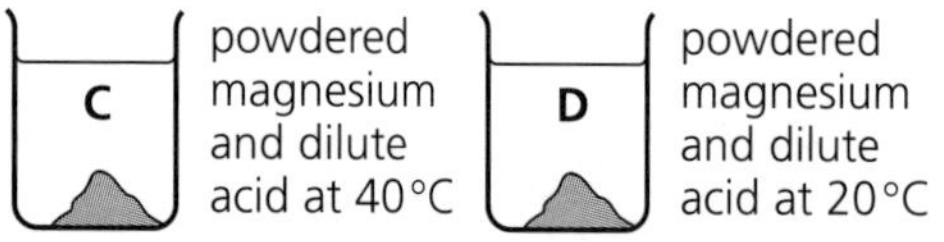

C: powdered magnesium and dilute acid at 40°C
D: powdered magnesium and dilute acid at 20°C

b Use the idea of particles to suggest and explain **two** reasons why the reaction in beaker C was faster than D. [4]

c Suggest **two** other ways of speeding reactions up. [2]

[8 marks]

7 Geologists think that a particular type of rock from South America was made from molten magma which came to the surface and quickly cooled.

a What do we call rocks formed when molten magma solidifies? [1]

b What can you see in the diagram that shows you that both these rocks were formed when molten rock cooled? [2]

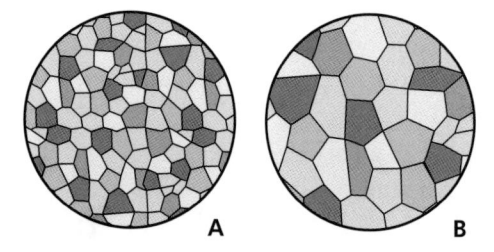

A   B

c Which of the rocks in the diagram could have cooled quickly? Explain how you can tell. [1]

d There is an identical type of rock in Africa. Geologists think that the two rocks were formed very close to each other. Use ideas about plate tectonics to explain why they are so far apart. [2]

[6 marks]

8 The thermit reaction uses a reactive metal to turn iron oxide into iron.

a What do we call a reaction were oxygen is removed from a compound? [1]

Here is part of the reactivity series:
aluminium, zinc, iron, copper, silver

b Which of these elements would convert iron oxide to iron? [1]

c Suggest one reason (apart from cost) why sodium is not used to do this. [1]

[3 marks]

9 The flow chart shows how ammonia is made.

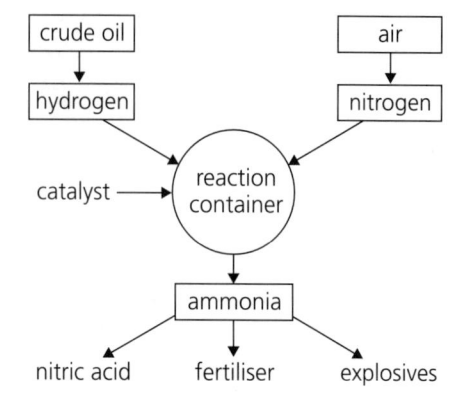

crude oil → hydrogen
air → nitrogen
catalyst → reaction container
→ ammonia
→ nitric acid, fertiliser, explosives

a i Air is a raw material used to make ammonia. Write down the name of the other raw material. [1]

ii Write down two uses of ammonia. [2]

iii What are three of the costs in making ammonia? [3]

b A catalyst is used in this reaction.
  i What is a catalyst? [2]
  ii Which catalyst is used in this process? [1]

c The Haber Process is a reversible reaction. What is meant by the term 'reversible reaction'? [1]

d The graph shows what percentage of ammonia is produced by the Haber Process at different pressures.

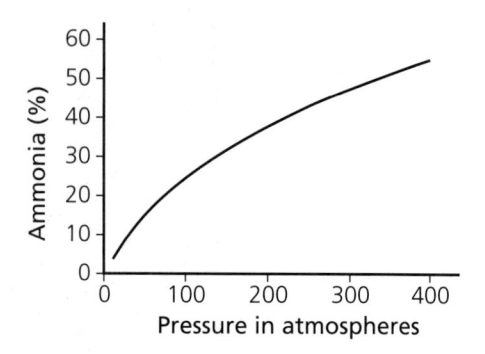

[graph: Ammonia (%) vs Pressure in atmospheres]

i The plant is usually operated at about 250 atmospheres pressure. What percentage of ammonia should this produce? [1]

ii It is too expensive to build a factory which works at a higher pressure, even though a higher percentage of ammonia would be produced. Suggest one reason why it is more expensive to use a higher pressure. [1]

e The equation for the Haber Process is
$$N_2 + 3H_2 \rightleftharpoons 2NH_3$$
What happens to the position of the equilibrium as the pressure is increased? [1]

[13 marks]

10 When the nuclear power station at Chernobyl released radioactive dust into the air, some of the dust fell on the Lake District in Britain. Sheep ate the dust that settled on the grass and produced radioactive milk. Sheep normally use calcium from the grass to make milk, but this time they were using strontium-90 from the dust as well.

a i Find strontium in the Periodic Table and decide how many protons are in the nucleus of a strontium atom. [1]

ii Strontium-90 is an isotope of strontium. What is the difference between two isotopes of the same element? [1]

b i Use the Periodic Table to decide how many electrons are in the outer shell of a strontium atom. [1]

ii Explain why sheep are likely to take in strontium as well as calcium. [2]

c An element has an atomic number of 13 and an atomic mass of 27.

i How many neutrons are in its nucleus? [1]

ii Write down the number of electrons in each shell, starting with the innermost shell. [1]

[7 marks]

11 Ammonia solution is an alkali. You can make fertiliser by neutralising ammonia solution with an acid. A student investigated neutralisation reactions by adding acid from a burette to alkali in a flask. She measured the pH during the investigation.

a i Suggest the pH of the alkali in the flask at the start. [1]

ii Suggest the pH of the solution when she had added just enough acid to neutralise the alkali. [1]

iii Suggest the pH of the solution if she added one drop too much of the acid. [1]

b Complete the equation
acid + alkali → _____ + water [1]

c The fertiliser that she made was ammonium nitrate, $(NH_4)_2NO_3$.

i How many atoms of nitrogen are in the formula of ammonium nitrate? [1]

ii How many different elements are in ammonium nitrate? [1]

iii The relative atomic mass (A_r) of hydrogen (H) is 1. The relative atomic mass (A_r) of nitrogen (N) is 14. The relative atomic mass (A_r) of oxygen (O) is 16. What is the relative formula mass of ammonium nitrate? [1]

d If fertilisers contaminate ponds or lakes, wildlife will be harmed.

i What do we call this effect? [1]

ii Briefly describe how the damage is done [3]

[11 marks]

12 Use this diagram of the Periodic Table to help you answer this question.

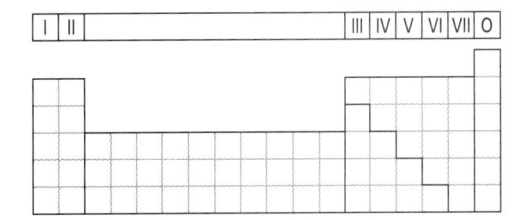

a i Where on the Periodic Table is the most reactive metal? [2]

ii Where on the Periodic Table is the most reactive non-metal? [2]

b Use ideas about electron shells to explain why the Noble Gases (Group 0) are not reactive. [1]

c Oxygen has eight electrons and is in Group VI.

i How many electrons are in the inner shell of an oxygen atom? [1]

ii How many electrons are in the outer shell of an oxygen atom? [1]

d Magnesium has two electrons in its outer shell. What is the charge on a magnesium ion? [2]

[9 marks]

13 Aluminium is produced by the electrolysis of aluminium oxide. Aluminium oxide is made up of Al^{+++} and O^{--} particles.

a What do we call Al^{+++} and O^{--} particles? [1]

b Cryolite is added to the aluminium oxide before it is melted. Explain why. [1]

c Explain why melted aluminium oxide will conduct electricity but the solid won't. [1]

d The sides and the bottom of the electrolysis cell are lined with carbon. This is connected to an electricity supply to make the negative electrode. Positive carbon electrodes are dipped into the liquid.

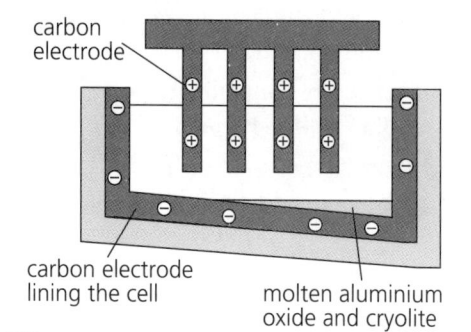

i What do we call a positive electrode? [1]
ii What do we call a negative electrode? [1]
iii What happens to the Al^{+++} particles when the current is switched on? [2]

[7 marks]

14 Ethane, C_2H_6, and ethene, C_2H_4, are hydrocarbons with slightly different formulae.

a How many atoms of carbon are in a molecule of ethane? [1]

b Hydrogen and carbon are both non-metals.
  i What happens to the electrons on the two atoms when they form a bond? [1]
  ii A carbon atom has a total of six electrons around its nucleus. How are they arranged in their shells? [2]

c Ethane is part of the alkane group.
  i What group is ethene part of? [1]
  ii What chemical test could you use to tell the difference between ethane and ethene? [1]
  iii What would you see if you tried this test on ethene? [1]
  iv State what you would see if you tried this test on ethane. [1]

d Ethene is used to make polythene, a polymer.
  i Use the symbol –E– for ethene to draw part of a polythene molecule. [1]
  ii Ethene does not form polythene without help. Give two things that you must do so that the ethene will react. [2]

[11 marks]

15 We think that wine was first produced by accident when wild yeasts landed on some crushed grapes and made them ferment.

a i What are the three important conditions for fermentation to go well? [3]
  ii What are the sugars in the grapes converted to during fermentation? [1]

b Yeast contains biological catalysts called enzymes.
  i What does a catalyst do to a reaction? [1]
  ii What can you say about a catalyst at the end of a reaction? [1]

c Yeast is also used in breadmaking. What does yeast produce to make the bread rise? [1]

d If bread is left in a cold place the yeast will only work very slowly. What will happen to the speed that the yeast works at as the temperature increases? Explain your answer. [4]

[11 marks]

16 Impure copper can be purified by electrolysis. The impure copper is used as the anode and pure copper is the cathode in an electrolysis cell. The cell is filled with copper sulphate solution. During the electrolysis the impure anode dissolves and the cathode gets heavier.

a i Where do the particles which make the cathode heavier come from? [1]
  ii Write an ionic equation for this process. [1]
b i Why does the cathode get lighter? [1]
  ii Write an ionic equation for this process. [1]

[4 marks]

AT4

Physical Processes

Electric circuits	96
Using electricity	102
Energy transfer	110
Forces, energy and motion	114
Waves	124
Earth in space	130
Concept map	134
Exam questions	135

Static electricity

Jo walks across the room. Her feet rub against the carpet, pulling tiny particles (**electrons**) off it. As the number of electrons on her builds up, Jo becomes **charged** with **static electricity**. She acquires a **negative charge** because she has gained some electrons. The carpet acquires a **positive charge** because it has lost electrons.

electrons transferred from carpet to Jo

carpet

electrons move quickly from Jo to handle

When Jo reaches the door, she touches the metal handle. All the electrons which she pulled off the carpet flow rapidly through her into the metal handle. She **discharges** herself, but gets an electric shock at the same time.

Conductors and insulators

Materials which allow electrons to move through them are **conductors**. Things which electrons can't move through are **insulators**. Metals and water are conductors. Most other materials (such as glass, wood and plastic) are insulators.

Now do this

1. What can move through conductors but not through insulators?
2. Name two materials which are insulators.
3. Name two materials which are conductors.
4. Copy and complete the following sentences. A nylon comb is an _____. When it passes through hair, _____ are pulled off the hair and carried away by the _____. This leaves the comb _____.

Types of charge

There are two sorts of charge, called **positive** and **negative**. The sort of charge picked up by objects when they are rubbed against each other depends on the two materials involved.

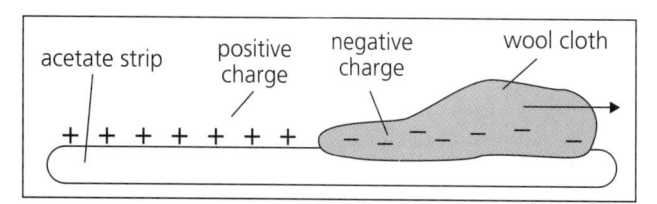

acetate strip   positive charge   negative charge   wool cloth

In this example, acetate becomes positive when rubbed with wool. This is because the electrons transferred from the acetate to the wool have a negative charge. The acetate becomes positive because it has lost some negative charge.

Polythene becomes negative when it is rubbed with wool. The wool becomes positive.

Now do this

5. Copy and complete the following sentences. Fur becomes positive when rubbed on glass. This is because electrons are transferred from the _____ to the _____ during the rubbing. Electrons have a _____ charge. Objects which have lost electrons have a _____ charge.
6. When glass is rubbed with silk, electrons are transferred from glass to silk. What are the charges of the glass and the silk after rubbing?

Electric circuits

Attraction and repulsion

Objects with any charge attract objects with no charge.
Objects with the same charge always repel each other.
Objects with different charges always attract each other.

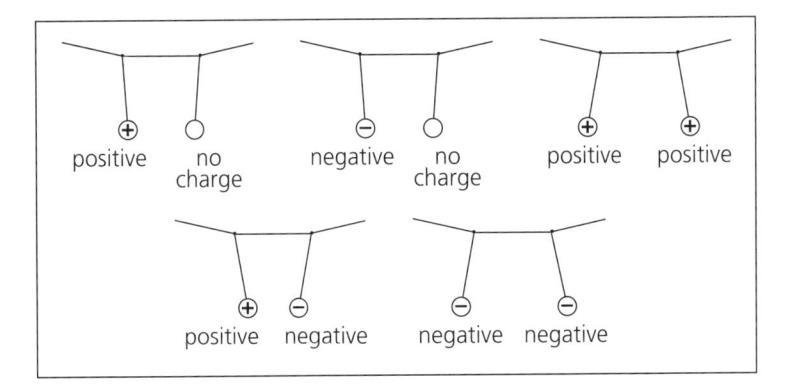

Now do this

7 The table shows the effect of bringing object L close to object R. Complete the table with the words attract and repel.

Charge on L	Charge on R	Effect
positive	negative	
positive	none	
negative	negative	

Using static electricity

Electrostatic forces are very useful.

Droplets of paint spray can be charged. They then repel each other, to give a fine mist which is strongly attracted to any uncharged metal objects nearby. The result is a very even coat of paint on the object, even round the back.

Photocopiers and laser printers use static electricity. Reflected light from a document is used to coat an insulating surface with a pattern of positive charge. This attracts tiny particles of negatively charged toner. The pattern of toner is then transferred to paper which has been strongly positively charged. The toner is fixed to the paper by heating to create a copy.

Electrostatic discharge can be dangerous.

Airplanes in flight become charged as they move rapidly through the air. The charge must be removed safely when the aircraft lands. Otherwise, there may be a **spark** between the airplane and the metal nozzle of the refuelling pipe. The spark (which is a rapid flow of electrons through the air) could ignite the fuel.

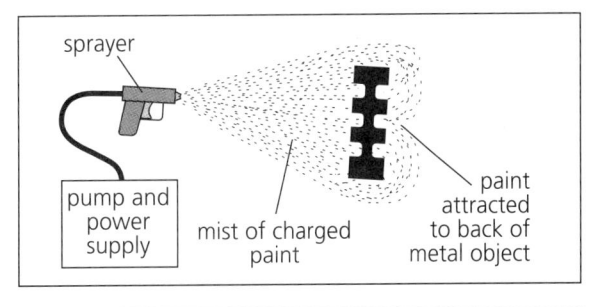

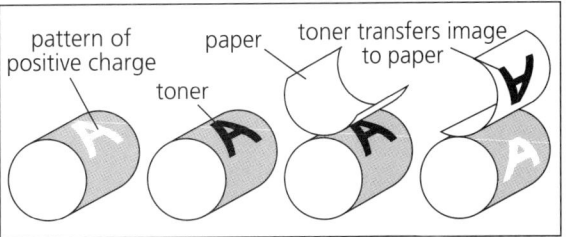

Now do this

8 Name two devices which use static electricity.

9 Explain why static charge can be dangerous when flammable substances are present.

10 Suggest why you can get an electric shock when you touch the body of a car after a journey.

Electrical circuits

Here is the **circuit diagram** for a **lamp** connected to a **battery** by a pair of **wires**.

Chemical energy in a cell makes electrons in the metal parts of the circuit flow from the negative terminal ⊖ to the positive one ⊕. A flow of electrons or charge is called a **current**. There is only a current if there is a complete conducting circuit between the terminals of the cell. Several cells make a **battery**. The current is the rate of flow of charge.

$$\text{current} = \frac{\text{charge}}{\text{time}} \qquad I = \frac{Q}{t}$$

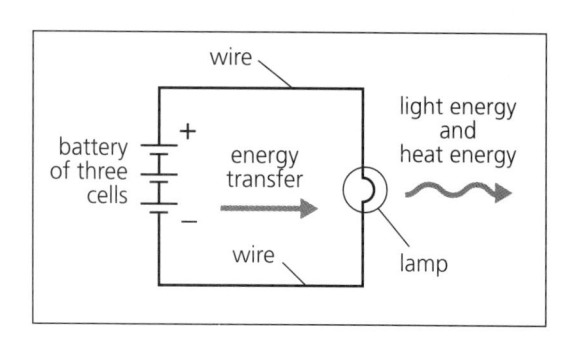

Symbol	Meaning	Units of measurement
I	current	ampere or A
Q	charge	coulomb or C
t	time	second or s

Worked example

Q A current of 250 mA flows in a lamp for 2 minutes. How much charge passes through the lamp?

A $I = 250$ mA $= 0.25$ A
$Q = ?$
$t = 2$ minutes $= 120$ s

$I = \dfrac{Q}{t}$

$Q = I\,t \qquad ? = 0.25 \times 120 = 30$ C

Now do this

1. Calculate the charge which flows through a 500 mA lamp in 30 s.
2. If 1200 C of charge passes through a motor in a minute, what is the current in it?

Component	Circuit symbol	Energy output
lamp	⊗	light and heat
resistor	▭	heat
buzzer	⌒	sound
motor	—(M)—	kinetic
LED	▶│	light

Now do this

3. Name five different electrical components. Draw their circuit symbols and state what type of energy they produce.
4. Draw the circuit diagram for a motor run off a battery.

Voltage

All electrical components have a **voltage rating**. This should be the same as the voltage of the electricity supply. You can run more than one component from one supply by connecting them in **parallel** with each other. If you put components in **series** with each other, low voltage components can be run off a high voltage supply.

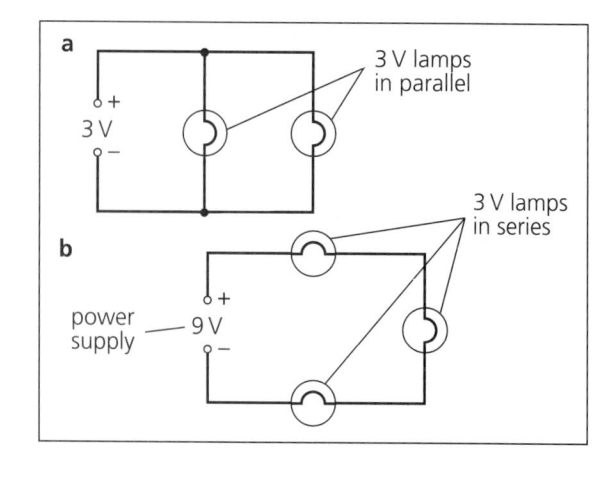

Electric circuits

Current

The amount of current in a component is measured with an **ammeter**. The meter is connected in **series** with the component.

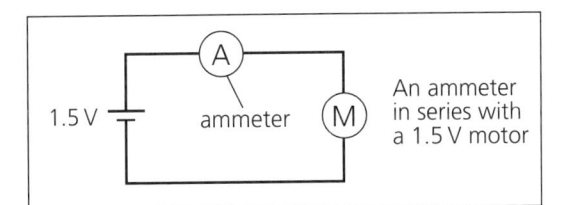

Current is measured in **amps** (**A**). It has the same value all the way round a series circuit. When components are connected in parallel, the current drawn from the electricity supply is the sum of the currents in the components.

components in series

components in parallel

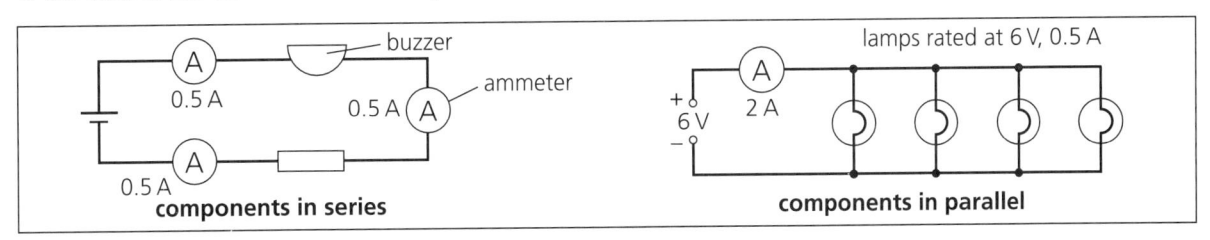

Measuring voltage

The voltage drop across a component is measured by connecting a **voltmeter** in **parallel** with it. Voltage (or **potential difference**) is measured in **volts** (**V**). The voltage at a point in a circuit is the energy of each coulomb of charge at that point.

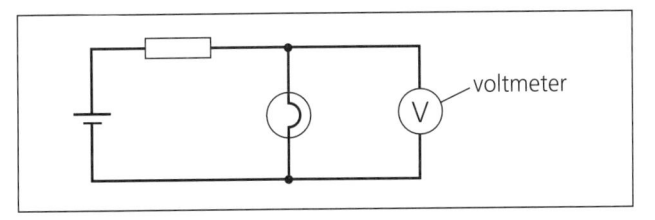

Types of electricity

There are two **sources** of electrical energy: **direct current** (or **d.c.**) and **alternating current** (or **a.c.**). Batteries supply d.c., dynamos and generators supply a.c.

A **cathode ray oscilloscope** (or CRO) can be used to show the difference between a.c. and d.c. supplies.

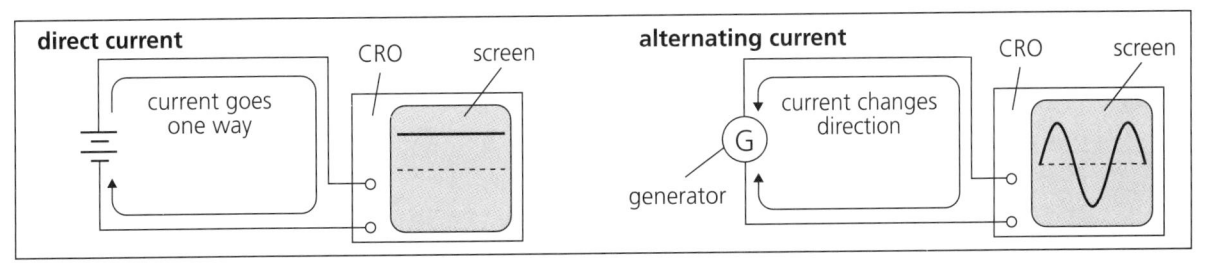

Now do this

5. Draw a diagram to show how to measure the current in a lamp being run off a 6 V battery.

6. Fill in the readings of the ammeters in this circuit.

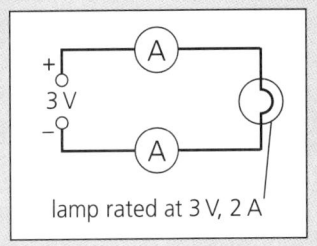

7. A single 60 W lamp draws a current of 0.25 A when connected to a 240 V supply. How much current will be drawn by 8 bulbs connected in parallel to 240 V?

Now do this

8. A resistor and a motor are connected in series with a 12 V battery. Draw a circuit diagram to show how the voltage across the motor can be measured.

9. There is a voltage drop of 12 V across a lamp. How much energy is delivered to the lamp when 8 C of charge flow through it?

Power

The **power** of an electrical component is given with this formula:

power = current × voltage $P = IV$

Symbol	Meaning	Units of measurement
P	power	joules/s or watts (W)
V	voltage	volts or V
I	current	amperes or A

Worked example

Q There is a current of 2 A in an electric drill connected to 230 V. Calculate the power of the drill.

A $P = ?$ $V = 230\,V$ $I = 2\,A$
$P = I \times V$
$? = 2 \times 230 = 460\,W$

Now do this

1. Write down the symbols and units for power, voltage and current. State the formula relating them.
2. There is a current of 5 A in a lamp connected to a 12 V battery. Calculate the power of the lamp.
3. Draw a circuit diagram to show how an ammeter and a voltmeter should be connected to measure the power of a motor.
4. A 100 W lamp is connected to a 250 V supply. Calculate the current in the lamp.

Resistance

Resistors control the current in a circuit. A big **resistance** means a small current. Two bulbs in series have a larger resistance than just one on its own. A **rheostat** is a variable resistor which controls the current in a circuit by altering its resistance.

As the voltage across a resistor increases, so does the current.

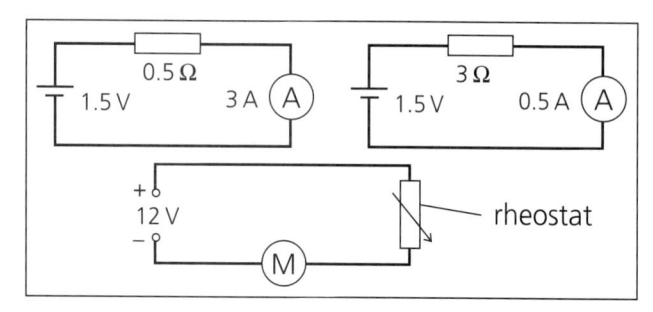

Now do this

5. Which of these circuits has the highest resistance?

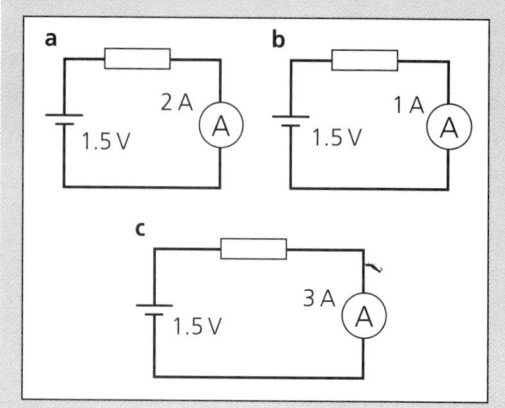

The **resistance** of an electrical component is calculated with this formula:

resistance = voltage / current $R = \dfrac{V}{I}$

Symbol	Meaning	Units of measurement
R	resistance	ohms or Ω
V	voltage	volts or V
I	current	amperes or A

Worked example

Q There is a current of 0.2 A in a resistor connected to a 3.0 V battery. Calculate the resistance.

A $R = ?$
$V = 3.0\,V$ $R = \dfrac{V}{I}$ $? = \dfrac{3.0}{0.2} = 15\,\Omega$
$I = 0.2\,A$

Electric circuits

Now do this

6. Write down the formula for electrical resistance. Explain the symbols and give their units.
7. A resistor has a current of 0.5 A when the voltage across it is 24 V. Calculate its resistance.
8. Show how a rheostat can be used to adjust the brightness of a lamp connected to a battery.
9. What is the current in a 3 Ω resistor when the voltage across it is 12 V?
10. What is the voltage across a 25 Ω resistor when there is a current of 4 A in it?

Switches

Switches are used to control the flow of electrical energy in a circuit. When the switch is **open** charge cannot flow through it. There can only be a current in a switch when it is **closed**.

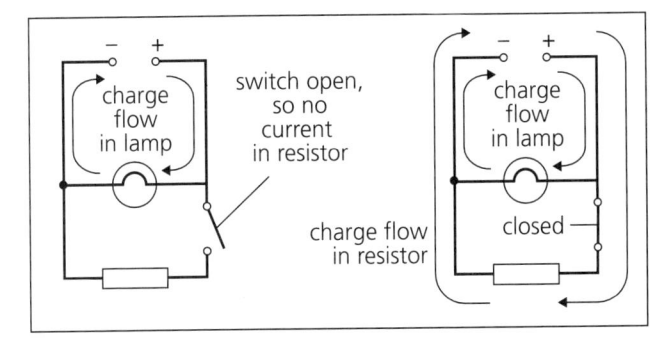

Now do this

11. Using the diagram, complete this table with the words **on** or **off**.

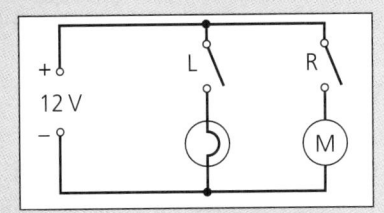

Switch L	Switch R	Lamp	Motor
open	open		
open	closed		
closed	open		
closed	closed		

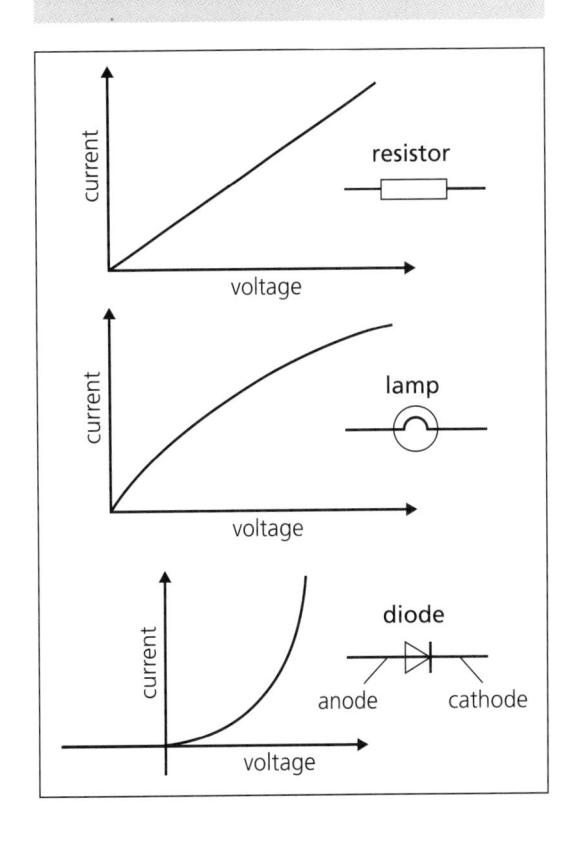

Temperature and light-sensitive components

Things which contain a lot of free electrons have a low resistance. The number of free electrons in a metal is fixed, but can be changed in a **semiconductor**. The electrons in thermistors and LDRs can be freed by giving them extra energy. Increased light reduces the resistance of a light-dependent resistor (LDR). Similarly, increased temperature reduces the resistance of a thermistor.

Voltage–current curves

These graphs show how the current in a wire resistor and a lamp depend on the voltage across them. Neither of these components have a polarity, so the graphs look exactly the same if the voltage is reversed.

The resistance of a **diode** depends on the voltage across it. The current rises steeply when the **anode** voltage rises above the **cathode** voltage.

Using electricity

Every electrical appliance should be marked with its **voltage** and **power rating**. The voltage rating is usually 230 V in Europe. The power is measured in **watts** (**W**) or **kilowatts** (**kW**).

1 kW = 1000 W

Calculating the cost

The power rating of an appliance can be used to calculate how much electrical energy it will need when it is switched on.

energy (kilowatt-hour) = **power** (kilowatt) × **time** (hour)

One kilowatt-hour (kWh) of energy is called a **unit** of electricity. It costs about 10p. Off-peak electricity at night costs less.

Worked example

Q A bulb has a power of 200 W. If a unit of electricity costs 8p, calculate the cost of running the bulb for a week.

A Power in kilowatts = $\frac{200}{1000}$ = 0.2 kW

time in hours = 24 × 7 = 168 h

units used = kilowatts × hours = 0.2 × 168 = 33.6 kWh

cost = units × 8 = 33.6 × 8 = 269p.

250 W microwave oven

3 kW heater

Now do this

1. A TV is rated at 230 V, 150 W. If a unit of electricity costs 9p, calculate how much it costs to run the TV for 5 hours.

2. If an off-peak unit of electricity costs 6p, calculate how much it costs to run a 2.5 kW water heater for 4 hours at night.

3. Suppose a unit of electricity costs 8p. How much money do you waste by leaving a 100 W bulb on for 10 minutes?

Electrical wiring

Electric currents in metals make them get hot. Thin, high-**resistance** wires get hotter than thick, low-resistance ones. Electrical appliances are connected to the 230 V mains supply by a pair of insulated metal wires. They are called **live** and **neutral**. If the appliance has a metal exterior, there will be a third **earth** wire as well.

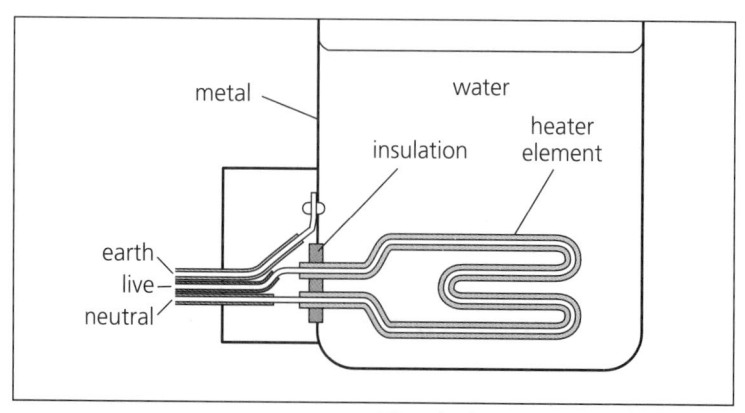

Electrical connections to a kettle

Each wire has a different coloured insulation

Wire	Insulation colour
live	brown
neutral	blue
earth	green and yellow

Using electricity

The live wire carries the energy from the supply to the appliance. The live wire is therefore the one which is most dangerous to touch, so it has the **switch**. The neutral wire completes the circuit for the electric current.

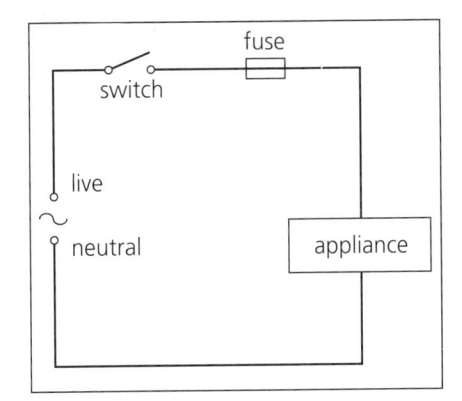

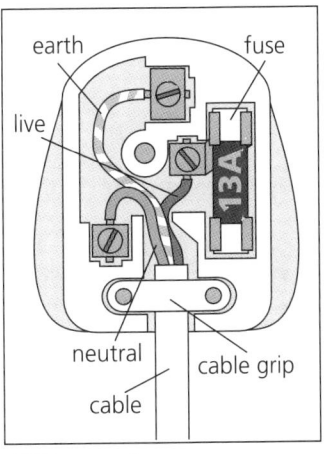

Wiring a plug

Now do this

4 Name the three wires connecting an electrical heater to the mains supply. State the colour of their insulation.

5 Explain why the wire in the heating element of a water heater is much thinner than the wire in the cable connecting the heater to the mains supply.

Fuses and safety

There should also be a **fuse** or **circuit breaker** in the live wire. This switches off the current automatically if it gets too high.

Large currents in a wire can cause it to get hot and damage its insulation. The fuse is the thinnest wire in the circuit, so it melts (blows) first, before the other wires are damaged.

The earth wire should always be connected to the metal outside of an appliance. This protects anyone using the appliance. If the live wire comes loose and touches the outside, a large current flows in the earth wire and the fuse blows.

Appliances which are **double insulated** do not need an earth wire. Should the live wire come loose, it can't touch any metal which is on the outside of the appliance. Any appliance which has a non-metallic case is definitely double insulated and doesn't need an earth wire.

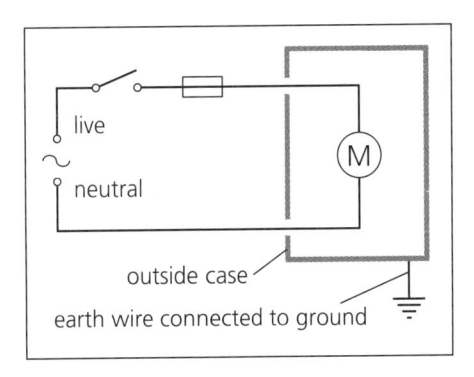

Now do this

6 State the function of each of the three wires connecting an appliance to the mains electricity supply.

7 Explain how a fuse or circuit breaker protects the insulation of mains wires.

8 Explain how a fuse can protect people from electric shock.

9 Where should the fuse and switch be connected?

10 What type of appliance does not need an earth wire?

11 Where should the earth wire be connected to an appliance? Why?

Electromagnetism

Magnets

Pieces of steel can be made into **magnets** by passing direct current through a coil wrapped around them.

Magnets attract **iron** and **steel** which has not been magnetised. They ignore all other metals except **cobalt** and **nickel**.

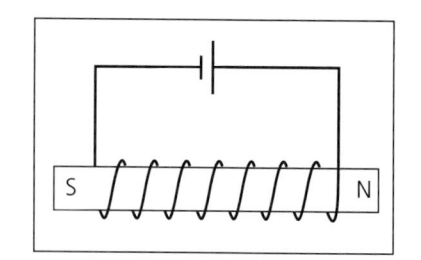

Magnetic fields

Here is the **magnetic field** around a bar magnet. Each **field line** has an arrow on it. The field lines tell you which way the needle of a **compass** points.

The two ends of a magnet have different names. One is called the **north pole**. The other is called **south pole**. The field lines come out of the north pole of the magnet and return at the south pole of the magnet.

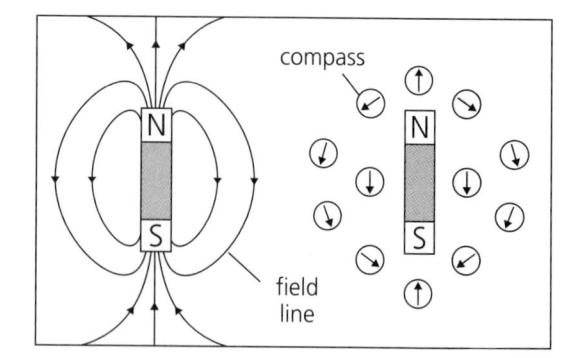

Now do this

1. Name the four materials which are attracted to magnets.
2. Name the pole at T on this magnet.
3. Which way will the compass needle point?

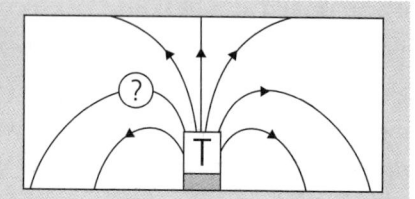

Either pole of a magnet will attract unmagnetised iron.
Poles which are the same always repel each other.
Poles which are different always attract each other.

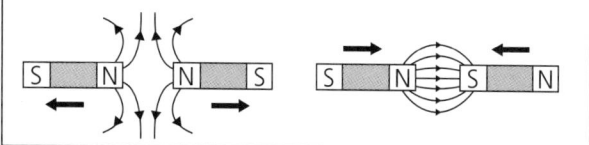

Now do this

4. Here are some pairs of objects. For each pair, state whether they repel, attract or ignore each other.

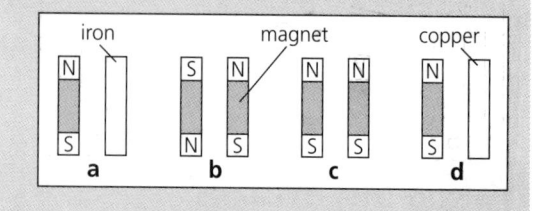

Forces on currents in magnetic fields

There is a **force** on a conductor which carries a current in a magnetic field. The force is at right angles to both the current and the field. The direction of the force can be reversed by reversing the direction of either the current or the field.

Now do this

5. The wire in diagram (a) is pushed to the left. Which way does the wire get pushed in diagrams (b), (c) and (d)?

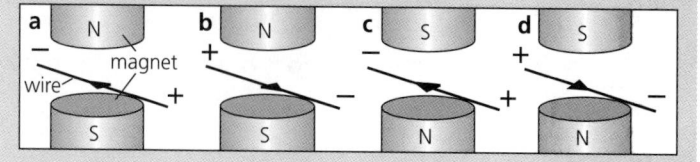

Using electricity

Electricity is **generated** whenever a wire is moved through a magnetic field. The voltage changes sign if the wire is moved the other way.

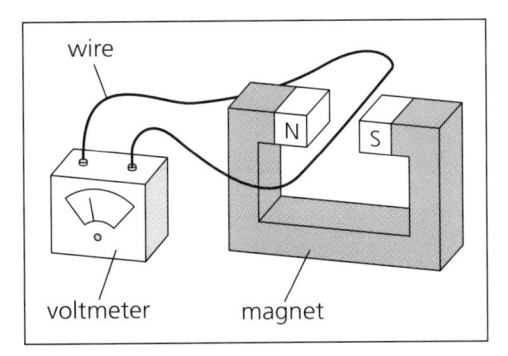

The size of the voltage can be increased by speeding up the motion and increasing the strength of the field.

A voltage is **induced** across the ends of a coil of wire whenever the magnetic field inside it changes. The sign of the induced voltage changes when the change of magnetic field is reversed.

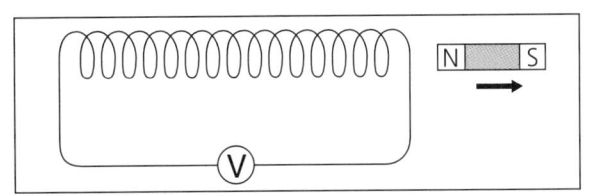

Electricity is generated on a large scale by spinning large coils of copper wire inside the fields of large magnets. The alternating current in the coil is brought out of the **generator** by **brushes** pressing on **slip rings**.

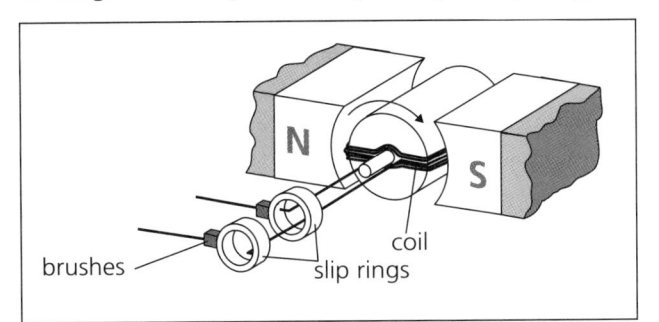

Now do this

6 The voltmeter reads +0.1V as the wire is pulled up through the poles of the magnet. What will it read when the wire is
 a pushed down
 b held still between the poles of the magnet?

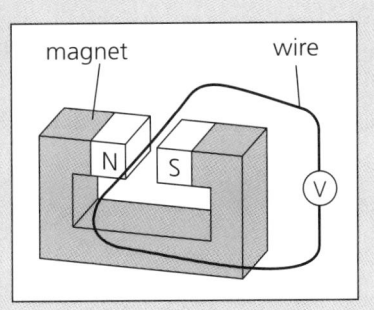

7 State two things you could do to increase the reading of the voltmeter in question 6.

The size of the voltage can be increased by:
- speeding up the change of magnetic field
- increasing the number of coils of wire
- increasing the area of the coil
- winding the coil around soft iron.

Now do this

8 Copy and complete the following sentences.
There is a positive voltage across a coil when a magnet is placed in it. The voltage is _____ when the magnet is left in the coil and becomes _____ as the magnet is removed from the coil.

9 State four ways of increasing the voltage induced in a coil when a magnet is brought close.

Now do this

10 A generator always contains lots of steel, soft iron and copper. Suggest what each material is used for in the generator.

11 Here is the voltage – time graph for a coil spinning in a magnetic field. How would the graph change if the coil spun round twice as fast?

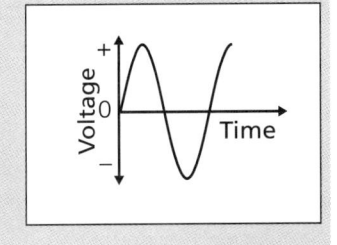

Generating electricity

Electricity is made on a large scale by boiling water to make high-pressure **steam**. The steam passes through a **turbine**, making it spin round. The turbine is connected to the shaft of a **generator**. Electromagnets are attached to the shaft. As it spins round, the magnetic field inside the coils of wire changes, generating electricity.

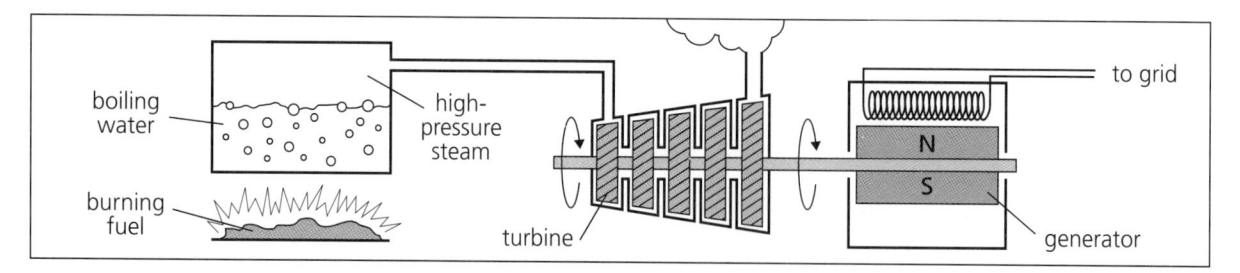

The water can be boiled by burning a fuel (such as coal, oil or gas) or by a nuclear reaction. Here is an energy flow diagram for a typical gas-fired electricity power station.

Efficiency

Each time the energy is **transformed**, some heat energy is lost. Overall, 1000 J of chemical energy in the gas becomes 400 J of electrical energy in the wires coming out of the generator. The remaining 600 J becomes heat energy at various places. The **efficiency** can be calculated with a formula.

$$\text{efficiency} = \frac{\text{useful output}}{\text{input}} \times 100$$

input = 1000 J
useful output = 400 J
efficiency = ?

$$\text{efficiency} = \frac{400}{1000} \times 100 = 40\%$$

The final value for the efficiency is quoted as a percentage. This is why it is sometimes called **percentage efficiency** (% efficiency).

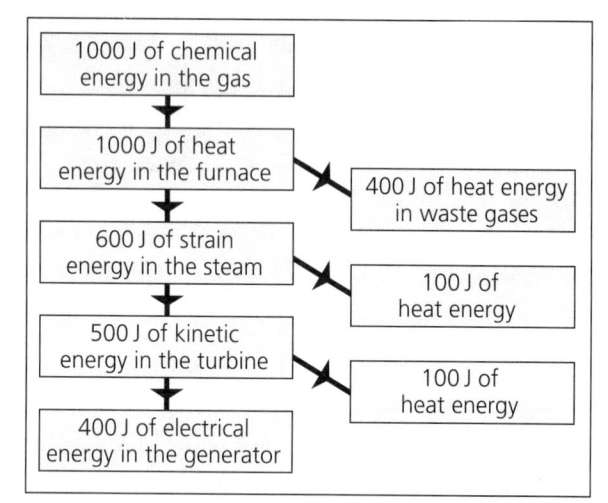

Now do this

1. Describe how electricity is generated from oil.
2. Draw an energy flow diagram for a power station.
3. State the places where heat energy is lost in a power station.
4. Write down the formula for calculating efficiency.
5. 200 J of chemical energy in coal becomes 50 J of electrical energy in a power station. Calculate the efficiency of the power station. What happens to the 150 J which doesn't become electricity?

Using electricity

Transporting electricity

Electricity is carried from power stations around the country by the **National Grid**. The electric current in this network of wires generates some heat energy. This is a waste of energy and it reduces the efficiency of the network. The efficiency is improved by keeping the wires in the grid at a very **high voltage**. This reduces the current in the wires, resulting in less wasteful heat energy.

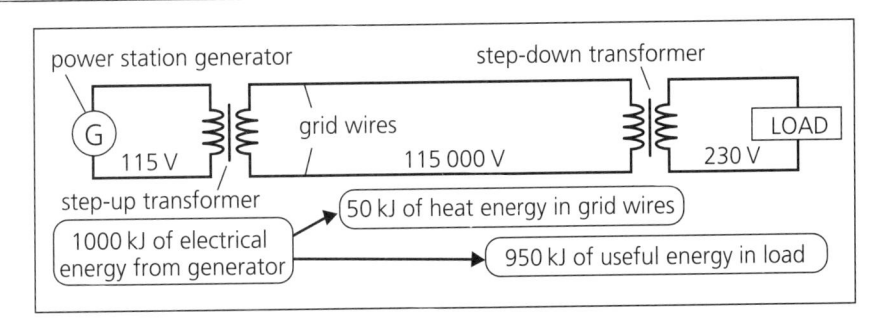

Diagram: power station generator (G) 115 V → step-up transformer → grid wires 115 000 V → step-down transformer → 230 V → LOAD. 1000 kJ of electrical energy from generator; 50 kJ of heat energy in grid wires; 950 kJ of useful energy in load.

Now do this

6. What is the National Grid? What does it do?
7. For every 1000 kJ of electricity fed into a grid, only 950 kJ can be extracted from it. What happens to the missing energy? Calculate the efficiency of the grid.
8. Explain why running the grid at a high voltage increases the efficiency of electricity transmission.

Transformers are used to raise and lower the voltage of the alternating current as it enters and leaves the grid.

A transformer is a loop of **soft iron**. Alternating current (a.c.) in the **primary coil** (made of **insulated copper**) continually changes the magnetism of the iron. This change of magnetism generates a voltage across the ends of the **secondary coil**.

Diagram: transformer with live 240 V ac, neutral, primary coil, iron core, copper secondary coil, 100 V lamp.

Transformers have a very high efficiency. Very little electricity gets converted to heat energy on the way through them.

$$\frac{\text{primary voltage}}{\text{secondary voltage}} = \frac{\text{primary turns}}{\text{secondary turns}}$$

$$\frac{V_p}{V_s} = \frac{n_p}{n_s}$$

Worked example

Q A transformer steps down 230 V to 12 V. If it has 60 turns of wire in its secondary coil, how many turns does it need in the primary coil?

A $\frac{V_p}{V_s} = \frac{n_p}{n_s}$ so $\frac{230}{12} = \frac{?}{60}$

therefore $? = 60 \times \frac{230}{12} = 1150$

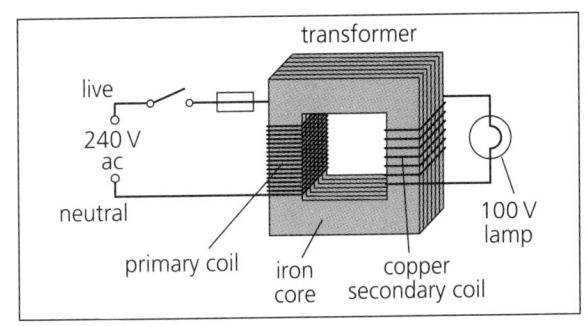

Now do this

9. Draw a labelled diagram of a transformer.
10. Explain why there is always a transformer between a generator and the National Grid.
11. Do transformers operate from a.c. or d.c.?
12. 1000 J of electricity enters the primary coil of a transformer. 20 J of heat energy appears in the transformer. Calculate the efficiency of the transformer.
13. The primary and secondary coils of a transformer have 920 and 48 turns of wire. If the primary coil is connected to a 230 V a.c. supply, what voltage appears at the secondary coil?

Electromagnets in action

There is a magnetic field around a coil of insulated wire carrying an electric current. The direction of the field reverses when the direction of the current is reversed.

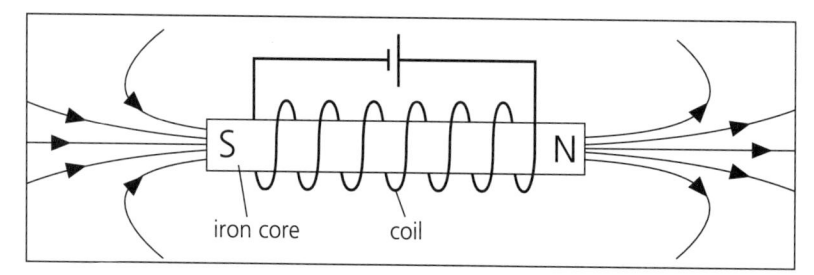

Electromagnets

A U-shaped **electromagnet** is useful for picking up objects made from iron. It only attracts them when the current in the coil is switched on.

An electromagnet becomes stronger if:
- more coils of wire are put on it
- the current in it is increased
- it is wound on a soft iron core.

Now do this

1. Sketch the magnetic field lines around a coil of wire which carries an electric current.
2. State three things which increase the strength of an electromagnet.

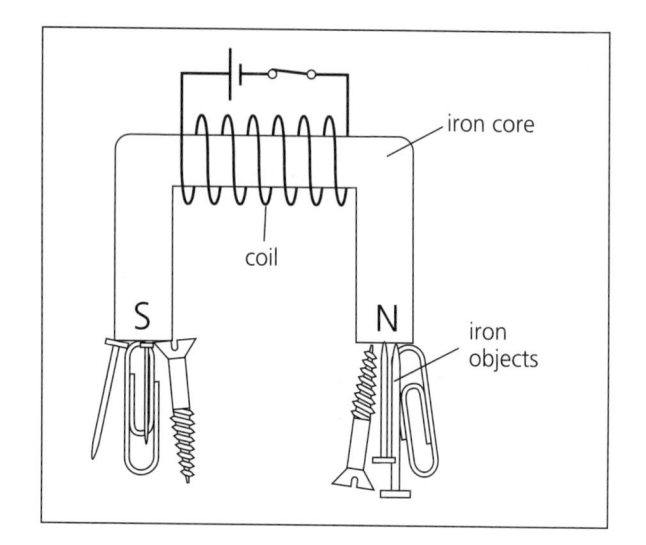

Relays

A **relay** uses an electromagnet to control an electrical switch. A small current in the **coil** attracts the iron **armature**, closing the copper **contacts**. The contacts open as soon as there is no current in the coil. The current in the contacts is often large or at a dangerous voltage.

Now do this

3. Draw a labelled diagram of a relay.
4. Describe and explain how to close and open the relay contacts.

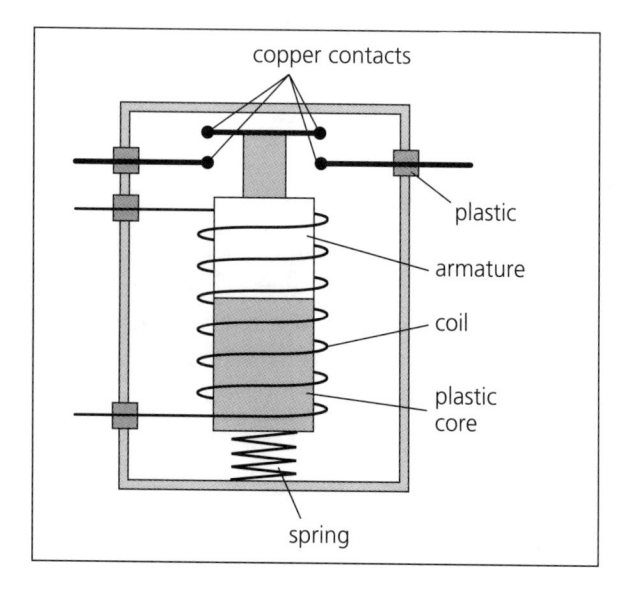

Using electricity

Electric bells

An electric **bell** works by using an electromagnet.

There can only be a current in the coil if the contacts are closed. This current will energise the electromagnet, causing the armature to move towards the electromagnet, opening the contacts. So the electromagnet is no longer energised, allowing the spring to pull the armature back again. Thus the armature moves up and down continually, hitting the bell.

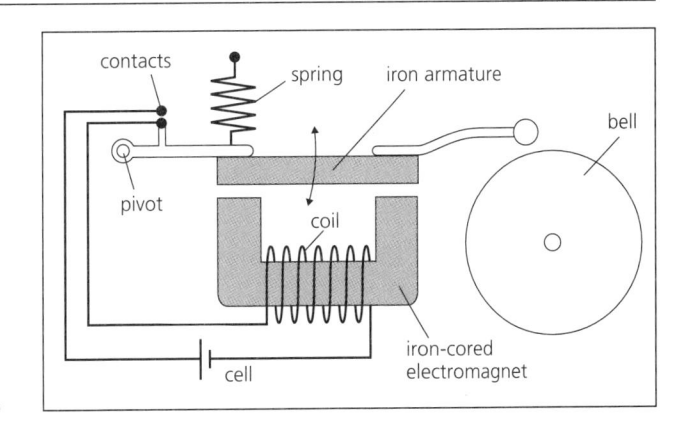

Now do this

5   Copy and complete the following sentences for an electric bell. Choose words from the following:

armature   open   off   close   comes on

When the contacts are closed, the electromagnet _____ . This attracts the _____ , so the contacts _____ . This turns the electromagnet _____ , the armature is pulled back by the spring and the contacts _____ once more.

Electric motor

An electric **motor** contains a coil of copper wire wound onto a soft iron cylinder. The cylinder is free to rotate on its axis, and it sits in a magnetic field from a permanent magnet or an electromagnet.

Electric current in the coil interacts with the magnetic field to create a pair of forces. These act in opposite directions, forcing the coil to turn round.

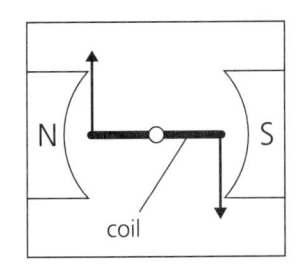

The current enters and leaves the coil via the **commutator** and **brushes**. These act as a switch which ensures that the forces on the coil always turn it in the same direction.

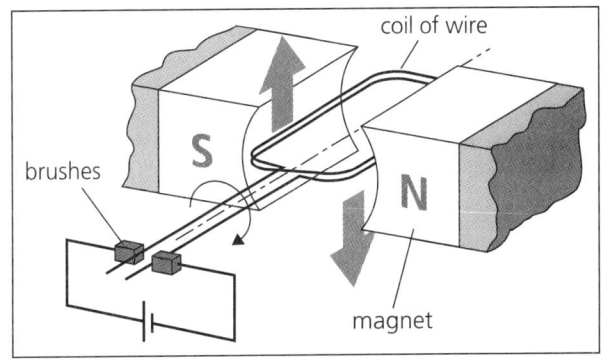

Now do this

6   What happens to the forces on a motor coil when the current direction is reversed?

7   Explain the function of the commutator in an electric motor.

8   Suggest three alterations to an electric motor which will increase its speed.

Heat energy transfer

A kettle is boiled and then left. The graph shows how its temperature changes with time. The kettle eventually settles to 20°C, the same temperature as the room.

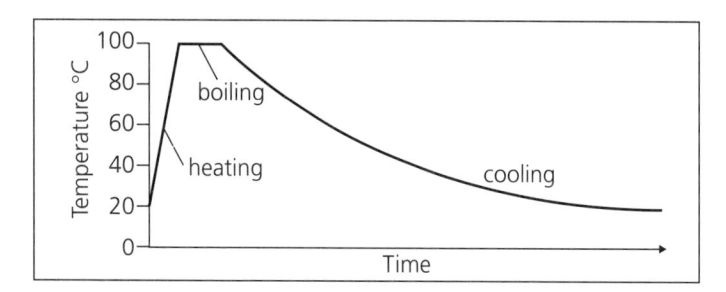

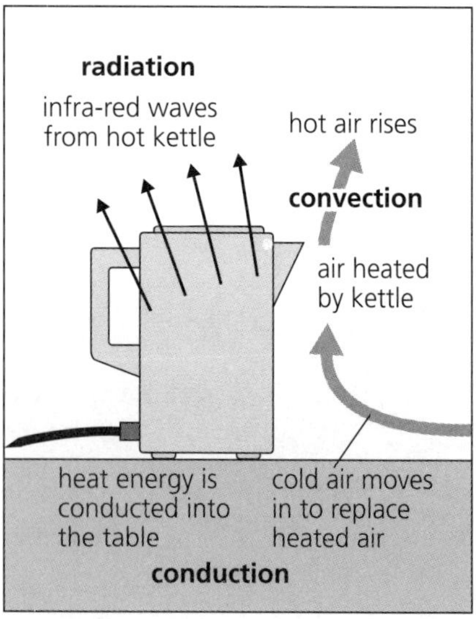

Heat energy flows from the hot kettle to the cold room until they are both at the same temperature.

There are three ways in which the kettle loses its heat energy:
- by **conduction** through the base into the table
- by **convection** as hot air rises from the sides
- by **radiation** as infra-red waves carry energy away.

Conduction

The **heat energy** of the kettle is just the **kinetic energy** of its particles. The particles in the solid kettle walls are always moving. They **vibrate**.

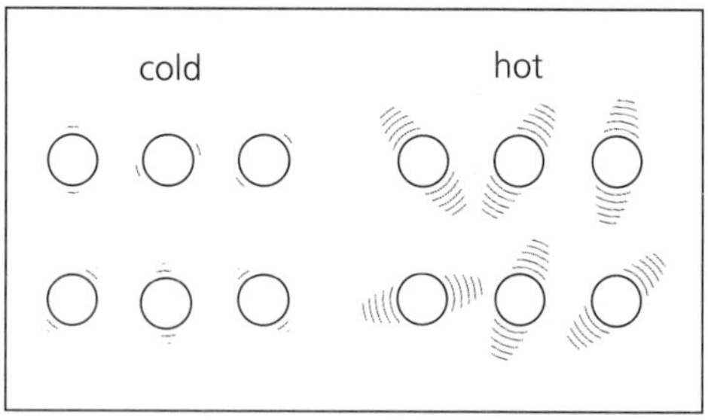

When one end of a solid is hotter than the other, the motion of the particles passes kinetic energy from the hot end to the cold end. The heat energy is **conducted**.

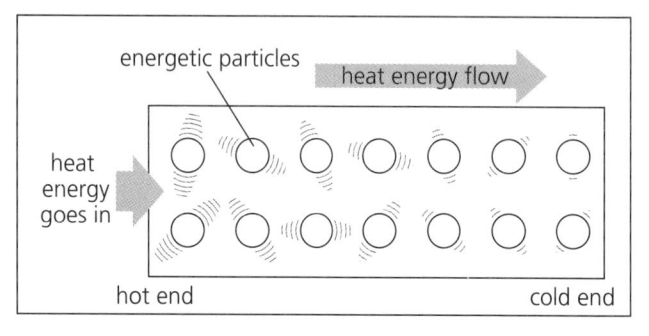

Now do this

1. A mug of coffee at 40°C is placed in a freezer at −20°C. State the final temperature of the mug. State the three ways in which heat energy leaves the mug.

Convection

Air particles which hit the hot surface of the kettle gain extra kinetic energy. So the air around the kettle heats up. This makes the air expand and rise up, carrying the extra heat energy with it. The heat energy is **convected** upwards.

Convection currents are set up around the kettle. There is a flow of cool air towards the kettle to replace the warm air moving upwards.

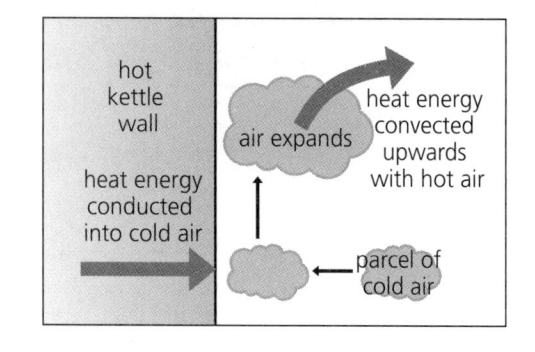

Energy transfer

Now do this

2. Copy and complete the following sentences.
   Particles in a solid have _____ energy which makes them _____.
   Particles in a hot solid have more _____ than particles in a cold solid.
   The process of heat transfer through a solid is called _____.

3. The cooling element inside a fridge is always at the top. What happens to the air particles when they hit the element? Describe and explain the convection currents inside the fridge.

Radiation

Like all hot objects, the surface of the kettle emits infra-red **radiation**. Black surfaces are much better at radiating heat than shiny ones. So a shiny kettle will lose heat energy less rapidly than a coloured one.

Remember
- **shiny** objects reflect infra-red rays, so they heat up slowly
- **black** objects absorb infra-red rays, so they heat up quickly.

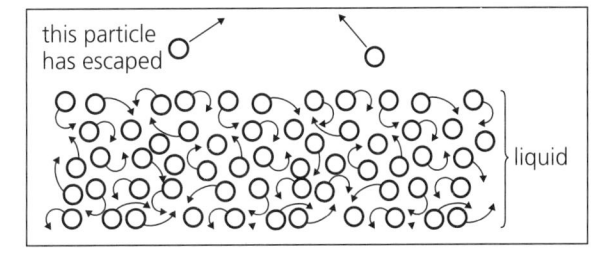

Evaporation

Liquids sometimes lose heat energy by **evaporation**. Particles at the surface of a liquid can escape if they have enough energy. So the particles with the most energy gradually leave the liquid. Only the less energetic particles are left behind, giving a colder liquid. A draught across the top of a liquid speeds up evaporation.

Insulation

Heat energy lost by conduction from a house can be reduced by trapping air in:
- layers of fluffy material in the roof
- cavities in the outside walls
- double glazing in the windows.

Heat energy lost by radiation from a house can be reduced by:
- painting roofs and walls shiny white
- using window glass which does not transmit infra-red radiation.

Heat energy lost by convection from a house can be reduced by:
- sheltering it from the wind
- keeping the surface area small.

Now do this

4. Copy and complete the following sentences with the words GOOD or BAD.
   Silver objects are _____ radiators and _____ absorbers of heat radiation. Black objects are _____ radiators and _____ absorbers of heat radiation.

5. What happens to the energy of the particles in a liquid as it cools?

6. Explain how evaporation can cool a liquid.

7. Describe and explain how the rate of heat loss from a house can be reduced.

Space heating

There are two main ways of heating a home. You can either use electricity or you can burn a fuel, such as wood, coal, oil or gas. The heat from the fuel is usually carried to each room in the home by hot water in pipes or by hot air in ducts.

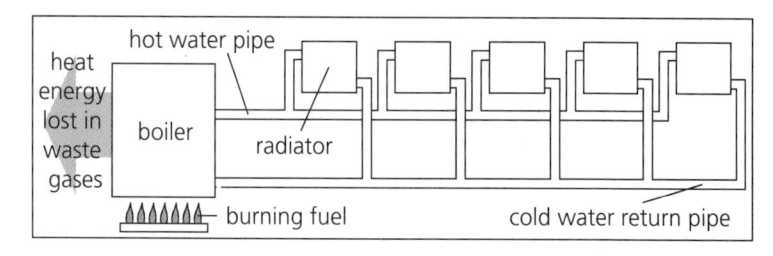

This **energy flow diagram** shows how the chemical energy in oil becomes heat energy in a room using a hot water radiator.

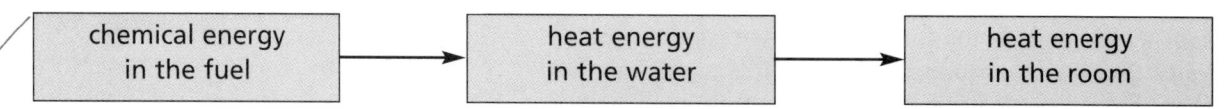

chemical energy in the fuel → heat energy in the water → heat energy in the room

Installing the pipes or ducts is expensive. It is often cheaper to put an electrical heater in each room instead. This also avoids using chimneys to vent the smoke and gases from the burnt fuel. The waste gases from the burnt fuel can **pollute** the environment.

However, making electricity often causes pollution, though it is easier to control this at the power station. Electricity is also expensive.

Now do this

1. Draw an energy flow diagram to show how the energy in gas can become heat energy in a room using hot air ducts.
2. Give two good reasons why electrical heaters should be used.
3. Give one good reason why fuels are better for heating than electricity.

Sources of electricity

Coal, oil and gas are **fossil fuels**. They are **non-renewable** sources of energy, particularly for making electricity. They will eventually be used up, and people are learning to use **renewable** sources, which use energy from the Sun. Energy is continually arriving from the Sun in the form of heat and light radiation.

Renewable sources of electricity include:
- **solar** energy, using solar cells to make electricity directly
- **wind** energy, caused by the heating of air by the Sun. Winds are convection currents, carrying cool air towards hot places
- **wave** energy, transferred to the oceans from the wind
- **plants**, which use **photosynthesis** to convert light energy into chemical energy

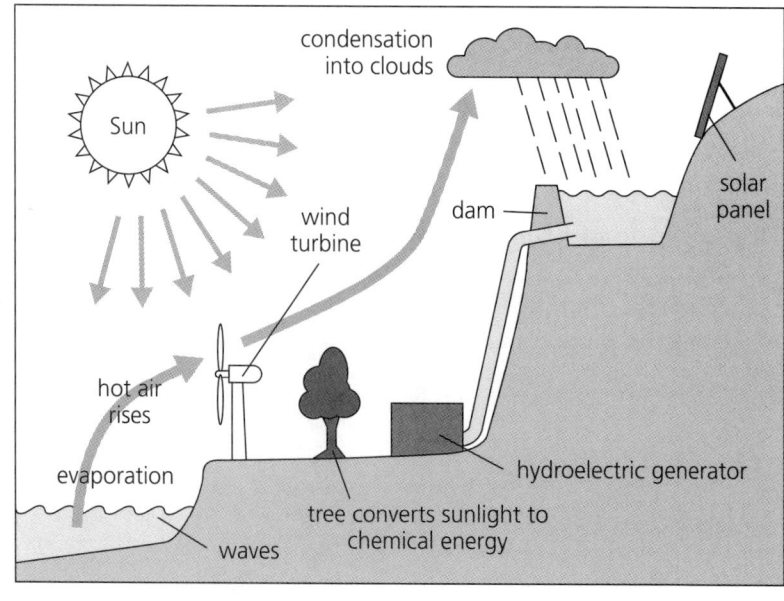

- **hydroelectric** energy, using rainwater which has fallen on mountains. The Sun evaporates the water from the sea and the wind carries the damp air above the mountains. As the air rises, it cools and the water turns to rain. The water is stored behind a dam. The stored water flows through a turbine to generate electricity.

Now do this

4. Name three non-renewable fuels for heating homes. State two reasons why it might be better to use electricity instead.
5. Name one renewable source of energy for heating a home.
6. Describe five renewable sources of electricity.

Insulation

It can be expensive to keep a building at a comfortable temperature. The only free energy is that which comes directly from the Sun. It pays to build houses which are **insulated**. Although you have to pay for the insulation, it can usually be paid for out of the saving made on buying energy to keep the house warm.

Now do this

7. The annual cost of heating a house drops from £800 to £600 when £1000 is spent on insulating the roof and walls. Calculate the pay-back time.

Worked example

Q It costs £5000 to double glaze all of the windows in a house. This cuts the annual heating bill from £750 to £500. How many years will it take before the double glazing pays for itself?

A Money saved in a year = £750 − £500 = £250, therefore pay-back time = $\frac{5000}{250}$ = 20 years.

Insulators and conductors

A material which is used to cut down the flow of heat energy is called an **insulator**. Most insulators contain a lot of air. Air is a poor conductor so it makes a good insulator when it is trapped. Clothes, curtains and double glazing all use trapped air to cut down heat energy loss.

Metals are good **conductors**. Heat energy flows quickly through them. They feel cold to the touch. Insulators feel warm.

Off-peak electricity

Electricity is produced by most power stations all of the time, night and day. The cheapest way of generating electricity is to keep producing it at a constant rate. However, there isn't much demand for electricity at night when most people are asleep. So electricity producers charge less for electricity at these **off-peak** times, to encourage people to use it. (Electricity is impossible to store directly, even for a few seconds.)

Automatic timers are used to switch on electrical devices at off-peak times, saving the consumer a lot of money. Cheap off-peak electricity can be used to:
- run storage heaters which heat bricks up at night and release their heat to air passed over them during the day
- operate washing machines and dishwashers overnight
- heat water overnight to be used during the next day.

Now do this

8. Copy and complete the following sentences.

Wool is an _____ because it contains trapped _____ .
Copper is a _____ because it is a _____ .

Measuring motion

Joe's car has a top speed of 35 metres per second (m/s). This means that it can move forwards 35 metres in each second, or 70 metres in two seconds.

The following formula can be used to calculate a speed if you know the distance and the time. (You must know this one by heart!)

$$\text{speed} = \frac{\text{distance}}{\text{time}}$$

$$v = \frac{s}{t}$$

Symbol	Meaning	Units of measurement
v	speed	metres per second or m/s
s	distance	metres or m
t	time	seconds or s

(v is for velocity, a word which can mean speed. s is for space, another word for distance. It is easy to get confused – don't!)

Worked example

Q A car at 30 m.p.h. travels 1.2 km in a minute. Calculate its speed in metres per second.

A $v = ?$ m/s
$s = 1.2$ km $= 1200$ m
$t = 1$ minute $= 60$ s

$$v = \frac{s}{t} = \frac{1200}{60} = 20 \text{ m/s}$$

Always make sure that you have the distance and the time in the correct units *before* you calculate the speed!

Now do this

1. Write down the symbols and units for speed, distance and time.
2. Write down the formula for speed using symbols.

Worked example

Q How far will a car with a speed of 15 m/s go in 10 minutes?

A $v = 15$ m/s
$s = ?$ m
$t = 600$ s

$$v = \frac{s}{t}$$

$s = vt$ $? = 15 \times 600 = 9000$ m

List the data … write the formula … draw the triangle … change the formula … insert the data.

Now do this

3. A car travels 400 m in 20 s. Calculate its speed.
4. Sound can travel 1.2 km in 4 s. How fast does it move?
5. Bill can walk 0.5 km in 5 minutes. How fast can he walk?
6. The legal top speed for a car is 110 km per hour. What is this in metres per second?

Now do this

7. A plane has a speed of 50 m/s. How far will it go in a minute?
8. A cheetah runs at 20 m/s. How long will it take to run 100 m?

Forces, energy and motion

Distance–time graphs

Distance–time graphs are a very good way of describing motion.

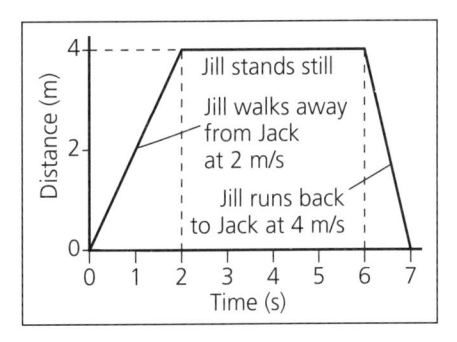

Graph: Distance (m) vs Time (s). Shows Jill walks away from Jack at 2 m/s, Jill stands still, Jill runs back to Jack at 4 m/s.

Now do this

9 Here are three different distance–time graphs. Match each one with a sentence from this list.
   a Going away then coming back again.
   b Starting off quickly and slowing to a halt.
   c Moving at a steady speed.
   d Moving away faster and faster.

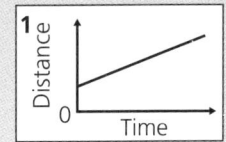

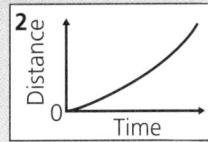

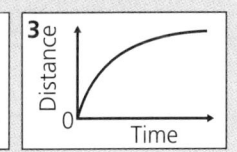

Three distance–time graphs labelled 1, 2, 3.

Speed–time graphs

Here are distance–time and speed–time graphs for Paul. He walks away slowly, stops for a while and then runs away quickly.

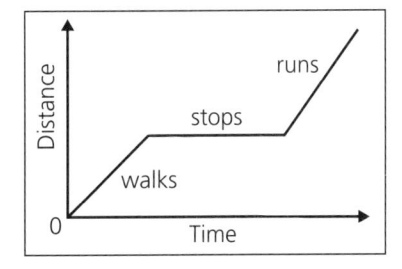

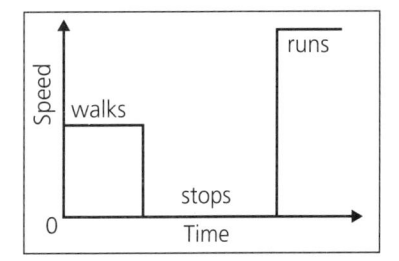

Distance–time graph showing walks, stops, runs. Speed–time graph showing walks, stops, runs.

Now do this

10 Here are three speed–time graphs. Match each one with a sentence from this list.
    a Speeding up to a steady speed.
    b Moving at a steady speed.
    c Moving at a steady speed and then slowing to a halt.

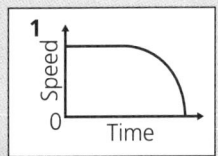

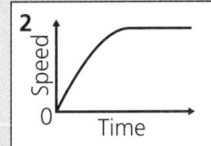

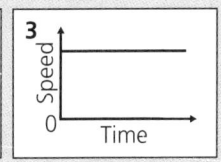

Three speed–time graphs labelled 1, 2, 3.

Here is a speed–time graph for Jake as he goes from rest to top speed on his bike.

The distance travelled is equal to the area under the line. The area is triangular in shape, with a base of 10 s and a height of 12 m/s.

distance = $\frac{1}{2}$ base × height = 0.5 × 10 × 12 = 60 m

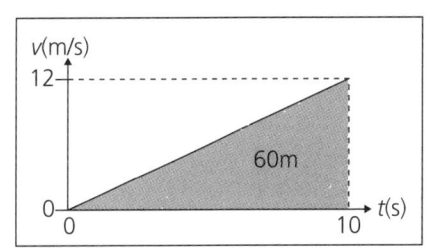

Speed–time graph: v (m/s) vs t (s), triangle from 0 to 10 s reaching 12 m/s, area 60 m.

Now do this

11 Use the speed–time graph to calculate the distance travelled between
    a 0 s and 5 s
    b 5 s and 15 s
    c 15 s and 25 s.

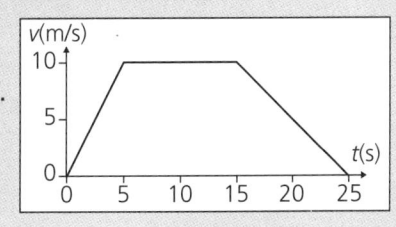

Speed–time graph: v (m/s) rises to 10 from 0–5 s, steady 5–15 s, falls to 0 by 25 s.

12 Use the distance–time graph to calculate the speed at
    a 5 s
    b 15 s
    c 25 s.

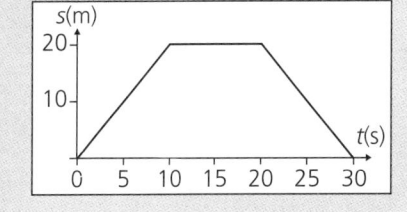

Distance–time graph: s (m) rises to 20 from 0–10 s, steady 10–20 s, falls to 0 by 30 s.

Speeding up and slowing down

Here is the speed–time graph for a bike which is **accelerating**.

Its speed increases as time goes on. The speed increases from 4 m/s to 10 m/s, a change of 6 m/s. This takes a time of 3 s. So the speed changes by 2 m/s each second.

The bike accelerates at 2 **m/s²** (**metres per second squared**).

Here is the formula for calculating acceleration. (You need to know it by heart!)

$$\text{acceleration} = \frac{\text{change of speed}}{\text{time taken}}$$

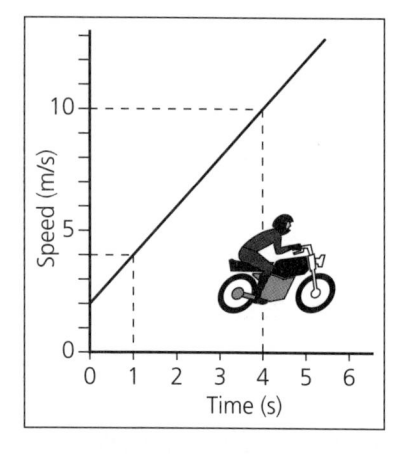

Now do this

1. Write down the formula for calculating acceleration. What are the units of acceleration?
2. A plane takes 4 s to get from a speed of 5 m/s to 45 m/s. Calculate its acceleration.
3. A car accelerates at 5 m/s². How long will it take to get from rest to a speed of 30 m/s?
4. A car at 20 m/s slows with an acceleration of –2 m/s². How fast will it be going after 5 s?

Friction

Jo pedals her bike along a level road. She stops pedalling. The force of **friction** slows her down until she stops. The friction comes from
- the air in front of the bike, which is pushed aside
- the contact between the tyres and the road
- the moving parts of the bike rubbing past each other.

The acceleration of the bike depends on the size of Jo's **thrust** compared with the friction.

Forces on the bike	Motion of the bike
thrust greater than friction	speed increases
thrust and friction the same	speed doesn't change
thrust smaller than friction	speed decreases

Now do this

5. State the sources of friction on a moving car.
6. Describe the motion of these objects:

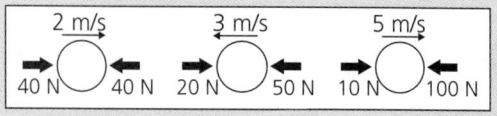

   2 m/s → ○ ← 40 N / 40 N
   3 m/s → ○ ← 20 N / 50 N
   5 m/s → ○ ← 10 N / 100 N

Mass and acceleration

The acceleration of any object depends on the overall (**resultant**) force and the mass.

force = mass × acceleration $F = ma$

Symbol	Meaning	Units of measurement
F	force	newtons or N
m	mass	kilograms or kg
a	acceleration	metres per second squared or m/s²

Forces, energy and motion

Worked example

Q A car has a mass of 800 kg. If the thrust is 600 N and the friction is 200 N, what is the acceleration of the car?

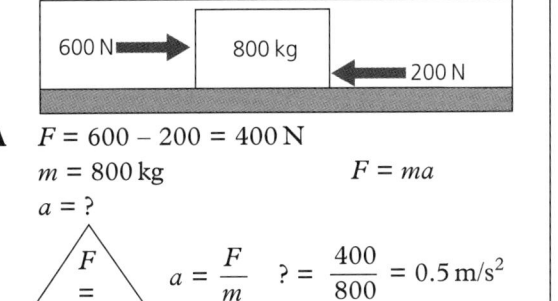

600 N → [800 kg] ← 200 N

A $F = 600 - 200 = 400$ N
$m = 800$ kg
$a = ?$

$F = ma$

$a = \dfrac{F}{m}$ $? = \dfrac{400}{800} = 0.5$ m/s^2

Now do this

7 A 1000 kg car accelerates at −6 m/s^2 when the brakes are on. Calculate the force needed.

8 A rocket has a mass of 5000 kg and a weight of 50 000 N. It accelerates upwards at 3 m/s^2. Calculate the upwards thrust from its engines.

9 The thrust on a 600 kg car is 1500 N. Calculate its acceleration when the friction is 300 N.

Road safety

Sam is driving along the road at a steady speed. He notices that there is a tree across the road. He puts on the brakes and stops. Here are speed–time and distance–time graphs for the car as it slows down.

The **thinking distance** is how far the car travels between Sam noticing the tree and the brakes starting to slow down the car.

It will increase if
- Sam is not concentrating
- Sam is tired
- Sam has been drinking alcohol.

The **braking distance** is how far the car travels once the brakes have started to slow it down. It will increase if
- the brakes are not adjusted correctly
- the road surface is wet or loose
- the tyres are inflated incorrectly
- the tyres don't have enough tread.

The gap between cars on the road needs to be more than the thinking distance, otherwise they will collide when the one in front stops suddenly.

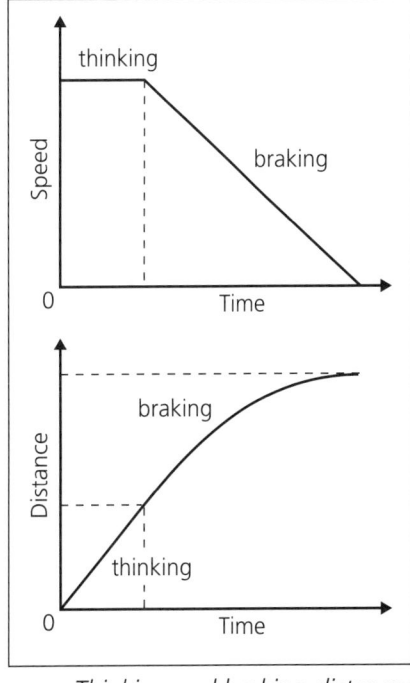

Thinking and braking distances

Now do this

10 Explain what the thinking distance is. State what will increase its value.

11 Explain what the braking distance is. State what will increase its value.

12 Thinking time is 0.7 s. Calculate the thinking distance for a car moving at 30 m/s (70 m.p.h.).

13 The acceleration of a car during braking is −6 m/s^2. For a car moving initially at 30 m/s, calculate
 a the braking time
 b the braking distance.

14 Repeat 12 and 13 for a car moving initially at 15 m/s.

Stretching and squeezing

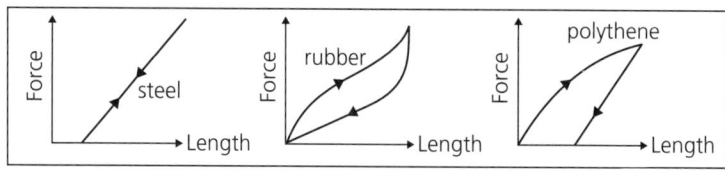

Jo stretches a rubber band. When she lets go of the band it returns to its original shape. Rubber is an **elastic** material.

Sam does the same experiment with a polythene bag. When he lets go of it, the bag stays deformed. Polythene is an **inelastic** material.

Now do this

1. Complete the sentences. Choose words from this list.

   inelastic   elastic   length   force   smaller   larger

   When a _force_ is applied to an object its _length_ changes. If the object is squashed, its length gets _smaller_. If the object is _elastic_, its length returns to its original value when the force is removed. If the object is _inelastic_, its length doesn't change when the _force_ is removed.

The force–length graph of many materials (such as springs) is a straight line. Their **extension** is proportional to the force applied.

Now do this

2. A 5 cm spring becomes 15 cm long when a force of 40 N is applied. How long is it for a force of 20 N?

   What force is required to give it a length of 20 cm?

Worked example

Q A spring goes from 10 cm to 15 cm when a force of 20 N is applied. What is its length when 30 N is applied?

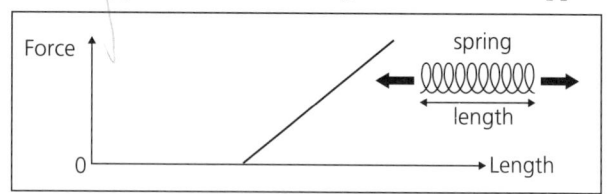

A 20 N gives an extension of 15 − 10 = 5 cm.
1 N gives an extension of 5/20 = 0.25 cm.
30 N gives an extension of 0.25 × 30 = 7.5 cm
So the length will be 10 + 7.5 = 17.5 cm.

Car safety

Inelastic materials are good at absorbing energy in car crashes. The **kinetic energy** of the car is used to squash the metal in the **crumple zone**.

Seat belts are inelastic if they are stretched enough. The kinetic energy of the driver permanently stretches the belt. This weakens the belt, so it should always be replaced after a bad crash. Gases are elastic. Car airbags are filled rapidly with gas in a collision. They provide a soft flat surface which cushions the driver's head.

Forces, energy and motion

The pressure of a gas increases as its volume decreases. So the force on the head increases steadily as it squashes the gas in the bag. The gas in the bag obeys this rule:

pressure × volume = constant

for a fixed mass of gas at constant temperature.

Calculating pressure

A material will change its shape permanently if the **pressure** is big enough.

$$\text{pressure} = \frac{\text{force}}{\text{area}}$$

$$P = \frac{F}{A}$$

Symbol	Meaning	Units of measurement
P	pressure	pascals or Pa
F	force	newtons or N
A	area	metres squared or m²

Now do this

3. Describe three safety features of a car which can protect the driver in a collision. Explain how they provide protection.

Worked example

Q A concrete block sits on the ground. The block weighs 5000 N. The base of the block is 0.5 m by 0.5 m. What is the pressure on the ground under the block?

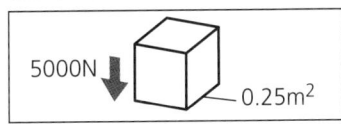

Q $P = ?$
$F = 5000$ N
$A = 0.5$ m × 0.5 m = 0.25 m²
$P = \frac{F}{A}$? = $\frac{5000}{0.25}$ = 20 000 Pa

Now do this

4. Write down the formula linking pressure, force and area. What are the units used?
5. A paving slab is 0.5 m by 0.8 m by 0.05 m. It weighs 400 N. It can be placed on the ground three different ways. Calculate the pressure for each way the slab can be placed on the ground. 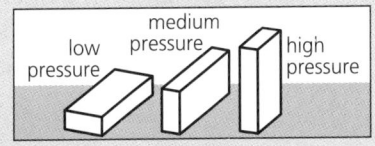
6. Write down a formula for calculating area from pressure and force.
7. A car weighs 10 000 N. If the pressure on each of its four tyres is 100 000 Pa, what is the area of contact between each tyre and the ground?

Large forces on surfaces can damage them. The pressure can be kept down to a safe value by making the area of contact large enough. Think about pushing on a drawing pin!

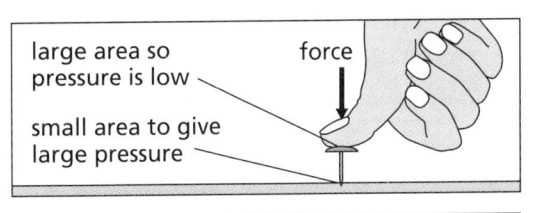

Hydraulic brakes

Liquids are **incompressible**. This makes them good at transmitting pressure from one place to another.

In car brakes all of the pressure from the master piston appears at the slave piston. So when the brake pedal is pushed, the brake pads are forced against the brake drum. A small force on the small area of the master piston results in a large force from the large area of the slave piston.

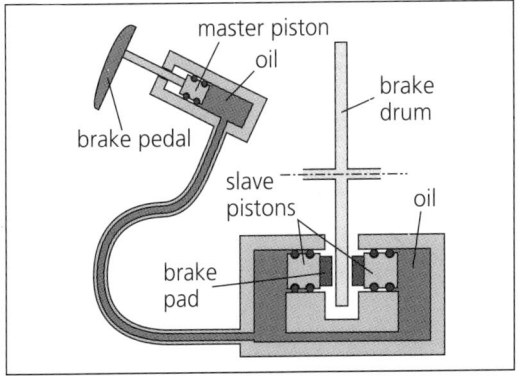

Work, energy and power

Jo lifts up a brick from the floor. She puts it on the table. This increases the **potential energy** (**PE**) of the brick. This extra energy comes from Jo.

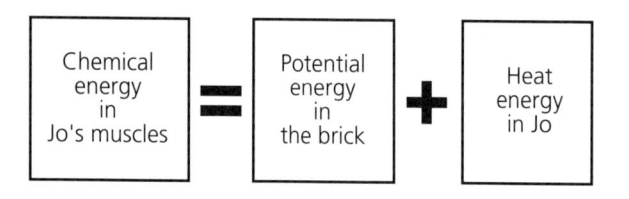

Chemical energy in Jo's muscles = Potential energy in the brick + Heat energy in Jo

Calculating work

The **work** done by Jo equals the PE gained by the brick.

work = force × distance $W = F \times s$

Symbol	Meaning	Units of measurement
W	work	joules or J
F	force	newtons or N
s	distance	metres or m

Worked example

Q Sam moves a table across the floor, pushing with a force of 20 N. How much work does he do if the table moves 4 m?

A $W = ?$ $F = 20$ N $s = 4$ m

$W = F \times s$ $? = 20 \times 4 = 80$ J

PE and KE

Moving objects have **kinetic energy** (**KE**). The faster they go, the more KE they have. Like all forms of energy, both PE and KE are measured in joules.

Now do this

1. Write down the formula for work. Explain the symbols and their units.
2. A brick weighs 25 N. Calculate the work needed to raise a brick by 3 m. How much PE does the brick gain in the process?
3. If 1000 J of work is done lifting a block of weight 50 N, through what height is it raised?
4. 50 000 J of work must be done to stop a car going at 10 m/s. If the car stops in a distance of 20 m, how big a force is required?

Now do this

5. Jo applies a force of 50 N to her bike. It moves forwards on level ground. How much KE has it gained after moving 10 m?
6. Which of these situations involve doing work:
   a lifting up a weight from the floor
   b stretching an elastic band
   c holding a weight still above your head
   d thinking out these answers?

Forces, energy and motion

Sam throws ball of clay into the air. As it rises, it **transforms** its KE into PE. The clay has maximum PE at the top of its flight. On the way down again, the PE is transformed back into KE. When the clay lands on the ground, all of the KE that Sam gave it becomes heat energy.

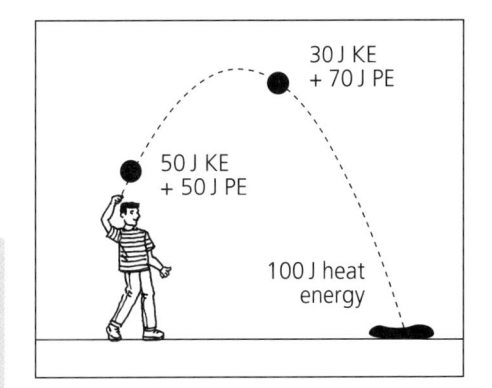

Now do this

7. Copy and complete the following sentences. Sally climbs up the ladder of a slide, transforming _chem_ energy into _Pot_ energy. As she moves down the slide, she transforms _Pot_ energy into _Kin_ energy. As she slides to a halt at the end, all of the KE has become _heat_ energy.

Calculating KE and PE

KE and PE can be calculated with the help of these formulae.

$$KE = \frac{1}{2}mv^2 \qquad PE = mgh$$

Symbol	Meaning	Unit
KE	kinetic energy	J
PE	potential energy	J
m	mass	kg
v	speed	m/s
g	acceleration of free fall	m/s²
h	height raised	m

Worked examples

Q Calculate the KE of a 500 kg car at 15 m/s.

A KE = ?   m = 500 kg   v = 15 m/s
   $KE = \frac{1}{2}mv^2$? = 0.5 × 500 × (15²) = 56 250 J

Q A ball has a mass of 0.5 kg. Calculate the increase in PE when it is thrown 20 m into the air. Assume that the acceleration of free fall is 10 m/s².

A PE = ? PE = mgh m = 0.5 kg g = 10 m/s² h = 20 m
   ? = 0.5 × 10 × 20 = 100 J

Now do this

8. Calculate the KE of a 70 kg man running at 10 m/s.
9. Calculate the increase in PE of a 50 kg girl who climbs a vertical distance of 5 m up a ladder.

Machines (such as motors) are often labelled with their **power**. This tells you how much work they can do in a second. A motor with a high power can deliver energy more quickly than one with a low power. So cars with high-power engines can accelerate and climb up hills faster than cars with low-power engines.

$$power = \frac{work}{time} \qquad P = \frac{W}{t}$$

Symbol	Meaning	Units
P	power	watts or W
W	work	joules or J
t	time	seconds or s

Worked example

Q Joe does 2000 J of work lifting bricks up a building. This takes him 50 s. Calculate his power.

A P = ?
   W = 2000 J $P = \frac{W}{t}$ $P = \frac{2000}{50}$ = 40 W
   t = 50 s

Now do this

10. A crane does 1600 J of work in 8 s. Calculate its power.

Gravity

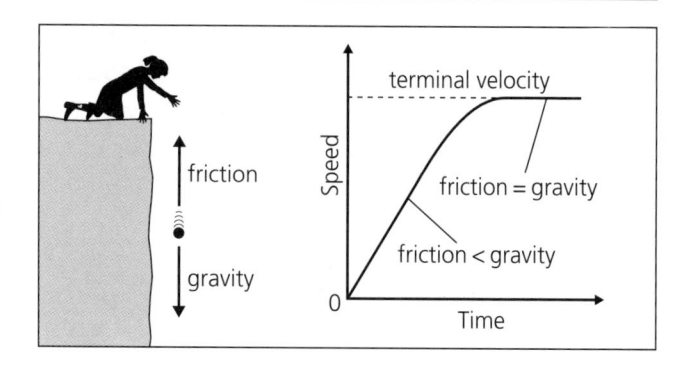

Terminal speed

Jo drops a ball over the edge of a high cliff. As it falls, the ball picks up speed until it reaches its **terminal speed**. The ball stays at that speed until it hits the ground.

Gravity tugs the ball downwards, towards the centre of the Earth. So the ball speeds up. But as it speeds up, **friction** increases. At the terminal speed, the friction force has the same size as the gravity force.

The two forces become **balanced** – they have the same strength, but act in opposite directions.

Free fall

In the absence of friction, all objects in free fall near the surface of the Earth have the same acceleration. The value of this acceleration g is about 10 m/s^2. So the speed increases by 10 m/s for every second that an object falls, if the friction is negligible.

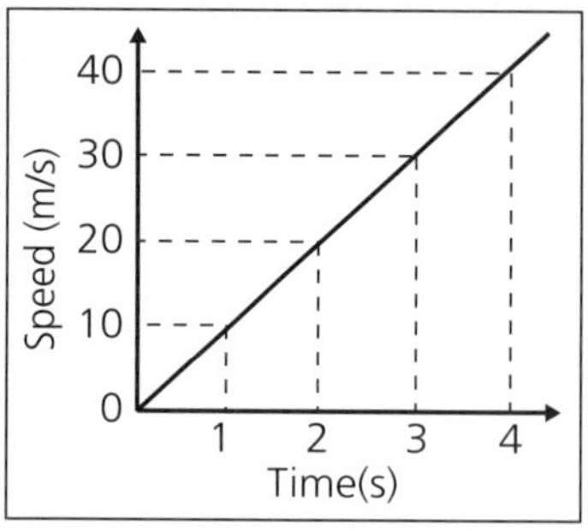

Gravity and weight

The force of gravity on an object is **weight**. It depends on the mass of the object and the acceleration of free fall, g.

weight	=	mass	×	g
(in newtons)		(in kilograms)		(in metres per second squared or newtons/kilogram)

The mass of an object does not depend on where it is. This is because mass is fixed by the number and type of atoms. However, the weight of an object changes as it moves from one place to another. This is because the value of g depends on the size and density of the planet. g is sometimes called the **gravitational field strength**.

Now do this

1 Name the two forces on a falling object. In which direction do they act?

2 Copy and complete the following sentences.
When an object is released _____ acts on it, so its _____ increases. The motion through the air produces the force _____ which acts _____. The friction _____ as the speed increases. At the terminal speed, the forces are _____ and the speed _____.

Now do this

3 A ball is dropped down a deep well. It is released from rest and hits the bottom after 3 s. If there is no friction with the air, calculate
 a the speed of the ball after 3 s
 b the average speed of the ball during its flight
 c the depth of the well.

Worked example

Q An astronaut has a weight of 800 N on Earth, where g is 10 m/s^2. What is his weight on the Moon where $g = 1.6 \text{ m/s}^2$?

A On the Earth: weight = mass × g
800 = mass × 10   so mass = 800/10 = 80 kg
On the Moon: weight = mass × g
weight = 80 × 1.6 = 128 N

Forces, energy and motion

Now do this

4. State the formula for calculating weight from mass. What are the units of weight and mass?
5. Explain why the weight of an object depends on its location but its mass does not.
6. Anita weighs 500 N on Earth. What are her mass and weight when she goes to Mars ($g = 4$ m/s^2)?

Velocity

The **velocity** of an object tells you two things about it:
- how fast it is moving, in m/s
- the direction in which it is moving.

An arrow gives the direction of velocity. The speed is given in m/s.

These objects have the same speed, but different velocities.

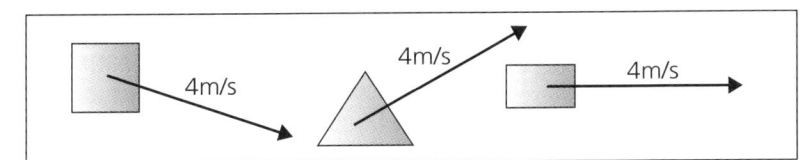

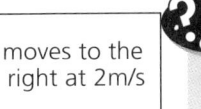

Now do this

7. What is the difference between speed and velocity?
8. The force of gravity on Joe from the Earth is 750 N towards the centre of the Earth. What is the size and direction of the force of gravity on the Earth from Joe?
9. Name two things that a force can do to an object.

Moments

Sam and Jo are sitting on a plank of wood. The centre of the plank is a pivot. Jo has a smaller weight than Sam, so she needs to sit further from the pivot to make the plank balance.

Sam provides a **clockwise moment** of 800 N × 3 m = 2400 Nm.

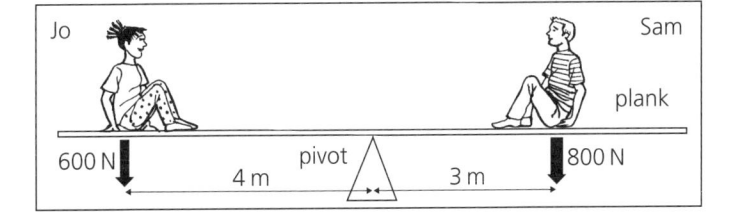

Jo must provide an **anticlockwise moment** of 2400 Nm for the plank to balance. Her weight is 600 N, so she must sit 4 m from the pivot (600 × 4 = 2400).

Sue pushes up on Sam's end of the plank with a force of 200 N, at a distance of 4 m from the pivot. This adds an extra anticlockwise moment of 200 × 4 = 800 Nm. The **total** clockwise moment must now be 2400 + 800 = 3200 Nm for balance. Sam has to move to 4 m from the pivot (800 N × 4 m = 3200 Nm).

Now do this

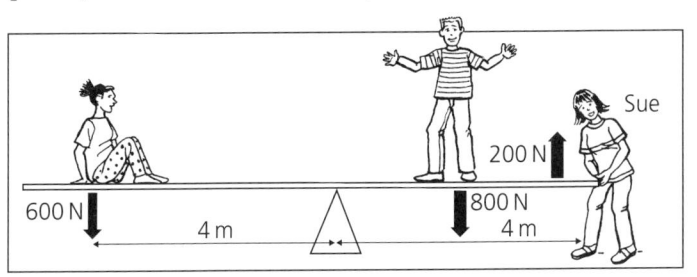

10. Calculate the values of x required for balance.

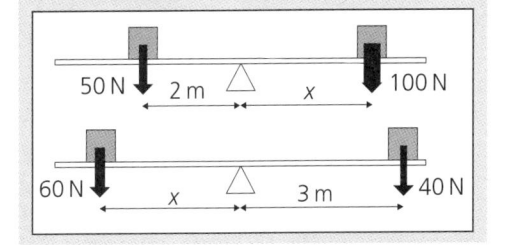

Making waves

Jo throws a brick at Sam. The brick (made from **matter**) transfers some **energy** from Jo to Sam.

Sam shouts at Jo. He makes a **sound wave**. The wave transfers some energy to Jo by making the air between them vibrate. There is no transfer of matter from Sam to Jo. There are two different types of wave. Sound is longitudinal and light is transverse.

Longitudinal waves

Sound is a **longitudinal wave**. It is caused by **vibrations** which squeeze and stretch the air. The pattern of high and low pressure travels through the air as a wave, carrying energy away from the source of the vibrations. The high-pressure regions are called **compressions**. The low-pressure regions are called **expansions** or **rarefactions**.

The **frequency** (in hertz (Hz)) of the wave is the number of vibrations per second. So if the source vibrates 1000 times in 5 s, the frequency is 1000/5 = 200 Hz.

The **wavelength** (in metres (m)) of the wave is the distance from one compression (or expansion) to the next. So if there are 20 compressions in 60 m, the wavelength is 60/20 = 3 m.

Now do this

1 Calculate the frequency of a wave whose source makes 12 000 vibrations in 6 s.

2 Calculate the wavelength of a wave which has 25 compressions in 100 m.

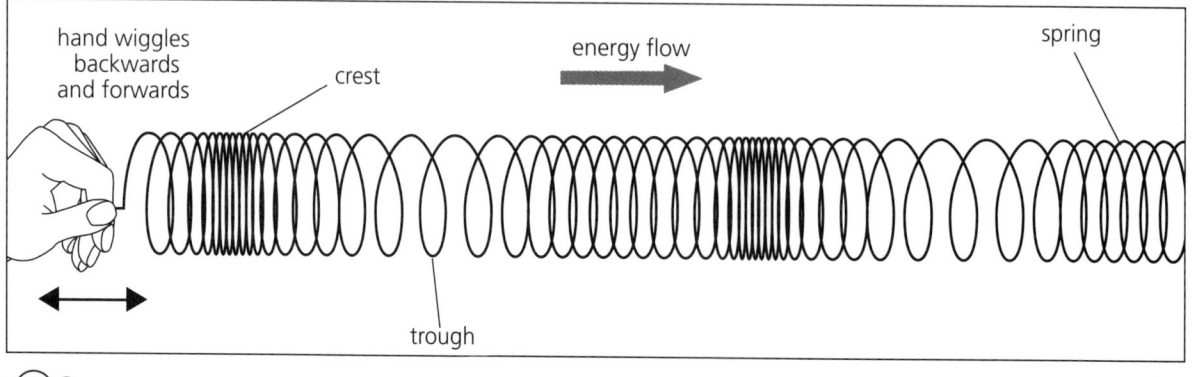

This diagram shows a longitudinal wave moving along a spring. Each coil vibrates back and forth in the same direction as the flow of energy. The compressions and rarefactions move from left to right.

Now do this

3 Copy and complete the following sentences.

Sound is created by _____. These create regions of high pressure (_____) and low pressure (_____) which move through the air. The number of vibrations per second is the _____ of the wave, measured in _____. The distance between compressions is the _____ of the wave, measured in _____. Sound is a _____ wave. It makes the air vibrate in the same direction as the _____ _____.

Transverse waves

Jo transmits a **transverse** wave to Sam along a stretched rope. As the wave travels from left to right, it makes each bit of the rope vibrate up and down. The **amplitude** of the wave is the maximum distance each part of the rope moves from its rest position.

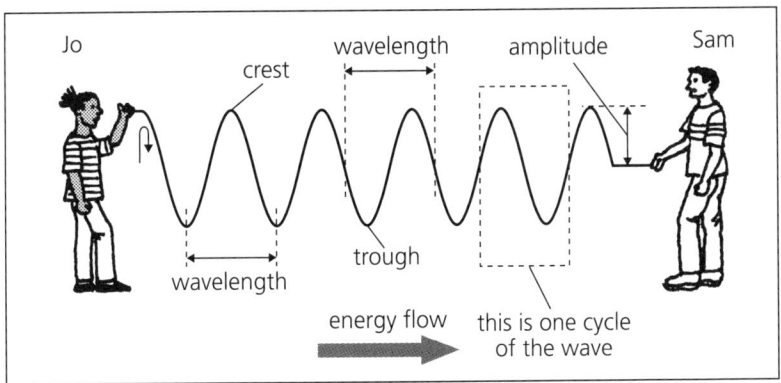

Now do this

4. Calculate values for the number of cycles, the wavelength and the amplitude of this wave in a stretched rope.

5. Explain why you can tell that the wave is a transverse one.

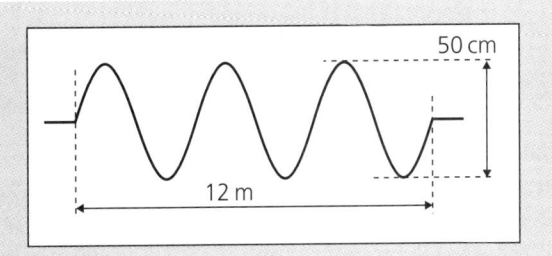

Speed, frequency and wavelength

The speed of a wave is linked to its frequency and wavelength with this formula.

speed = frequency × wavelength $v = fL$

Symbol	Meaning	Units of measurement
v	speed	metres per second or m/s
f	frequency	hertz or Hz
L	wavelength	metres or m

Now do this

6. State the formula linking speed, wavelength and frequency of a wave.

7. A wave in water has a frequency of 6 Hz and a wavelength of 4 m. Calculate its speed.

8. A radio wave has a speed of 300 000 000 m/s. If it has a frequency of 6 000 000 Hz, what is its wavelength? If its wavelength is 500 m, what is its frequency?

Worked example

Q Sound has a speed in air of 300 m/s. Calculate the wavelength of a 1200 Hz sound wave in air.

A v = 300 m/s
   f = 1200 Hz $v = fL$
   L = ? m

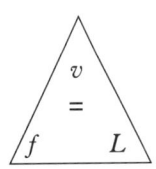

List the data... write the formula... draw the triangle... change the formula... insert the data.

$L = \dfrac{v}{f}$ $? = \dfrac{300}{1200} = 0.25$ m

Using light waves

Reflection

Light waves travel in straight lines. These are drawn as **rays**.

When light rays reflect off a shiny surface, the **angle of reflection**, r, is the same as the **angle of incidence**, i. Both angles are measured from the **normal**. This is a line at right angles to the reflector at the point where the ray hits it.

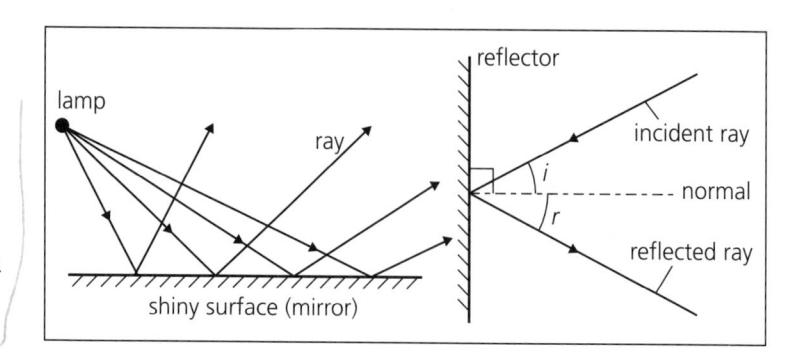

Now do this

1 What are the values for the angles of incidence and reflection for these rays of light?

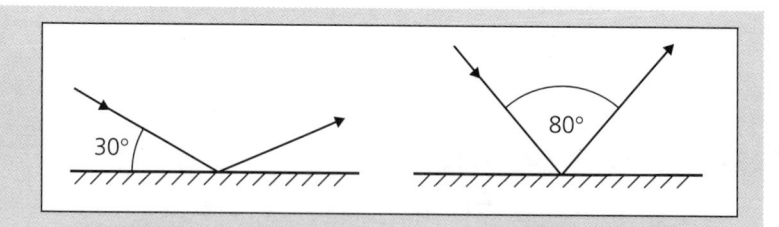

Light reflected from a flat mirror appears to come from behind the mirror. If you look at the reflected light, you see an **image** of the **object** which produced the light. The distance from the image to the mirror is the same as the distance from the object to the mirror.

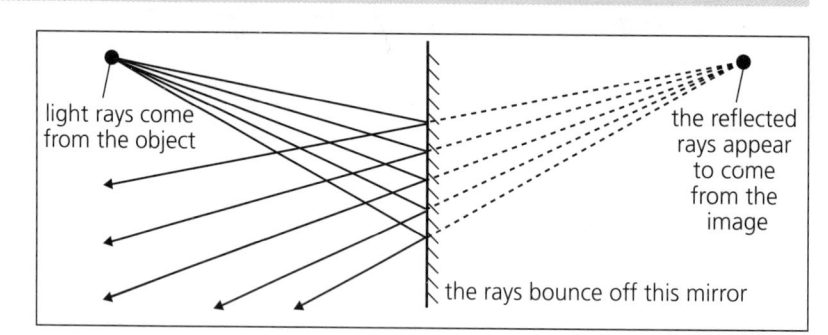

Refraction

When light goes from air into a transparent material (such as glass) it changes direction. It is **refracted**.

On the way into the material the **angle of refraction** is always smaller than the **angle of incidence**. Both angles are measured from the **normal**.

On the way out of the material the angle of refraction is always larger than the angle of incidence.

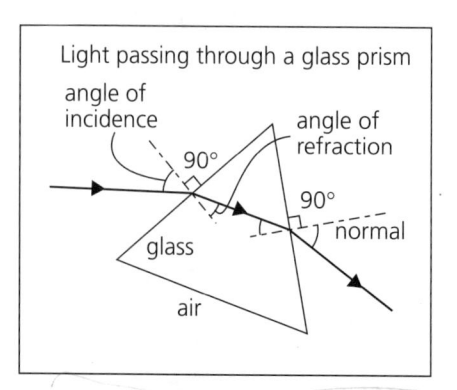

Now do this

2 How big are the values of the angles of incidence and refraction for this ray of light?

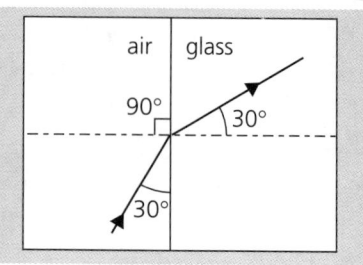

If the angle of incidence is large enough, rays of light will not refract out. They are **totally internally reflected**. This is used in optical fibres. Light which goes in at one end has to reflect off the edge of the fibre until it gets to the other end.

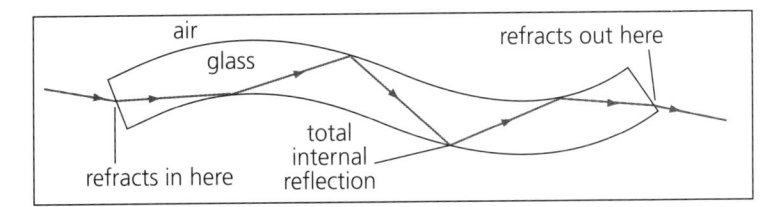

Now do this

3. A ray of light enters a prism. The ray is totally internally reflected at X. In what direction will it emerge from the prism?

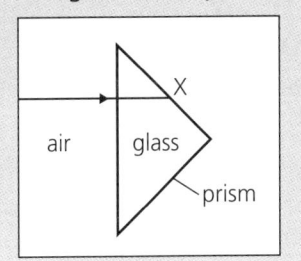

Water waves

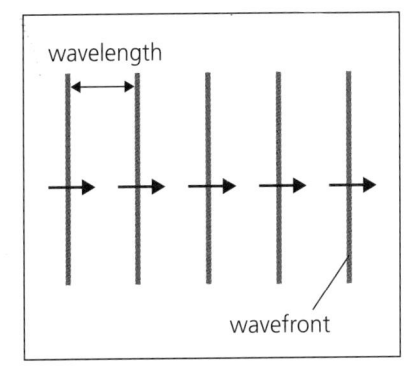

Waves on the surface of water are represented with **wavefronts**. Each wavefront shows the position of a crest, so the distance between wavefronts is the wavelength.

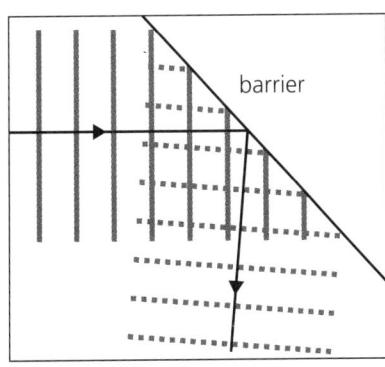

Like sound waves and light waves, water waves are reflected when they hit barriers.

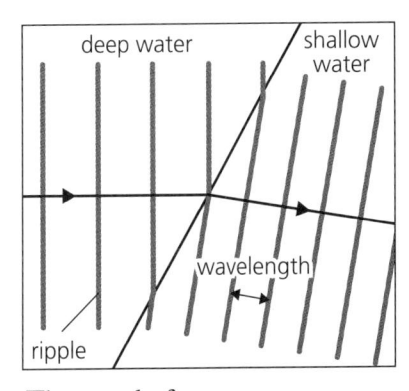

The speed of water waves depends on the depth of the water. The waves go faster in deep water. So water waves are **refracted** when they move from one depth to another.

Diffraction

When water waves pass through a gap they are **diffracted**. Plane waves which approach the gap emerge as circular waves if the gap is smaller than the wavelength. All waves (sound and light) are diffracted, but the gap has to be smaller than the wavelength for the effect to be noticeable.

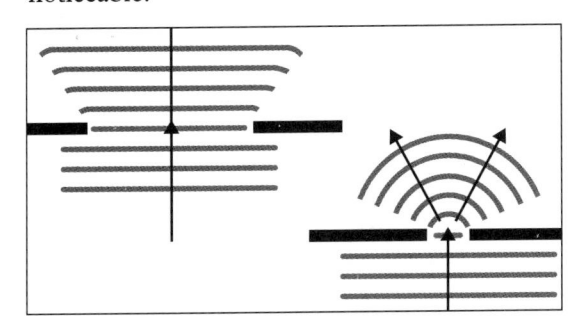

Now do this

4. Draw diagrams to show plane water waves being reflected from a straight barrier and a curved barrier.

5. Draw a diagram to show water waves being refracted as they move from deep water to shallow water.

6. A sound wave has a wavelength of 20 cm. Draw diagrams to show what happens to the wave when it passes through a gap of width
a 200 cm b 2 cm.

Ultrasound

The highest frequency sound that humans can hear is about 20 000 Hz (or 20 kHz). Sound with higher frequency than 20 kHz is called **ultrasound**. It is very useful.

Ships use **pulses** of ultrasound to detect what is underneath them. Each pulse **reflects** off solid objects in the water. A special microphone under the ship listens for these **echoes**. The time delay between the pulse and its echo is used to calculate the distance to the solid reflector.

Sound travels at 1500 m/s in water. So a time delay of 0.1 s means that the pulse travelled $1500 \times 0.1 = 150$ m. The reflector must therefore be $\frac{1}{2} \times 150 = 75$ m below the ship.

Now do this

2 A submarine sends out pulses of ultrasound. Echoes arrive back 0.05 s after each pulse. How far away is the source of the echoes?

Ultrasound can also be used to look inside the human body without the need for surgery. Pulses of ultrasound are fed in through the skin. Each time a pulse passes from one organ into another, some of it is reflected back to the skin.

These echoes can be used to form a picture of what lies under the skin. Ultrasound is often used to scan babies before they are born.

Now do this

3 Describe a use of ultrasound in medicine.

Seismic waves

Earthquakes produce two different low-frequency waves which travel through the Earth:
- **p-waves** are longitudinal and can therefore travel through both solids and liquids
- **s-waves** are transverse and can therefore only travel through solids.

The Earth has a liquid core which s-waves cannot pass through. The size of this core can be found by finding those places which receive only p-waves from an earthquake.

Now do this

1 Here are the frequencies of five different sound waves. List them in order of increasing frequency. Which of them will be ultrasound?

12 000 Hz   24 kHz   47 Hz   50 000 Hz   900 Hz

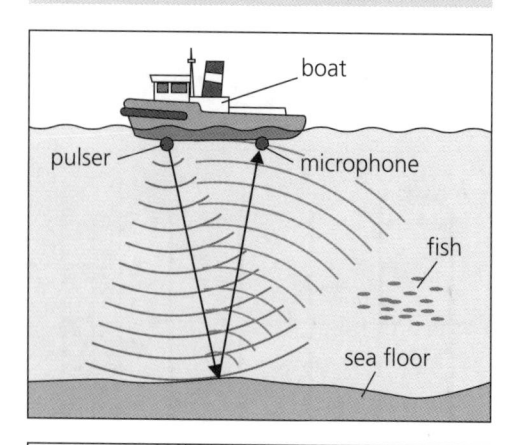

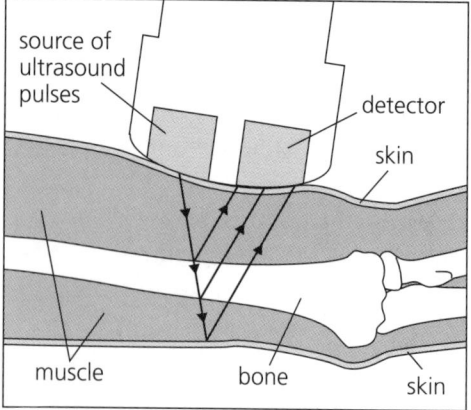

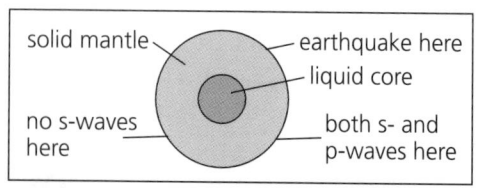

Now do this

4 Describe the differences between s-waves and p-waves.

Electromagnetic waves

The **electromagnetic spectrum** is a family of waves which can pass through empty space at the colossal speed of 300 000 000 m/s. Here is the spectrum of waves, with the longest wavelength listed first.

We use electromagnetic waves in many different ways. The energy delivered by an electromagnetic wave increases with decreasing wavelength.

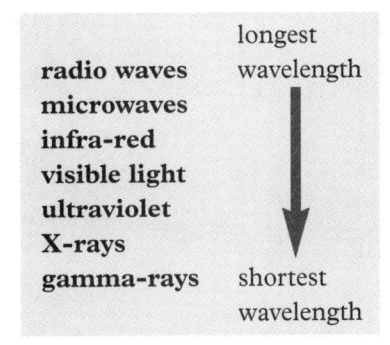

radio waves — longest wavelength
microwaves
infra-red
visible light
ultraviolet
X-rays
gamma-rays — shortest wavelength

Now do this

5 Write down the seven parts of the electromagnetic spectrum in order of increasing wavelength.

Radio waves are used to carry information about sound (music and speech) as well as pictures (TV).

Microwaves can be made into beams by curved reflectors. As well as being used to communicate with satellites in space, pulsed microwaves are used to detect aircraft and ships. Microwaves with one particular wavelength are strongly absorbed by water and can be used to heat up food.

Infra-red waves carry heat energy. They are emitted by hot objects, such as the Sun. They can also carry information down optical fibres and allow hand-held remote controls to communicate with TVs and video recorders.

Ultraviolet waves damage living cells and can cause skin cancer. Dark skin will absorb ultraviolet waves and protect the living cells underneath.

X-rays pass through flesh but are strongly absorbed by bone. They allow photographs to be made of the inside of the body. X-rays also kill living cells and can cause cancer.

Gamma rays can pass through steel and concrete. They are very dangerous, but can be used to destroy cancer cells. Gamma rays are emitted by radioactive atoms. A short-lived radioactive substance can act as a tracer when it is injected into someone – the gamma rays emitted by the tracer can be picked up outside the body, showing the passage of the tracer through the person.

- Radio waves create alternating currents of electrons in electrical conductors.
- Infra-red waves can set whole atoms and molecules vibrating.
- Visible light waves can cause chemical reactions in some substances.
- Ultraviolet waves can damage living cells and knock electrons out of metals.
- X-rays and gamma-rays can knock electrons out of atoms and kill living cells.

Radioactivity

Some atoms have a nucleus which is unstable. It can break up, spitting out fragments which have a lot of energy. This process is called **radioactivity**.

All atoms contain a small **nucleus** at their centre. Most of the **mass** and all of the **positive charge** of an atom are in this nucleus. The rest of the mass and all of the **negative charge** are in the **electrons** which move around the rest of the atom.

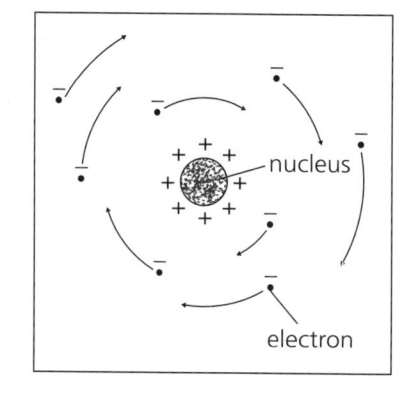

Now do this
1. Describe the structure of an atom.
2. What is the charge of a nucleus?
3. What is the charge of an electron?
4. What is radioactivity?

Types of radiation

There are three different **nuclear radiations** from radioactive substances:
- **alpha (α) particle,** which is a heavy, positive helium nucleus
- **beta (β) particle**, which is a light, negative electron
- **gamma (γ) ray**, which is an electromagnetic wave with no charge.

All three radiations cause **ionisation** of the matter they pass through. They do this by knocking electrons out of the atoms which they pass through, leaving **ions**. The ions are positively charged.

Alpha particles are the least penetrating radiation. They can be stopped by a sheet of paper. Beta particles are stopped by a few millimetres of aluminium. Gamma rays can pass through several centimetres of lead, so they are the most penetrating.

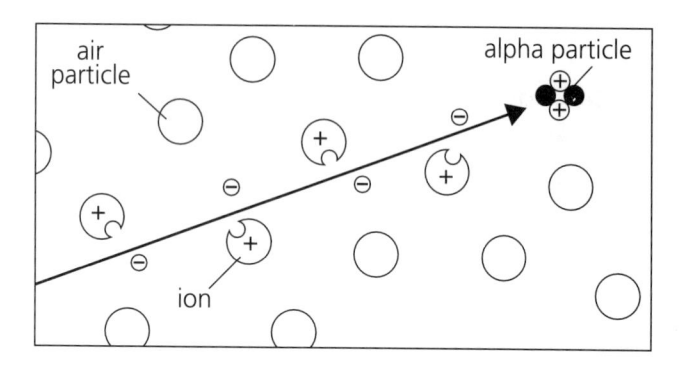

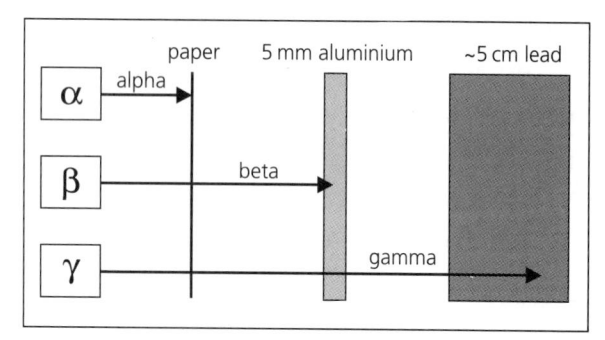

Dangers of radiation

Nuclear radiations are dangerous to living things. The ionisation that they cause can kill cells or change their genetic structure. Too much exposure to nuclear radiation can result in cancer.

Now do this
5. Name the three different nuclear radiations.
6. Which part of an atom does nuclear radiation come from?
7. State the charge of each of the nuclear radiations.
8. Name the radiation which a has the greatest mass b is a wave c is a nucleus d is an electron.
9. Here is a list of radiations. Write them down in order of ability to penetrate solids. Start with the least penetrating power.
    beta   gamma   alpha

Earth in space

Background radiation

We are exposed to radiation all the time. There are several causes of this background nuclear radiation:
- radioactive atoms, such as uranium, in rocks
- radioactive gases, such as radon, from the soil
- fallout from nuclear bomb tests and nuclear power stations
- cosmic rays from space.

Radioactive decay

The **activity** of a radioactive material goes down as time goes on. When the last unstable nucleus has split, the material is no longer radioactive. Some materials take a long time to decay, others are only radioactive for a short while.

Activity is measured in **becquerels** (**Bq**). It tells you the rate at which atoms are changing. So if the activity is 365 Bq, there are, on average 365 atoms decaying in one second.

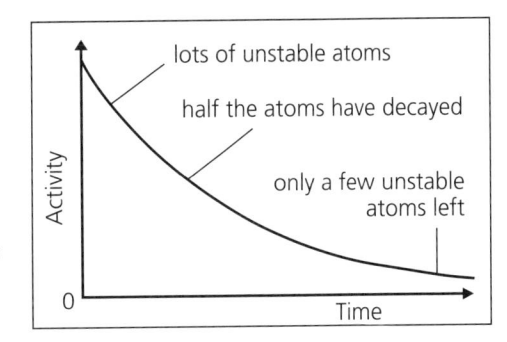

Now do this

10 Name the four sources of background radiation.

11 A radioactive source has an activity of 100 Bq. How many atoms in it decay in a minute?

12 How does the activity of a radioactive material change with time? Explain why.

The **half-life** of an element is the amount of time it takes for half of the atoms to decay. Each element has its own half-life.

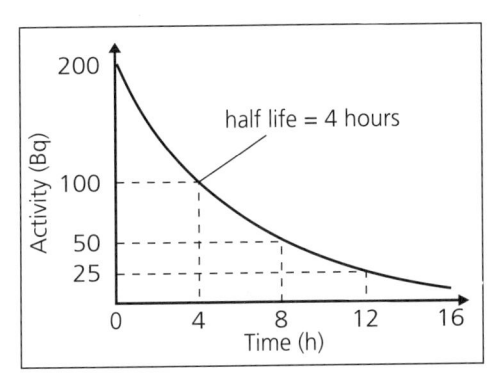

Worked example

Q A radioactive source has a half-life of 3 hours. If its activity is 400 Bq now, what will it be in 12 hours time?

A

Time (hours)	0	3	6	9	12
Activity (Bq)	400	200	100	50	25

so the final activity will be 25 Bq

Uses of radioactivity

Here are some uses of nuclear radiation and radioactive substances.
- Uranium can be used to boil water in a nuclear power station.
- Gamma rays can be used to sterilise surgical instruments.
- Alpha particle sources are used in smoke alarms.
- Beta particle sources can be used to measure the thickness of sheets of material.
- Gamma rays can be used to kill cancer tumours.
- Radioactive materials make good tracers in plants and people.
- The age of rocks can be measured with radioactivity.

Now do this

13 State one use for
  a alpha particles
  b beta particles
  c gamma rays
  d uranium.

Physical Processes

Space

The Earth we live on is a **planet**. It is a sphere of rock, surrounded by a very thin skin of gas and liquid (the atmosphere and oceans). Gravity pulls everything on the Earth towards its centre.

The **Sun** is much larger than the Earth. The Sun is our nearest **star**, a ball of hot gases (mostly hydrogen) which radiates a lot of light and heat energy. That energy comes from **fusion** reactions at the hot centre of the star. These reactions convert hydrogen into helium.

The Earth is only one of several planets which orbit the Sun.

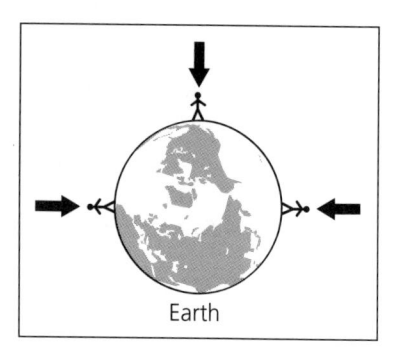

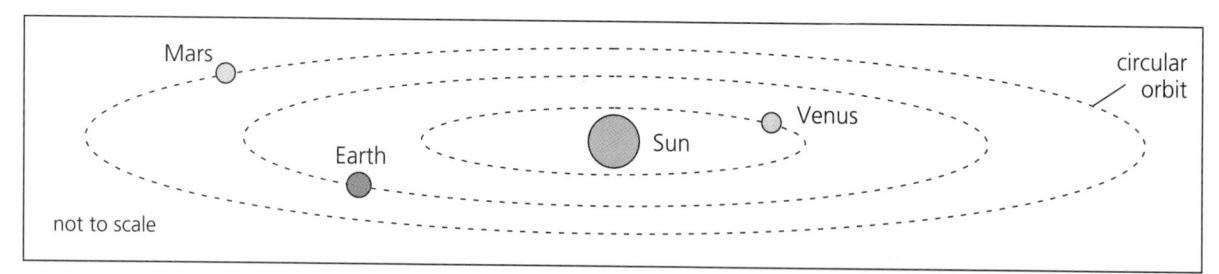

Gravity tugs each planet towards the Sun. This force keeps each planet moving in either a **circle** or an **ellipse** around the Sun.

There is no friction in space, so orbits can keep going for billions of years.

Earth has just one **moon**. It goes once around the Earth in a month. A moon is a smaller lump of rock which orbits around a planet. Many planets have more than one moon.

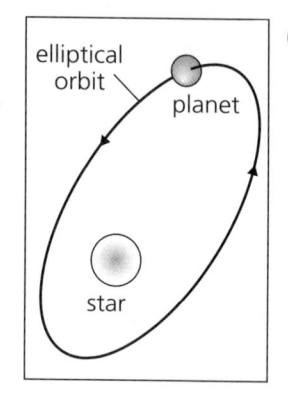

Now do this
1 Describe a planet.
2 Describe a star.
3 Describe the motion of a planet around a star. Why does it move this way?

The Universe

The Sun, its planets and their moons make up a **solar system**. There are billions of solar systems clumped together in our local **galaxy**, the Milky Way. The **Universe** contains billions of different galaxies, separated by empty space.

We now know that:
- the Earth orbits the Sun, taking one year to go round once
- day and night are caused by the Earth spinning taking 24 hours to spin round once
- the stars are far away, at various distances, and only move very slowly.

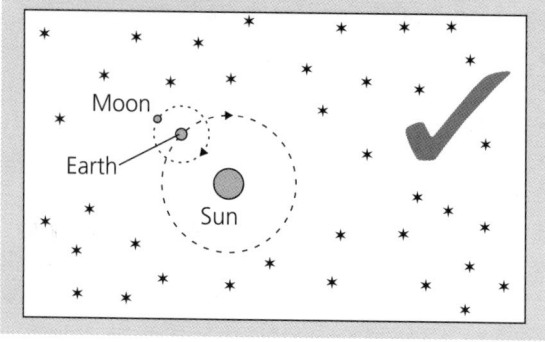

Now do this
4 Here is a list of objects. Write it out in order of size. Start with the smallest.
galaxy   moon   star   solar system   Universe   planet
5 What is the difference between a planet and moon?
6 Explain why the stars appear to move across the sky at night.

The origin of the Universe

The Universe is about 15 billion years old. Scientists have evidence that it started with a Big Bang and has evolved into what we see around us today. Here are the main events in its life so far.

To start with, space is completely empty ...
 ... then all the matter and energy suddenly appears at one point ...
  ... the Universe expands rapidly, getting cooler as it does so ...
   ... until, after 300 000 years, stable atoms of hydrogen and helium condense out ...
    ... gravity makes these clouds of gas shrink, heating them up at the same time ...
     ... until the temperature of the star reaches 15 million °C ...
      ... and nuclear fusion begins to convert hydrogen into helium ...
       ... and the heat generated stops the star collapsing further ...
        ... after 10 billion years most of the hydrogen in the star's core is used up ...
         ... so gravity collapses it a bit more, and helium atoms fuse to form heavier elements ...
          ... when the core is mostly iron it becomes unstable and the star explodes as a supernova ...
           ... the energy of the explosion creates a vast quantity of different atoms ...
            ... which form a large cloud of dust and hydrogen ...
             ... which gravity pulls in to form more stars ...
              ... with planets orbiting around them.

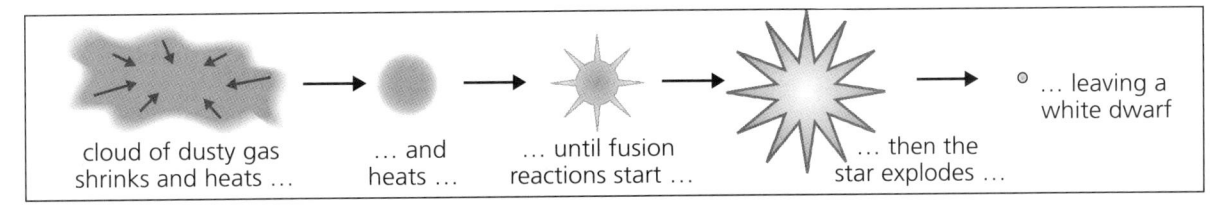

cloud of dusty gas shrinks and heats ... → ... and heats ... → ... until fusion reactions start ... → ... then the star explodes ... → ... leaving a white dwarf

Now do this

7 Write out a brief history of the Universe from the Big Bang to the present day.

Only very large stars explode. Smaller ones (like our Sun) will just run out of fuel and collapse into a cold lump.

We know that the Universe is expanding because of the **red shift** of the light from other galaxies. When light is emitted by a galaxy moving away from us, its wavelength becomes longer. The increase in wavelength can be used to measure the speed of the galaxy.

Galaxies that are far away from us have a greater red shift than those which are close by. Red shift and distance measurements provide evidence that all of the galaxies started off in the same place about 15 billion years ago. If there is enough material in the Universe, gravity will stop its expansion and force it to shrink down into a single point – the **big crunch**! Otherwise, the Universe will carry on expanding for ever.

Now do this

8 What is the red shift? What can it tell us about a galaxy?

9 What is the big crunch? What may cause it?

Physical Processes

Concept map

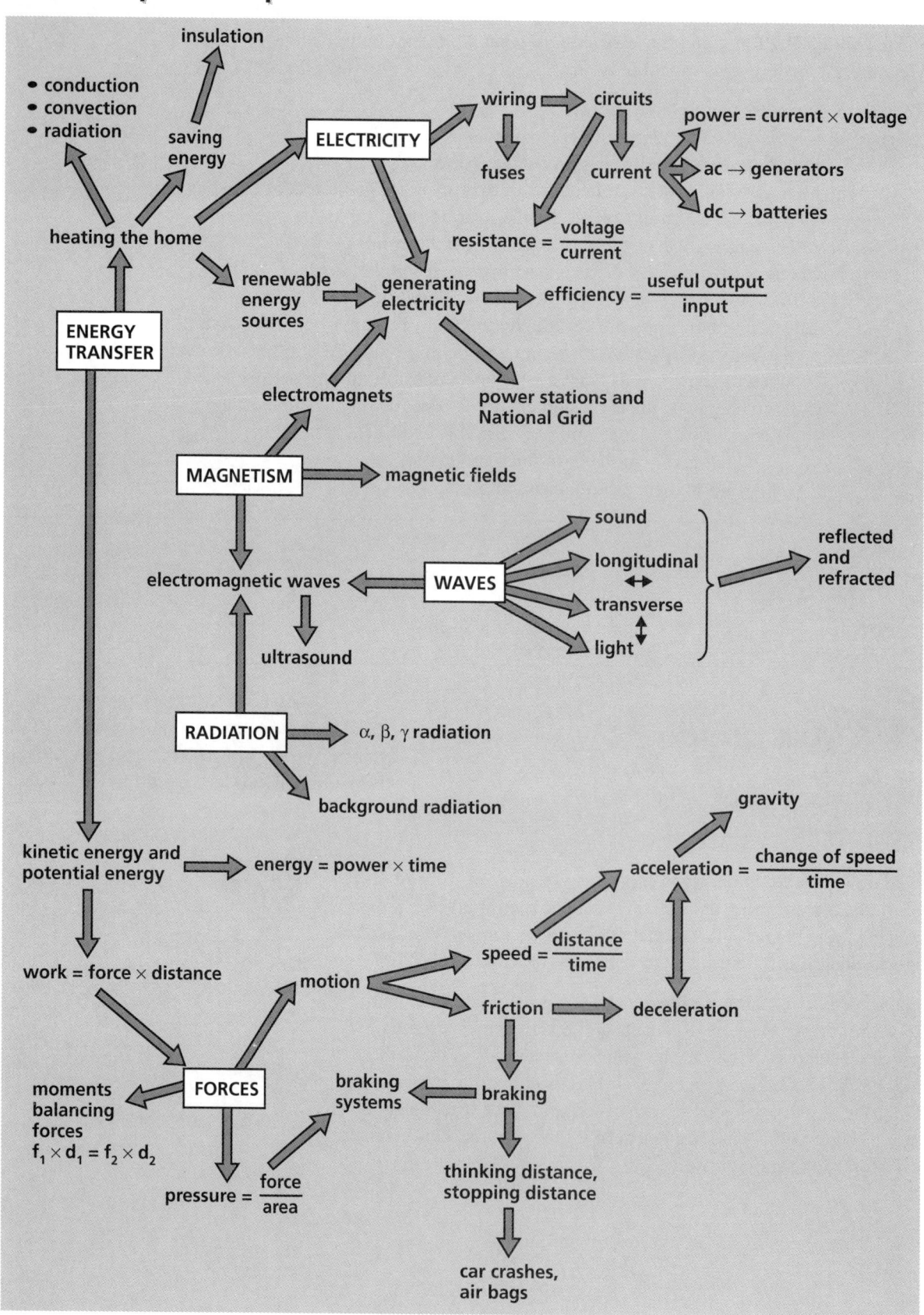

- conduction
- convection
- radiation

ENERGY TRANSFER

saving energy → insulation

heating the home

ELECTRICITY → wiring → circuits
- fuses
- current
- resistance = $\dfrac{\text{voltage}}{\text{current}}$
- power = current × voltage
- ac → generators
- dc → batteries

renewable energy sources → generating electricity → efficiency = $\dfrac{\text{useful output}}{\text{input}}$

electromagnets → power stations and National Grid

MAGNETISM → magnetic fields

WAVES:
- sound
- longitudinal ↔
- transverse
- light ↕
- electromagnetic waves
- ultrasound

→ reflected and refracted

RADIATION → α, β, γ radiation
→ background radiation

kinetic energy and potential energy → energy = power × time

work = force × distance → motion

speed = $\dfrac{\text{distance}}{\text{time}}$

acceleration = $\dfrac{\text{change of speed}}{\text{time}}$ → gravity

friction → deceleration

FORCES
- moments balancing forces $f_1 \times d_1 = f_2 \times d_2$
- pressure = $\dfrac{\text{force}}{\text{area}}$
- braking systems ← braking
- thinking distance, stopping distance
- car crashes, air bags

Exam questions

1 Tom sends a wave to Jill along a rope. Look at the diagram.

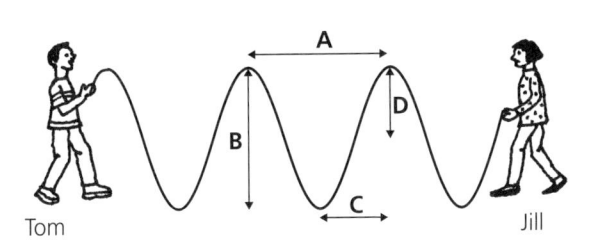

a i State the type of wave. Explain how you can tell. [2]

ii Which letter shows the wavelength of the wave? [1]

iii Tom moves his hand up and down six times in two seconds. Calculate the frequency of the wave. [2]

iv The wavelength is 0.5 m. Calculate the speed of the wave. [2]

b Jill uses two paper cups to send a different wave along the rope. Look at the diagram.

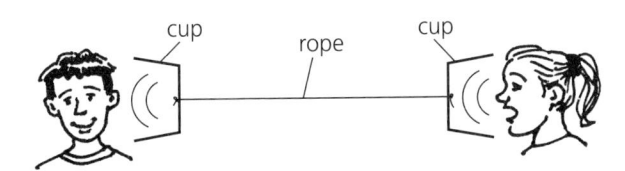

Jill speaks into her cup. Explain why Tom hears a sound from his cup. [3]

[10 marks]

2 Sanjay shines his torch on a mirror. The light reflects off the mirror. Look at the diagram.

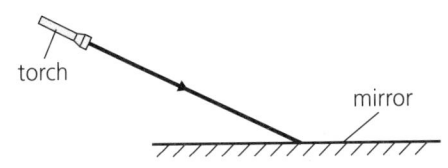

a Draw on the diagram the path taken by the ray. [1]

b Some reflected light reaches Susan. Susan sees an image of Sanjay's torch behind the mirror. Explain why she sees the image there. [2]

c Sanjay's torch has a mirror behind the lamp. Look at the diagrams.

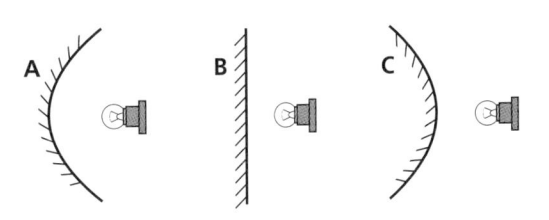

i Which diagram shows the correct type of mirror? [1]

ii Explain why it is the correct type. [2]

[6 marks]

3 Freddie spends £100 a month to keep her house warm. Look at the table.

How the heat escapes	Value
through the windows	£10
through the floor	£15
through the roof	£25
through the walls	£35
by draughts	£15

a The most heat escapes through the walls. Use your idea of particles to describe how the heat travels through a wall. [2]

b Freddie decides to save money by reducing heat lost through the roof.

i What is the best insulating material to put in the loft? Choose from: brick wood fibre wool steel tile [1]

ii Explain why the material you have chosen is a good insulator. [2]

c Freddie draughtproofs her house.

i What could she could do to stop the draughts? [1]

ii The cost of heat wasted through draughts is now only £5 a month. The draughtproofing cost £80. How long does it take for the money saved to pay for the draughtproofing? [2]

d Freddie wants to save even more money on her heating bills. Explain two ways in which she could do this. [4]

[12 marks]

Physical Processes

4 Julie has five electrical appliances in her room. Look at the table.

Appliance	Power in kW
hair dryer	1.2
lamp	0.1
heater	2.0
TV	0.2
computer	0.4

a Julie turns on her computer for 3 hours.
  i Calculate how many units of electricity this uses, in kilowatt-hours. [1]
  ii Each unit of electricity costs 8p. Calculate how much it costs for Julie to run her computer. [1]
b The heater is connected to the mains supply by three wires. Complete the sentences below.
Electrical energy flows to the heater from the mains along the ____ wire. The ____ wire completes the electrical circuit. The ____ wire prevents Julie being electrocuted. [3]

[5 marks]

5 Melissa cycles along the road. Look at the graph below.

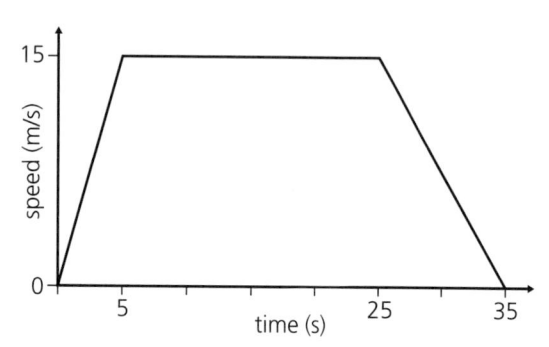

(speed (m/s) vs time (s) graph: rises from 0 at t=5 to 15 m/s, constant until t=25, falls to 0 at t=35)

a Melissa starts off by accelerating.
  i Calculate her acceleration. [2]
  ii The overall pushing force on Melissa during acceleration is 180 N. Calculate Melissa's mass. [2]
b Melissa travels at a top speed of 15 m/s. Calculate how far she moves at that speed. [2]
c Melissa stops pedalling after 25 s. Explain why she stops moving at 35 s. Use your idea of forces. [3]
d Melissa wears a cycle helmet. This will protect her if she falls off her cycle. Use your idea of pressure to explain this. [3]

[12 marks]

6 A student assembles the circuit shown below.

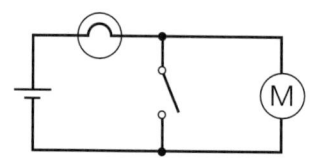

(circuit diagram: battery, lamp, switch, motor M)

The switch is open. The lamp glows dimly. The motor rotates slowly.

a The student presses the switch. Explain what happens to the lamp and the motor. [3]
b The table gives data for the lamp and the motor.

component	power	voltage
lamp	6 W	12 V
motor	24 W	12 V

  i The lamp and motor run off the same 12 V battery. Draw a circuit diagram to show how. [1]
  ii Which will have the greatest current? Explain your answer. [2]
  iii Calculate the current drawn from the battery. [3]

[9 marks]

7 Mel measures the power of a motor connected to a cell.

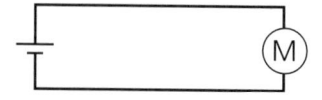

(circuit diagram: cell and motor M)

a She uses a voltmeter and an ammeter. Draw a circuit to show this. [2]
b The voltmeter reads 1.2 V. The ammeter reads 0.6 A.
  i Calculate the power of the motor. [3]
  ii Calculate the resistance of the motor. [3]
c Mel puts a rheostat in series with the motor. This allows her to change its speed. Use your idea of resistance to explain this. [3]

[11 marks]

Exam questions

8 Sam combs his hair. His hair becomes positively charged.
  a Explain why his hair becomes charged. [3]
  b Sam's hair stands on end after it is combed. Explain why. [2]
  c Sam uses a plastic comb. Julie uses a metal comb. Her hair does not get charged. Explain why. [2]
  [7 marks]

9 a Jane is driving a car. She puts on the brakes.

  i Complete the sentence.
  The brakes transfer the _____ energy of the car into _____ energy. [2]
  The brakes exert a force of 500 N on the car. It stops in a distance of 20 m.
  ii Calculate the work done on the car by the brakes. [3]
  iii The car can stop in less than 20 m when it goes uphill. Use the ideas of energy conservation to explain why. [3]
  b Jane pushes hard on the accelerator for 10 s. The engine transfers 50 000 J of kinetic energy to the car.
  i Calculate the power of the engine. [3]
  ii 200 000 J of chemical energy was transferred into the engine during the 10 s. Calculate the efficiency of the engine. [3]
  [14 marks]

10 Here is an electromagnet surrounded by three compasses.

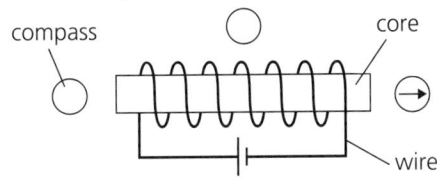

  a What is the best material to use for the core? [1]
  b Write down **two** things you could do to increase the strength of the electromagnet. [2]
  c There are three compasses near the electromagnet. The needle has been drawn for one compass.
  i Draw in the other two needles. [2]
  ii Write down what you could do to make the needles face in the opposite direction. [1]
  [6 marks]

11 A power station burns coal to make electricity.

  a Complete the sentences, choosing from:.
  generator   turbine   furnace
  transformer   boiler
  The coal is burnt in the _____. The heat energy turns water into steam in the _____. The steam passes through the _____ to make kinetic energy. This is transferred to electrical energy by the _____. The voltage of the electricity is raised by a _____. [5]
  b The station uses 250 MJ of chemical energy in the coal to make 75 MJ of electrical energy. Calculate the efficiency of the power station. [2]
  c Useless heat energy appears at various places in the power station.
  i Describe three of the places. [3]
  ii Explain why the heat energy is useless [1]
  [11 marks]

12 The diagram shows the Solar System. The planets orbit the star. (The diagram is not drawn to scale.)

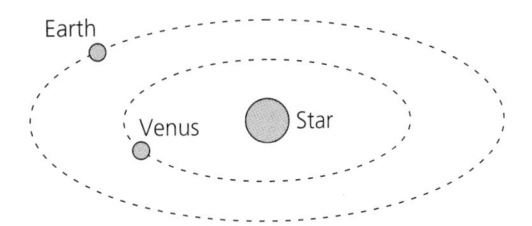

  a What is the difference between a planet and a star? [1]
  b Stars are kept hot by fusion. Describe the fusion reaction. [3]
  c Stars start off as a large cloud of dust and gas. Explain how this can become a star. [4]

d Suggest what will happen to a star when its fusion reactions stop. Give an explanation. [2]

[10 marks]

13 There are satellites in orbit around the Earth.
a Name the force which keeps a satellite in orbit around the Earth. [1]
b Explain why there are satellites around the Earth. [2]
c The MEG satellite takes 90 minutes to orbit the Earth. It is 200 km above the Earth. The OCR satellite is 3000 km above the Earth.
   i What is its orbit time? Choose from:
   less than 90 minutes   exactly 90 minutes   more than 90 minutes [1]
   ii Explain your answer. [2]

[6 marks]

14 Radioactivity is dangerous.
a Why is radioactivity dangerous? [2]
b Explain why a piece of radioactive material becomes less dangerous as time goes on. [3]
c A radioactive source has an activity of 500 Bq now. Its half-life is 10 days. Calculate the activity of the source in 30 days time. [3]

[8 marks]

15 The Highway Code states the distance required to stop an average car in good weather on a normal road.
Look at the information.

For a typical driver at an initial speed of 30 m/s:
   thinking distance = 20 m
   braking distance = 85 m
   stopping distance = 105 m

a i Explain what is meant by **thinking distance**. [1]
   ii Use the information to calculate the thinking time of a typical driver. [2]
   iii State two things which could increase the thinking distance. [2]
b A car initially travelling at 30 m/s takes 5.6 s to travel the braking distance.
   i Calculate the acceleration of the car as it is stopped. [3]

   ii The braking force on a typical car is 5000 N. Calculate the mass of a typical car. [3]

[11 marks]

16 A transformer has 1150 turns in its primary coil and 30 turns in its secondary coil. Both coils are wound on a metal core.
a Suggest the best material for the core. Explain why it is the best. [2]
b If the primary coil is connected to a 230 V supply, calculate the voltage across the secondary coil. [2]
c Use the idea of changing magnetic fields to explain how a transformer works. [3]

[7 marks]

17 Julie throws a ball high into the air. The ball has a mass of 0.3 kg. The ball leaves Julie's hand with 60 J of kinetic energy and 30 J of potential energy.
a Show that the ball leaves Julie's hand with a speed of 20 m/s. [2]
b At the top of its flight, the ball has 80 J of potential energy.
   i How much kinetic enegy does it have? [1]
   ii How high above the ground does the ball rise? [3]
c If the ball stays on the ground when it hits it, what happens to its energy? [1]

[7 marks]

18 An LED is connected in series with a 3 V battery and a resistor.
a Draw the circuit diagram [1]
b Complete the sentences.
Choose from:
heat   light   sound   chemical   electrical

_____ energy in the battery becomes _____ energy in the wires. The LED transforms _____ energy into _____ energy [4]
c A voltage across the LED is 2 V when the current in it is 0.05 A.
   i Explain why the voltage across the resistor is 1 V. [1]
   ii Calculate the resistance of the resistor. [3]

[9 marks]

Answers to Now Do This Questions

Pages 2 and 3

2 Maggots, grass, oak tree.
3 **a** chloroplasts **b** cell membrane **c** cell wall.
4 To allow more room to take up oxygen.

Pages 4 and 5

1 Digestion is the breakdown of large food molecules into small soluble ones.
2 Bile is produced in the liver. It is released into the intestine to emulsify fats.
3 Enzymes speed up the breakdown of food.
4 Stomach acid provides the right conditions for stomach enzymes to work: kills microbes on food.
5 Stomach, pancreas.
6 If it is too cold enzymes do not move around very quickly and therefore they do not work very efficiently; too hot, and they are destroyed (denatured).
7 The small intestine is long, with lots of thin-walled villi to increase the surface area for absorption.
8 Peristalsis is the muscular contractions which squeeze food through the digestive system. It is so important because it ensures that food does not normally get stuck in the digestive system.

Pages 6 and 7

1 Any three from: water, digested food (e.g. glucose), hormones, waste products, urea, carbon dioxide.
2 They contain the oxygen carrier haemoglobin; they have no nucleus, therefore more room for haemoglobin, and they have a large surface area to take up more oxygen.
3 Oxygen enters in the lungs and leaves at respiring cells; carbon dioxide enters at respiring cells and leaves at the lungs; food enters at the small intestine and leaves at respiring cells.
4 It allows oxygen to be given up easily when the oxyhaemoglobin arrives at respiring cells.
5 Any two from: arteries have a narrow lumen; thick, elastic, muscular walls; contain blood at high pressure; do not contain valves. Veins have a wide lumen; thin, muscular walls; walls lack elastic fibres; blood at low pressure; contain valves.
6 It allows oxygenated blood to be sent from the heart at a higher pressure, giving a greater rate of flow to the tissues.
7 Right ventricle, left ventricle.
8 To prevent blood flowing backwards when the heart contracts.
9 There are valves in veins, to prevent the backflow of blood.

Pages 8 and 9

1 We need oxygen to release energy from food in respiration.
2 In the alveoli there is a higher concentration of oxygen than in the blood. Therefore oxygen moves down the diffusion gradient into the blood.
3 Three from: large surface area; thin walls; moist surface to aid diffusion; good transport system to carry the gases away.
4 Inhalation – diaphragm contracts and flattens, rib cage lifts, moving out and up; this increases the volume of the chest cavity and sucks air in. Exhalation – the diaphragm domes upwards, the ribs are lowered, the volume of the chest cavity decreases; therefore air is forced out.
5 The bronchi and larger bronchioles have cartilage to support them so that they do not collapse when the air pressure changes during exhalation.
6 Some of the chemicals in cigarette smoke are corrosive and attack the delicate lining of the alveoli, others stop the cilia beating; this causes mucus and trapped bacteria and dirt to accumulate in the lungs and set up infections.

Pages 10 and 11

1 Pressure receptors in the skin; chemical receptors in the nose; light receptors in the eye; pressure receptors in the ear, and the semi-circular canals.
2 Retina contains the light-sensitive cells to respond to the different patterns of light; iris controls the amount of light entering the eye; optic nerve carries messages to the brain; lens bends the light so that it can come to a focus on the retina.
3 Circular muscles in the iris contract and the radial muscles relax to make the pupil small.
4 Motor neurones are very long, enabling them to cover long distances in the body; often insulated to speed up transmission of the message; end at effectors such as muscles or glands.
5 Synapse is the tiny gap between two different neurones. Synapses ensure that messages can only pass in one direction along a neurone.

Answers to Now Do This Questions

6 Stimulus, pain of dog bite – pain receptor in skin – sensory neurone – central nervous system – motor neurone – arm muscle – hand moves away from the dog.

Pages 12 and 13

1 Three from: start their menstrual cycle (have periods); develop breasts; grow pubic and underarm hair; grow taller.
2 Hormones are released into the blood and travel to their target sites in the blood as it travels around the body, whereas nervous messages travel in a direct route.
3 A pregnant woman maintains a high level of progesterone to keep the uterus lining in place for the baby to develop in, therefore the uterus lining cannot come away as menstruation.
4 It prevents the ovaries releasing eggs.
5 Oestrogen helps to repair and build up the lining of the uterus.

Pages 14 and 15

1 Two from: regulate plant shoot and root growth; control ripening of fruits; control flowering.
2 Auxins dissolve in water to move around the plant.
3 Light and gravity. Light is needed so that the plants can photosynthesise and produce the materials needed for them to grow; gravity ensures that whichever way a seed is planted, the roots will always grow down into the soil to obtain water and minerals.
4 Two from: rooting compound to ensure cuttings start to produce roots and shoots; selective weedkiller because it can accelerate the growth of certain plants to such an extent that they become too weak and die; enables farmers to pick fruit before fully ripe and then to complete ripening when required.
5 A selective weedkiller is one which kills only certain types of plants, and leaves others unharmed.
6 The shoot is positively phototropic and grows up towards the light; the root grows down towards gravity.

Page 16

1 The habitat – non-living part; the populations – the living part.
2 a Insects and other very small creatures.
 b Plants.
 c Small nocturnal animals.

Pages 18 and 19

1 a Producer – heather; primary consumer – rabbit, grouse, bees, deer; predator – fox, eagle.
 b Any two starting with heather, e.g. heather → grouse → fox.
 c Should show a normal pyramid shape.
2 Light energy.
3 A food chain shows only one feeding relationship, whereas a food web is more realistic and shows many more feeding relationships.
4 In a pyramid of numbers, one oak tree is represented as the same as one grass plant, or one mouse. If you use the mass of each, you take account of their relative sizes.
5 Energy is lost at each trophic level, therefore there is insufficient energy to sustain more than four or five trophic levels.

Pages 20 and 21

1 Fungi and bacteria.
2 Decomposers recycle nutrients which would otherwise be locked away inside dead things.
3 Deforestation involves removal of trees, which would otherwise be removing carbon dioxide from the atmosphere for photosynthesis; burning these trees, or increased burning of fossil fuels, is increasing carbon dioxide in the atmosphere; increase in population leading to increased demand for cars, higher standard of living etc. leading to more fossil fuels being burnt and more carbon dioxide in the atmosphere.
4 Photosynthesis.
5 Nitrogen-fixing bacteria change nitrogen into nitrates; denitrifying bacteria convert nitrates into nitrogen; nitrifying bacteria convert ammonia into nitrates.
6 Beans have root nodules with nitrogen-fixing bacteria in. They therefore put a lot of nitrates back into the soil when ploughed in.

Pages 22 and 23

1 Use – fertilisers to increase growth; pesticides to reduce crop damage and loss; herbicides to reduce losses caused by competition; intensive practices; biological control.
2 Pesticide increases yield, but may get into the food chain and kill other organisms which would naturally eat some of the pest species, leading to more pesticide required in subsequent years. It is also costly.
3 Nitrate rich materials drain through the soil and into waterways. Here they encourage growth of surface algae cutting off light to the

Answers to Now Do This Questions

plants below. These plants die and decompose, leading to the death of all the other living things in the waterway.

4   For example – more household waste, overcome by increasing public awareness and recycling facilities. Increased car use adding to the greenhouse gases, overcome by increased public awareness and improved public transport systems.

Pages 24 and 25

1   Green plants use light energy to change carbon dioxide and water into sugars (food).
    carbon dioxide + water → glucose + oxygen
              chlorophyll and light energy
2   Carbon dioxide comes from the atmosphere; water from the soil via the root hairs.
3   Three from: broad; thin; lots of chlorophyll; good transport system; stomata.
4   Oxygen and water vapour.
5   No, because they need light to photosynthesise.
6   Plants appear green because they reflect green light. Light that they reflect cannot be used for photosynthesis, therefore green light is not very good for photosynthesis and plants do not grow well.

Pages 26 and 27

1   Three from: changed into sucrose for transport; changed into cellulose; changed into proteins; respired to release energy; changed into starch for storage.
2   It allows some materials to pass through it, but not others.
3   There is more water inside the chips than there is in the concentrated sugar solution around them, therefore water will move from a high concentration to a low concentration, leaving the cells and making them smaller; in the dilute sugar solution, the osmotic gradient is the other way round, with water moving into the cells and causing the chip to become longer.
4   The xylem, to transport absorbed water and minerals; the phloem to transport dissolved sucrose.
5   Magnesium is used to make chlorophyll, which makes plants look green. Chlorophyll is essential for photosynthesis, which makes the materials necessary for the plant to grow.
6   One crop will rapidly use up certain minerals in the soil, and if the crop is harvested rather than ploughed back into the soil, the minerals are removed as well. Farmers have to use fertilisers to replenish the lost minerals.
7   To absorb water and dissolved minerals.

Page 29

1   A vascular bundle is a group of tissues concerned with transport, therefore it contains xylem and phloem.
2   Prevents the plant losing too much water by evaporation.
3   Transpiration is the evaporation of water from the leaves of a plant and its replacement by water from the xylem.
4   Three from: provides water for photosynthesis; cools the plant down; helps to move minerals up the plant; provides support because the cells are stiff when full of water.
5 a Carbon dioxide diffuses in through open stomata.
  b Oxygen diffuses out through the stomata from a high concentration to a relatively lower concentration in the atmosphere.

Page 31

1   Respiration is the release of energy from glucose (food).
2   $C_6H_{12}O_6 + 6O_2 \rightarrow 6CO_2 + 6H_2O +$ energy
3   Two from: aerobic produces more energy; aerobic produces carbon dioxide; anaerobic produces lactic acid; only aerobic uses oxygen.
4   Respiration occurs in all the cells in the body.
5   Two from: breathing rate increases; heart beat increases; aerobic respiration increases.
6   Breathing rate, more oxygen; heart beat, faster delivery of oxygen and glucose to cells; more respiration, more energy to work the muscles.
7   Glucose → lactic acid + some energy
8   During vigorous exercise the muscles have to respire anaerobically. This forms lactic acid. To get rid of lactic acid, oxygen is needed, therefore at the end of the exercise you have built up a lot of lactic acid which must be broken down. The oxygen needed to break it down is referred to as the oxygen debt.
9   Aerobic respiration breaks down glucose all the way to carbon dioxide and water, whereas anaerobic respiration only breaks down glucose to lactic acid, which still contains a lot of stored energy.

Pages 32 and 33

1   Homeostasis means maintaining conditions in your body at a steady state (optimum level).
2   Pancreas, liver.
3   Water, urea, and salt as urine.
4   Carbon dioxide dissolves in the blood to form

Answers to Now Do This Questions

carbonic acid. A change in the blood pH will affect enzyme activity around the body.

5 On a hot sunny day you lose water through sweating, therefore there is less water in the body to be lost in the urine, so you produce more concentrated urine.

6 Brain.

7 Sweat uses some of our body heat to evaporate it from the skin, therefore some of the body heat is used up.

Pages 34 and 35

1 Tears contain antiseptic which destroys microbes.

2 Blood blocks the hole (platelets) and white blood cells launch a counter attack.

3 An antibody is a chemical produced to attack something our body recognises as foreign (antigen).

4 White blood cells leave the blood to reach any invading microbes so that they can launch an attack.

5 A drug is a substance that changes the way your body works.

6 Chemicals in cigarette smoke stop the cilia beating, therefore mucus and microbes lodge in the lungs rather than constantly being removed. In the lungs microbes can cause infections.

7 Depressant – slows down brain activity, e.g. alcohol.
   Stimulant – speeds up brain activity, e.g. caffeine.

Page 37

1 Growth needs the production of identical cells, all carrying all the chromosomes. Only mitosis does this.

2

Mitosis	Meiosis
Occurs in growth and asexual reproduction.	Occurs in gamete formation.
Produces two identical cells.	Produces four non-identical cells.
Same number of chromosomes as parent cell.	Half the number of chromosomes as parent cell.

3 Down's syndrome.

4 Two or more genetically identical individuals.

5 Mitosis.

Page 39

1 50% blue, 50% brown; Bb × bb = Bb, Bb (both brown), bb, bb (both blue).

2 50% rollers, 50% non-rollers. Ratio 1 : 1.

3

Gametes	X	X^c
X^c	XX^c	X^cX^c — colour-blind girl
Y	XY	X^cY

or

Gametes	X^c	X^c
X^c	X^cX^c	X^cX^c — all girls colour blind
Y	X^cY	X^cY

4 Weight and body shape

Page 41

1 Some body parts do not fossilise; only some organisms were in the right place at the right time, some may have died and been eaten; there are still fossils which we have not yet found.

2 Natural selection means that the environment determines which genotype survives and reproduces.

3 When tree trunks became darker it was the darker version of the moth which avoided predation and therefore was more likely to breed and pass its genes on. They survived because they were better adapted to their environment than their pale counterparts.

4 Any species unable to compete successfully as the environment changes, will become extinct because the individuals will be unable to adapt themselves successfully to the changes.

Pages 42 and 43

1 **a** speed.
   b Selective breeding – pick two speedy parents, breed them and pick the fastest foal, repeat.

2 Animals reproduce by sexual reproduction, whereas plants can also reproduce asexually to produce genetically identical offspring.

3 *see next page*

4 A, T, G, C. They pair up A to T and G to C.

5 One side of the DNA is used as a template for the bases to attach to, therefore each new piece of DNA will always contain one of the original sides of the ladder, and one newly formed side.

6 DNA carries the genetic code (genes) which controls all the activities of the cell. Therefore it is vital that this code is not changed in any way, or the information it contains might be changed too.

Answers to Now Do This Questions

3

Selective breeding	Genetic engineering
Advantages • Gradually produce living things with more and more desirable characteristics.	*Advantages* • Outcome is known. • Once set up it is quicker than selective breeding. • Can transfer genes from one species to another. • Can make large amounts of useful products, e.g. insulin.
Disadvantages • Time consuming. • Outcome not predictable.	*Disadvantages* • Expensive to set up. • Worries about transferred gene escaping into other species. • Worries about effects of eating genetically altered individuals. • Ethical worries, including how it might be applied to human beings.

Pages 50 and 51

1 Hydrogen sulphide, sugar, nitric acid.
2 Salt and sand, salty water.
3 Evaporate; filter; filter, evaporate; dissolve, filter, evaporate.

Pages 52 and 53

1 Particles can move through the container. Particles are randomly arranged.
2 Particles are held in position and can't move closer.
3 Gets warm, difficult to change back again.
4 Condensed, dissolve, solvent, solution.

Pages 54 and 55

1

Formula	No. of atoms in formula	No. of different elements
HCl	2	2
H_2O	3	2
CH_4	5	2
$AlCl_3$	4	2
H_2SO_4	7	3
$C_6H_{12}O_6$	24	3

2 H_2S
3 NH_3
4 $MgCl_2$, Fe_2O_3
5 Reactant side: 1 atom of Mg, 2 atoms of O.
Product side: 2 atoms of Mg, 2 atoms of O.
Equation doesn't balance.
Reactant side: 1 atom of C, 4 atoms of H and 4 atoms of O.
Product side: 1 atom of C, 2 atoms of O and 4 atoms of H, 2 atoms of O.
Equation balances.
6 2, 2, 3, 4, 3

Page 57

1 Increase temperature, increase concentration of acid, increase surface area of the carbonate (use smaller pieces).
2 Increase temperature and concentration.
3 A. The slope is the steepest.
4 C

Pages 58 and 59

1 **a** Broken:
$4 \times$ C—H $= 4 \times 435 =$ 1740 kJ
$1 \times$ Cl—Cl $=$ 243 $=$ 243 kJ
Total energy to break bonds 1983 kJ
b Made:
$3 \times$ C—H $= 3 \times 435 =$ 1305 kJ
$1 \times$ C—Cl $=$ 346 $=$ 346 kJ
$1 \times$ H—Cl $=$ 432 $=$ 432 kJ
Total energy on making bonds 2083 kJ
2 **a** 2083 − 1983 = 100 kJ **b** Exothermic
3 $400 \times 4.5 \times 4.2 = 7560$ J
4 Carbon dioxide, greenhouse, ultraviolet, infra-red, sulphur dioxide.

Pages 60 and 61

1 Respiration, combustion.
2 Photosynthesis.
3 80%, 20%, 0.04%, oxygen, carbon dioxide, respiration, combustion.

Pages 62 and 63

1–3 See page 40.
4 **a** Underneath, into the mantle **b** They melt.
5 They get older.

Pages 64 and 65

1 Large, igneous, metamorphic.
2 Weathering, sedimentary, metamorphic, upthrust.

Pages 66 and 67

1 300°C, 100°C, 200°C.
2 Because it has a lower boiling point.
3 Because it has more carbon atoms.
4 Propane + oxygen → carbon dioxide + water
5 $C_3H_8 + 5O_2 \rightarrow 3CO_2 + 4H_2O$
6 $C_5H_{12} + 8O_2 \rightarrow 5CO_2 + 6H_2O$

Answers to Now Do This Questions

Pages 68 and 69

1. Zinc + copper oxide → zinc oxide + copper
2. Copper oxide, silver oxide, the metal and water will be formed.
3. CABD
4. Reduced – iron oxide, oxidised – aluminium.
5. Reduction
6. Carbon + copper oxide → carbon dioxide + copper
7. **a** Zinc **b** Zinc is more reactive than iron.

Pages 70 and 71

1. Positive.
2. Negative.
3. Mg^{++}
4. The ions can't move through the solid.
5. Negative electrode (cathode).
6. **a** Positive **b** negative.
7. Negative electrode (cathode).
8. Negative electrode (cathode).

Pages 72 and 73

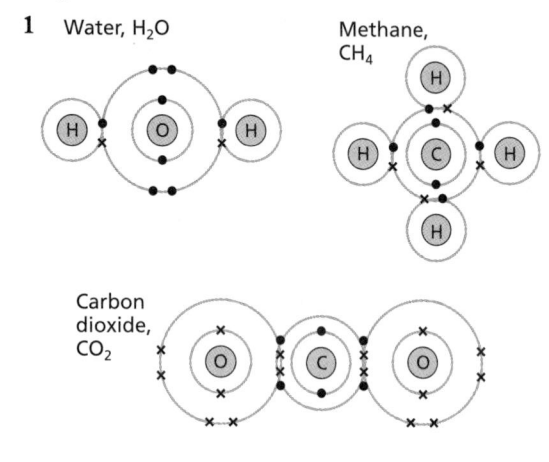

1. Water, H_2O; Methane, CH_4; Carbon dioxide, CO_2; Nitrogen, N_2 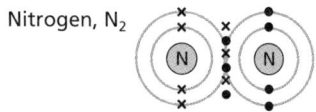
2. Molecular structure.
3. Giant structure.
4. Covalent bonds.
5. Weak forces.

Page 74 and 75

1. 1
2. 6
3. [diagram]
4. It has many weak forces.
5. 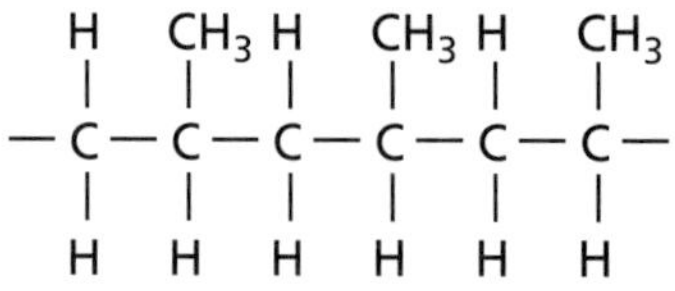
```
    H   CH3  H   CH3  H   CH3
    |   |    |   |    |   |
  — C — C  — C — C  — C — C —
    |   |    |   |    |   |
    H   H    H   H    H   H
```
6.
```
    H   CN
    |   |
    C = C
    |   |
    H   H
```

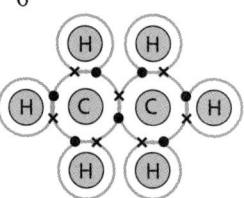

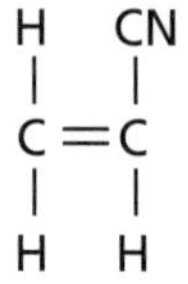

Page 77

1. **a** It increases
   b It slows down and stops.
2. It is damaged (denatured).
3. Alcohol, carbon dioxide.
4. **a** Oxygen in the air.
   b Acid in the lemon juice denatures the enzyme.
   c The high temperature during cooking denatures the enzyme.
   d Less air can get to the apple.

Page 79

1. Falls.
2. Baking soda.
3. Iron sulphate.
4. **a** Magnesium chloride and hydrogen.
   b $Mg + 2HCl \rightarrow MgCl_2 + H_2$

Pages 80 and 81

1. A reaction that will go in either direction.
2. Nitrogen and hydrogen.
3. Ammonium sulphate, $(NH_4)_2SO_4$
4. $2NH_4OH + H_2SO_4 \rightarrow (NH_4)_2SO_4 + H_2O$
5. Too much fertiliser increases plant growth. This cuts out the light, so plants at the bottom rot and use up oxygen.

Pages 82 and 83

1. **a** 24 g **b** 64 g
2. 64%
3. Cu_2O
4. CuO

Pages 84 and 85

1. Oxygen-18 has two more neutrons than oxygen-16.
2. 26
3. 30
4. **a** 7 **b** 7 **c** 2 in the first shell, 5 in the next.
5. 2 : 8 : 1
6. 2 : 8 : 8 : 1

Answers to Now Do This Questions

Pages 86 and 87

1. They have two outer electrons, which they lose to leave a stable shell.
2. Group 0 elements have a stable outer electron shell.
3. Sodium + water → sodium hydroxide + hydrogen
4. $2Na + 2H_2O \rightarrow 2NaOH + H_2$

Page 88

1. Hydrogen + chlorine → hydrogen chloride
2. $2Na + Cl_2 \rightarrow 2NaCl$

Pages 96 and 97

1. Electrons.
2. Glass, wood.
3. Metals, water.
4. Insulator, electrons, comb, charged.
5. Fur, glass, negative, positive.
6. Glass is positive, silk is negative.
7. Attract, attract, repel.
8. Paint sprayers, photocopiers.
9. The sparks may ignite the substance.
10. The car discharges itself through you.

Pages 98 and 99

1. 15 C
2. 20 A
3. See the table on page 98.
4. [circuit diagram with cell and motor M]
5. [circuit diagram with ammeter A, 6 V source]
6. They all read 2 A
7. 2 A
8. [circuit diagram with 12 V source, resistor, motor M, voltmeter V]
9. 96 J

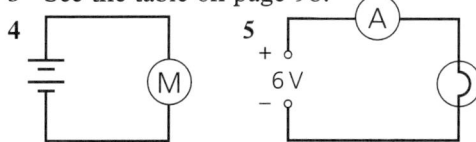

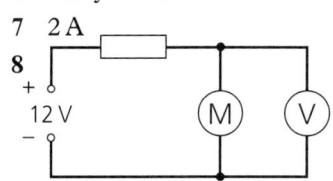

Pages 100 and 101

1. $P(W) = I(A) \times V(V)$
2. 60 W
3. [circuit diagram with ammeter A, motor M, voltmeter V]
4. 0.4 A
5. b
6. $R(\Omega) = V(V)/I(A)$
7. 48 Ω
8. [circuit diagram with cell, variable resistor, lamp]
9. 4 A
10. 100 V
11. off + off, off + on, on + off, on + on

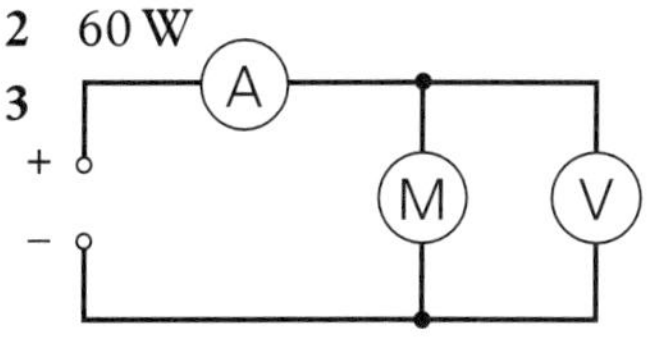

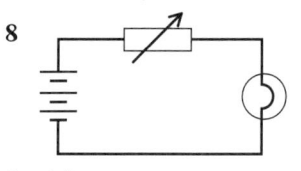

Pages 102 and 103

1. 6.75p
2. 60p
3. 0.13p (!)
4. Live (brown), neutral (blue), earth (green and yellow).
5. Thin wires get hot. The cable would get damaged if it got too hot.
6. Live carries energy to the appliance. Neutral completes the electrical circuit. Earth prevents electrocution.
7. Cuts off the current if it gets large enough to heat up the wires.
8. It blows if the live comes into contact with the earth wire, disconnecting the appliance from the live wire.
9. In the live connection.
10. Double insulated appliances.
11. To the metal outside. It stops the outside becoming live and killing someone.

Pages 104 and 105

1. Iron, steel, cobalt, nickel.
2. North
3. Left
4. Attract, attract, repel, ignore.
5. Right, right, left.
6. **a** –0.1 V **b** 0 V.
7. Move the wire faster, use stronger magnets.
8. Zero, negative.
9. Speed up magnet, more coils, stronger magnet, iron in coil.
10. Steel for the magnets, copper for the coils which spin inside the magnets, iron to wind the coils on.
11. Twice as many cycles on the graph, maximum voltage doubled.

Pages 106 and 107

1. Oil is burnt to make steam from water. The steam rotates the turbine. The turbine rotates the generator to make electricity.
2. Chemical energy in the fuel → heat energy in the steam → kinetic energy in the turbine → electrical energy in the generator.

Answers to Now Do This Questions

3 Chimney for gases from burnt fuel, pipes carrying steam, friction in the turbine and generator.
4 Efficiency = (useful output/input) × 100
5 25%, heat energy.
6 Wires which carry electricity away from power stations.
7 Heat energy, 95%.
8 To increase efficiency by reducing current which creates wasteful heat energy.
9 See page 107.
10 Increases the voltage and reduce the current in the grid wires.
11 a.c.
12 98%
13 12 V a.c.

Pages 108 and 109
1 See page 108.
2 Use an iron core, increase number of coils, increase the current.
3 Page 108
4 The contacts are opened by a spring. Current in the coil magnetises the core, attracting the iron armature and pulling the contacts together.
5 Comes on, armature, open, off, close.
6 Coil changes direction.
7 Allow current in and out of the coil such that forces on it always twist it round the same way.
8 More current, stronger magnets, more turns in the coil.

Pages 110 and 111
1 −20°C. Conduction, convection and radiation.
2 Kinetic, vibrate, energy, conduction.
3 Lose energy. Air at the top cools, shrinks and falls. It is replaced by a flow of hot air from the base of the fridge.
4 Bad, bad, good, good.
5 Gets less.
6 Only particles with more than average energy can escape. Leaves particles with less than average energy behind in the liquid.
7 Wall cavities, double glazing and roof insulation reduce conduction. White walls and special window glass reduce radiation. Sheltered location and small surface area reduces convection.

Pages 112 and 113
1 Chemical energy in gas → heat energy in the air duct → heat energy in the room.
2 Cheap to install, no waste gases.
3 Electricity is expensive.
4 Coal, oil, natural gas. Less pollution, can be made from renewable sources.
5 Wood (from plants).
6 Look at the bottom of page 112.
7 5 years.
8 Insulator, air, conductor, metal.

Pages 114 and 115
1 v (m/s), s (m), t (s)
2 $v = s/t$
3 20 m/s
4 300 m/s
5 1.67 m/s
6 30.6 m/s
7 3000 m
8 5 s
9 1 = c, 2 = d, 3 = b
10 1 = c, 2 = a, 3 = b
11 **a** 25 m **b** 100 m **c** 50 m
12 **a** 2 m/s **b** 0 m/s **c** 2 m/s

Pages 116 and 117
1 Acceleration = change of speed/time taken, m/s^2
2 10 m/s^2
3 6 s
4 10 m/s
5 Air resistance, contact between tyres and road, moving parts in the wheels.
6 Steady speed, getting faster, slowing down.
7 6000 N
8 15 000 N
9 2 m/s^2
10 Distance moved before the brakes start to slow the car down. Lack of concentration, tiredness, intoxication.
11 Distance moved while the brakes are on. Incorrect adjustment, rain, bald tyres, badly inflated tyres.
12 21 m
13 **a** 5 s **b** 75 m
14 10.5 m, 2.5 s, 18.8 m

Pages 118 and 119
1 Force, length, smaller, elastic, inelastic, force.
2 10 cm, 60 N
3 Crumple zones absorb kinetic energy. Seat belts slow people down securely. Air bags provide a soft cushion.
4 Pressure (Pa) = force (N)/area (m^2)
5 1000 Pa, 10 000 Pa, 16 000 Pa.
6 $A = F/P$
7 0.025 m^2

Answers to Now Do This Questions

Pages 120 and 121
1. $W(J) = F(N) \times s(m)$
2. 75 J, 75 J.
3. 20 m
4. 2500 N
5. 500 J
6. a, b
7. Chemical, potential, potential, kinetic, heat.
8. 3500 J
9. 2500 J
10. 200 W

Pages 122 and 123
1. Gravity downwards, friction upwards.
2. Gravity, speed, friction, upwards, increases, balanced, stays the same.
3. **a** 30 m/s **b** 15 m/s **c** 45 m
4. Weight (N) = mass (kg) × gravity (N/kg or m/s^2)
5. Mass is fixed by number of atoms, g is fixed by planet.
6. 50 kg, 200 N
7. Velocity is both speed and direction.
8. 750 N from the centre of the Earth to Sue.
9. Change its speed and its direction of motion.
10. 1 m, 2 m

Pages 124 and 125
1. 2000 Hz
2. 4 m
3. Vibrations, compressions, rarefactions, frequency, hertz or Hz, wavelength, metres, longitudinal, energy flow.
4. 3, 4 m, 25 cm
5. The energy frows from left to right but the wiggles are up and down.
6. $v = fL$
7. 24 m/s
8. 50 m, 600 000 Hz

Pages 126 and 127
1. 60°, 60°; 40°, 40°
2. 60°, 30°
3. Opposite to the way it entered the prism.
4. See page 127
5. See page 127
6. **a** Plane waves emerge from the gap
   b Circular waves emerge from the gap.

Pages 128 and 129
1. 47 Hz, 900 Hz, 12 000 Hz, 24 kHz, 50 000 Hz, The last two.
2. 37.5 m
3. Looking inside people.
4. p-waves are longitudinal, s-waves are transverse.
5. See the top of page 129.

Pages 130 and 131
1. A small central nucleus with electrons moving around it.
2. Positive.
3. Negative.
4. The break up of a nucleus.
5. Alpha, beta and gamma.
6. Nucleus.
7. Alpha is positive, beta is negative and gamma has no charge.
8. **a** Alpha **b** Gamma **c** Alpha **d** Beta.
9. Alpha, beta, gamma.
10. Uranium in rocks, radon in the air, nuclear fallout from bomb tests, cosmic rays from space.
11. 6000
12. Goes down, as the number of unstable atoms decreases.
13. **a** Smoke alarms **b** Thickness measurement
    c Sterilising instruments, killing cancers
    d Generating electricity.

Pages 132 and 133
1. A sphere of rock or gas which orbits a star.
2. A ball of gases kept hot by fusion reactions.
3. The planet goes in a circle or ellipse around the star. Gravity pulls on it.
4. Moon, planet, star, solar system, galaxy, universe.
5. A moon is lighter than the planet which it orbits around.
6. The Earth is spinning round.
7. See page 133!
8. The increase in wavelength of light emitted by a galaxy moving away from us. It can be used to measure the speed of the galaxy.
9. Shrinking of the Universe down to a single point; if there is enough material, gravity will stop expansion.

Answers to Exam Questions

AT2

Question			Answer	Marks	Total
1	a		C	1	
	b	i	Work very quickly so we respond to stimuli very rapidly.	1	
		ii	Any two suitable examples – e.g. swallowing, blinking, coughing, suckling, sneezing.	2	
	c		Electrical message reaches synapse; causes release of chemical messenger; diffuses across synapse and stimulates production of an electrical message on the other side of the synapse.	3	**7 marks**
2	a		Any three of: permeable; moist; large surface area; good blood supply.	3	
	b		Diaphragm contracts; intercostals contract and raise ribs; pressure in lungs decreases as volume increases; gases move into lungs.	4	**7 marks**
3	a		−3.9	1	
	b		*[Graph: Change in length (mm) vs sugar concentration (mol/dm³); curve passing from +3 at 0 through zero around 0.32, down to approximately −5 at 0.8]*	4	
	c		The point at which the two lines cross. On this graph it is 0.32.	1	
	d		Osmosis; water moves from a high concentration; through a cell membrane; to a lower concentration; rhubarb shrank as water moved out of the cells; rhubarb became longer as water moved into the cells. *Any 4 – but must mention osmosis.*	4	**10 marks**
4	a		0.2	1	
	b	i	Emulsifies fats.	1	
		ii	Increases the surface area of fats; so that lipases can break them down more quickly.	2	**4 marks**
5	a		Any three of: thick fur to trap still air and prevent heat loss; white fur to camouflage for easier hunting; large body mass to reduce heat loss; blubber/fat for insulation.	3	
	b		Any two of: vasoconstriction to reduce heat loss by radiation; shivering to release extra heat from respiration; increase metabolic rate; behavioural response such as putting on extra clothing.	2	
	c		Receptors in the brain monitoring blood temperature.	1	
	d		Either of: enzymes kept at optimum temperature for action; can survive in much wider range of habitats.	1	**7 marks**
6	a		$6CO_2$; $6O_2$	2	
	b		Light; chlorophyll.	2	
	c		*[Diagram: coloured filter between light source and water plant in flask; bicarbonate solution to provide plenty of CO_2; oxygen collecting tube — count the number of bubbles per minute; wavelength (blue light)]* Diagram or description based on the diagram; measure rate of oxygen production; using different coloured light; all other factors to remain the same.	5	**9 marks**

Answers to Exam Questions

Question			Answer	Marks	Total
7	a		Exercise involves muscles working; to do this they require oxygen to respire and release energy.	2	
	b	i	Glucose → lactic acid + some energy	3	
		ii	The lactic acid produced is toxic and has to be broken down; oxygen is needed to break it down; the amount of extra oxygen needed is called the oxygen debt.	3	
		iii	C to D	1	9 marks
8			Any four of: nitrates encourage growth of surface algae; these cut off light to plants below; these plants cannot photosynthesise therefore they die; decomposers move in and rot the dead plants; they use up oxygen in the water; all other living things suffocate; waterway becomes largely uninhabited.	4	4 marks
9	a		Hormones.	1	
	b		Any four from: increases heart rate; increases breathing rate; therefore more blood with oxygen and glucose delivered to the muscles; converts glycogen to glucose to increase glucose availability; diverts blood to muscles and brain away from gut and other less important areas.	4	5 marks
10	a		Phototropism.	1	
	b		Enables them to take up light; needed for photosynthesis.	2	
	c		Produced at the tip and diffuses back down the shoot; on the light side the auxin is destroyed; on the shaded side the auxin causes the cells to elongate; this side therefore grows whereas the side in the light stops growing.	3	6 marks
11	a	i	Replication.	1	
		ii	Any five of: an enzyme is separating the two sides; free bases move in; from the nucleus; A-T; C-G; complementary bases pair up; the new bases join together; forming two new strands of DNA; identical to the original strand.	5	
	b		They carry the genetic code. c A change in the genetic code.	1 1	8 marks
12	a		The gene is on the X (or Y) chromosome.	1	
	b		A form of a gene; which is only expressed in the homozygous state.	2	
	c	i	Sarah or his mother; his father was not a haemophiliac and therefore could not have given him the allele. He only inherits an X chromosome from his mother.	2	
		ii	No; he only passes his Y chromosome on to his son. iii 50%	2 1	8 marks
13	a		Homeostasis.	1	
	b		Three of water; salt; pH; temperature; glucose; carbon dioxide; urea.	3	
	c		Blood is filtered; useful molecules; such as glucose, are reabsorbed; urea and left over water remain; in the kidney tubule to form urine.	4	
	d		On a hot day you would sweat; therefore less water needs to be lost from the body in urine; small volume of concentrated urine; reverse argument for cold day.	3	11 marks
14	a		To make into proteins/nucleic acids.	1	
	b		Nitrogen is unreactive; most living things need soluble nitrates.	2	
	c		Conversion of nitrogen to nitrates.	1	

Answers to Exam Questions

Question			Answer	Marks	Total
	d		add a fertiliser; plant a crop with root nodules	2	
	e		Nitrates; leached from the soil; promote growth of algae; cuts off light to plants below; suffocates all other living things; leads to stagnant waterways; may get into drinking water; nitrate pollution.	5	11 marks
15	a		Lining of the uterus comes away/menstruation	1	
	b		It causes the lining of the uterus to thicken. c 14	1 1	
	d		Level will stay high; because the yellow body stays active.	2	
	e		Other things may cause the body temperature to increase – for example a fever or 'flu.	1	6 marks
16	a		Nucleus; contains genetic information to control activities of the cell.	2	
	b		To leave more room to transport oxygen.	1	
	c	i	To release energy by respiration ii To release the energy for it to swim.	1 1	
	d		Oxygen e Water (can accept a named mineral)	1 1	
	f		A and D. Both have cell walls/both have a large vacuole.	1	10 marks
17	a		Speed up; the breakdown food; or break down large insoluble food molecules into; small soluble ones.	2	
	b		The enzyme has broken down the starch into glucose; which has passed through the semi-permeable membrane.	2	
	c		Blood. d Starch is too big to pass through the membrane.	1 1	
	e		Nothing; boiling has destroyed the enzyme; therefore no glucose can be produced.	3	
	f		Mouth salivary glands/pancreas.	1	10 marks

AT3

Question			Answer	Marks	Total
1	a		B	1	
	b	i	It will go in.	1	
		ii	Particles are far apart, so can be pushed closer together.	2	
	c	i	Plunger will not go in.	1	
		ii	Particles are close together so cannot be pushed any closer.	2	
	d		Energy is needed to overcome the forces between the molecules so that the liquid can evaporate. This energy is called the latent heat of evaporation.	3	10 marks
2	a		calcium + oxygen → calcium oxide *One mark for the reactants, one mark for the product.*	2	
	c		$2Ca + O_2 \rightarrow 2CaO$ *One mark for the reactants, one mark for the product.*	2	4 marks
3	a		Rose up the filter paper. b No, the spots are different.	1 1	
	c	i	Two. ii Three.	1 1	4 marks
4	a		They have different boiling points.	1	
	b	i	Oxidation. ii Carbon dioxide and water.	1 2	
		iii	$CH_4 + 2O_2 \rightarrow CO_2 + 2H_2O$ *One mark for correct formulae, one mark for correct balancing.*	2	

Answers to Exam Questions

Question		Answer	Marks	Total
	iv	Carbon monoxide and water.	2	
	v	$CH_4 + 1.5O_2 \rightarrow CO + 2H_2O$ *or* $2CH_4 + 3O_2 \rightarrow 2CO + 4H_2O$ *One mark for correct formulae, one mark for correct balancing.*	2	**10 marks**
5 a		Exothermic. **b** Joules or kilojoules	1 1	
c		Any three from: ultraviolet (short wavelength) radiation comes in from the Sun; the Earth gives out infra-red (long wavelength) radiation; greenhouse gases trap this long wavelength radiation, preventing heat loss.	3	**5 marks**
6 a		Collisions: greater surface area/more places for collision.	2	
b		Particles move faster, collide more often. Particles have more energy so can break bonds more easily.	4	
c		Increase the concentration, use a catalyst.	2	**8 marks**
7 a		Igneous. **b** Interlocking crystals.	1 2	
c		Rock A. It has small crystals.	1	
d		The plate split, and the two halves moved apart.	2	**6 marks**
8 a		Reduction. **b** Aluminium and zinc.	1 1	
c		Sodium is too dangerous or too reactive.	1	**3 marks**
9 a	i	Crude oil. **ii** To make nitric acid *or* fertiliser *or* explosives.	1 2	
	iii	Wages, raw materials, energy, building the factory, etc.	3	
b	i	A substance which speeds up a reaction and can be recovered.	2	
	ii	Iron.	1	
c		The reaction will go in either (and both) direction.	1	
d	i	43% **ii** Cost of compressors *or* need for thicker walled reaction vessel.	1 1	
e		Moves to the right.	1	**13 marks**
10 a	i	38 **ii** The number of neutrons. **b i** Two	1 1 1	
	ii	Strontium and calcium are in the same group/have the same number of outer electrons, so will have very similar properties.	2	
c	i	14 **ii** 2, 8, 3	1 1	**7 marks**
11 a	i	Between 9 and 14. **ii** 7 **iii** Between 6 and 4. **b** Salt	1 1 1 1	
c	i	Two **ii** Three **iii** 80 **d i** Eutrophication	1 1 1 1	
	ii	Any three from: algae grow on the surface; this cuts the light to the lower plants; plants die and rot; using up oxygen from the water; killing animals such as fish.	3	**11 marks**
12 a	i	Bottom of Group I. **ii** Top of Group VII.	2 2	
b		They have a stable outer shell. **c i** 2 **ii** 6	1 1 1	
d		Double positive.	2	**9 marks**
13 a		Ions. **b** To lower the melting point.	1 1	
c		Ions can travel through the liquid but not the solid.	1	
d	i	Anode. **ii** Cathode.	1 1	
	iii	They go to the cathode and turn into atoms (they are neutralised).	2	**7 Marks**
14 a		Two. **b i** They are shared.	1 1	
	ii	Two electrons in the first shell, four in the second.	2	

Answers to Exam Questions

Question		Answer	Marks	Total
c	i	Alkene group. ii Bromine water. iii Goes colourless.	1 1 1	
	iv	Stays orange/brown.	1	
d	i	–E–E–E–E–E–E–E–E–E–E– ii Use high pressure and a catalyst.	1 2	**11 marks**
15 a	i	Sugar, moisture, warmth. ii Alcohol (ethanol).	3 1	
b	i	Speeds up the reaction. ii It can be recovered.	1 1	
c		Carbon dioxide gas.	1	
d		Speeds up, to reach its maximum rate at 37°C, then slows down as the yeast is killed and stops.	4	**11 marks**
16 a	i	From the copper sulphate solution. ii Cu^{++} (aq) + $2e^-$ → Cu (s)	1 1	
b	i	Copper dissolves, it turns into ions. ii Cu (s) → Cu^{++} (aq) + $2e^-$	1 1	**4 marks**

AT4

Question		Answer	Marks	Total
1 a	i	Transverse. Energy flow at right angles to displacement.	2	
	ii	A iii 3 Hz iv 1.5 m/s	1 2 2	
b		Jill's voice vibrates her cup. This sends a longitudinal wave along the string. This vibrates Tom's cup, creating a sound wave.	3	**10 marks**
2 a			1	
b		All the reflected rays appear to come from a single point behind the mirror.	2	
c	i	A	1	
	ii	Rays from the lamp which reflect from the mirror emerge in the same direction, making a beam of light.	2	**6 marks**
3 a		Heat energy increases vibration of particles in the wall. Particles in solids touch each other, so the energy of vibration is passed from one particle to another.	2	
b	i	Fibre wool ii It contains air, which is a poor conductor.	1 2	
c	i	Block up gaps in windows and doors. ii 8 months	1 2	
d		Double glaze windows to reduce heat conducting through. Reduce the temperature of the house to reduce heat flow to the cold outside.	4	**12 marks**
4 a	i	1.2 kWh ii 9.6p b Live, neutral, earth.	1 1 3	**5 marks**
5 a	i	3 m/s² ii 60 kg b 300 m	2 2 2	
c		Friction is the only horizontal force, acting against her velocity. So she has a negative acceleration.	3	
d		The helmet spreads the force of impact over a large area, reducing the pressure on her skull.	3	**12 marks**
6 a		The motor stops because all the current takes the low resistance path through the switch. The lamp glows brightly because there is more current in the circuit, since the resistance of the motor has been removed.	3	

Answers to Exam Questions

Question			Answer	Marks	Total
	b	i	[circuit diagram: 12 V battery with ammeter and motor M in parallel arrangement]	1	
		ii	$P = IV$, so motor has 2 A, lamp has only 0.5 A **iii** 2.5 A	2 3	**9 marks**
7	a		[circuit diagram: battery with ammeter A, motor M and voltmeter V] **b i** 0.72 W **ii** 2 Ω	2 3 3	
	c		As the resistance of the rheostat increases the current decreases, lowering the power of the motor, so reducing its speed.	3	**11 marks**
8	a		The comb pulls electrons off his hair. Electrons are negative, leaving the hair positive.	3	
	b		Like charges repel. Each hair is repelled by all the other hairs, forcing it upright.	2	
	c		Plastic is an insulator, so carries the electrons away from the hair. Electrons removed from hair by a metal comb can flow through it back to the hair.	2	**7 marks**
9	a	i	Kinetic, heat. **ii** 10 000 J	2 3	
		iii	Some of the KE can become PE as the car moves up, so the brakes need to do less work.	3	
	b	i	5000 W **ii** 25%	3 3	**14 marks**
10	a		Soft iron. **b** Increase current, wrap more coils of wire.	1 2	
	c	i	[diagram of solenoid with arrows showing magnetic field direction] **ii** Reverse the direction of the current in the wire.	2 1	**6 marks**
11	a		Furnace, boiler, turbine, generator, transformer. **b** 30%	5 2	
	c	i	Waste gas from the furnace, from the cooling tower where the steam condenses, heat radiated from the hot boiler.	3	
		ii	Because it is too spread out to be converted into electricity.	1	**11 marks**
12	a		Stars generate heat energy within them.	1	
	b		Hydrogen atoms collide and join to form helium atoms.	3	
	c		Gravity pulls the particles towards each other, giving them kinetic energy. So the cloud collapses and heats up. Eventually, the pressure and temperature are high enough for fusion to start.	4	
	d		The heat of the star will radiate into space, so it will cool down.	2	**10 marks**
13	a		Gravity	1	
	b		To allow communication between different parts of the Earth, to monitor the climate and weather.	2	
	c	i	More than 90 minutes	1	
		ii	Gravity gets weaker as you go away from the Earth, and the satellite has a much larger distance to cover in one orbit.	2	**6 marks**
14	a		The emissions can break up molecules in living cells, killing them or damaging their DNA.	2	

Answers to Exam Questions

Question			Answer				Marks	Total
	b		Each nucleus can only decay once. As time goes on, there are fewer and fewer nuclei left to decay.				3	
	c		63 Bq				3	8 marks
15	a	i	The time it takes for the driver to apply the brakes	ii	0.67 s		1 2	
		iii	Tiredness, inebriation.				2	
	b	i	-5.4 m/s^2	ii	933 kg		3 3	11 marks
17	a		Use KE = $1/2\, mv^2$				2	
	b	i	10 J	ii	27 m.	c Heat energy	1 3 1	7 marks
18	a						1	
	b		Chemical, electrical, electrical, light				4	
	c	i	3V from battery is shared between LED and resistor.	ii	20 Ω		1 3	9 marks

Index

A
absorption of food 5
acceleration 116
 free fall 122
acid rain, and sulphur
  dioxide 23, 59
acids
 and metals 79
 and pH 78
 stomach acid 4
active transport 26
adapting to survive 17
addictive drugs 35
adrenal glands 13
adrenaline 13
aerobic respiration 30
air
 breathing, change in
  composition 8
 carbon cycle 20, 60
 component gases 60
 origins 61
 pollution 23, 59
air sacs 8
airplanes, charge 97
alcohol
 brewing 76
 effects 35
 fermentation 31
alkali metals (Group I) 87
alkalis 78
alkanes 67, 74
alkenes 74
alpha radiation 130
alternating current (a.c.) 99
aluminium
 extraction 71
 reactivity 68
alveoli 8
amino acids 4–5
ammonia 80
 Haber process 80
ammonium compounds 80
amperes (A) 99
amplitude, waves 125
amylase 4
anaerobic respiration 30
analgesics 35
angle of incidence 126–7
angle of reflection 126–7
animal cells
 red/white blood cells 6, 34
 structure 2
anode 70
answers, exam questions 149–56
answers, Now Do This 139–48
antibodies 34
antigens 34
area
 pressure measurement 119
 see also surface area
argon 89
armature 108
arteries 6
artificial selection 42
aseptic technique 37
asexual reproduction 36
atmosphere see air
atomic mass 82
atoms
atomic or proton number 84
 giant structures 72
 molecules and elements 50
atrio-ventricular valves 7
atrium, heart 7
auxins, plant growth 14–15

B
background radiation 131
bacteria
 decay 20
 and disease 34
 nitrifying 21
baking 76
balance 10
bases
 DNA 43
 reactions 78
battery 98
Benedict's solution 5
beta radiation 130
big bang 133
big crunch 133
bile duct 4
biodegradable plastics 75
biological controls 22
biomass, pyramid 19
biotechnology 76
biuret solution 5
blast furnace 69
blood
 and body temperature 33
 circulation 6
 oxygenation 8
 platelets 6
 red/white cells 3, 6, 34
blood vessels 6–9
body temperature 33
boiling 52
boiling points, oils 66
bonds
 covalent 72
 in fats 75
 ionic 70, 72
brain 11
brakes, liquid pressure 119
braking distance 117
breathing (gas exchange) 8
breeding, selective 42
brewing 76
bromine 88
bronchiole 8
bronchus 8
Buckminster Fullerene 73
burning, fossil fuels 23, 60, 67
butane 74
buzzer 98

C
caffeine, effects 35
calcium 68
camouflage 17
capillaries 6
 lungs 8
 villi 5
carbon
 forms 73
 isotopes 84
carbon compounds 20, 74
carbon cycle 20, 60
carbon dioxide
 atmosphere 59
 decay 20
 greenhouse effect 23, 59
 lab production 57
 lungs/blood 8
 photosynthesis 23, 24–5
 test 60
carbon monoxide 67
 iron extraction 69
carbonates 79
carnivores 18
cars
 braking distance 117
 braking force 119
 materials and safety 118
 speed measurement 114
 thinking distance 117
catalyst
 enzymes 5
 and reactants 56
cathode 70
cell membrane 2
cell structure 2–3
cellulose cell wall, plants 2, 28
central nervous system 11
centripetal force 131
charge, positive/negative 96, 98
chemical calculations,
  formula mass 82
chemical energy 58–9
chemical equations 55
chemical formulae,
  calculation 83
chemical reactions 53
 endothermic/exothermic 58
 metals 78
 percentage yields 83
 products 55
 rates 56
 reactants 55
 reactivity series 68
 reduction 68
 reversible reactions 80
chemical symbols 54
chlorine 53, 73, 84, 88
 isotopes 84
chlorophyll 2
chloroplasts 2
chromatography 51
chromosomes 37
cilia 9, 35
circuit breakers 103
circuits, electrical 99
circulation, double 7
clone 37
coal 59
cobalt 104
colour blindness 39
comets 132
community, ecosystems 16
competition 17
compounds 50
concentration of reactants 56
condensation 51, 52
conduction
 electricity 96
 heat energy 110
conductors 113
consumers, primary,
  secondary 18
continental drift 62
contraceptive pill 13
convection 110
copper, extraction 71
cornea 10
covalent bonding 72
covalent molecules 73
crop rotation 27
crystallisation 51
current 99
 and magnets 104–5
 measurement 99
cuttings 15
cytoplasm, cell 2

D
Darwin, Charles 41
decay
 biological 20, 76
 radioactive 131
decomposers 20
dehydration 32
depressant drugs 35
diabetes 12
diamond 73
diaphragm 8
diesel fuel 66
diffraction 127
diffusion
 oxygen in lungs 8
 plants 26
digestion 4–5
digestive system 4
dinosaurs 90–1
diode 101
direct current (d.c.) 99
dissolving 53
distance/time measurements
  115
distillation 51
DNA 43
dominance 38
double circulation 7
double glazing 113
Down's syndrome 37
drugs 35
dwarfism 13
dynamo 99

E
ears 10
Earth
 greenhouse effect 23, 59
 mantle, magma, core 62
 plate tectonics 62
 resources 112
 rocks 64–6
 structure 62
earth wire, electrical
  appliances 103
earthquake 63
 seismic waves 128
 zones 62
ecology and ecosystems 16–17
effectors 11
efficiency, formula 106
egg (ovum) 13
elastic materials
 car safety 118
 stretching and squeezing
  118
electric bell 109
electric motor 98, 105, 109
electrical appliances 102–3
electricity 96–7, 102–3, 106–7
 alternating current (a.c.) 99
 amperes (A) 99
 circuits 98
 current or charge 99
 direct current (d.c.) 99
 electrostatic forces 97
 generating 106–7
 magnetism 104–7
 making 58
 measurement 99, 102
 off-peak 113
 positive and negative
  charge 96
 power 100
 resistance (ohms) 100
 rheostat or variable
  resistor 100
 safety 102–3
 sources 112
 static 96
 switches 103
 transformers 107

Index

transmitting 107
unit 102
voltage (V) 98
electrolysis 70–1
electromagnetic waves 129
electromagnets 104–8
electrons
   in atoms 84–5
   and positive/negative charge 96
   static electricity 96
electrostatic forces 97
elements 50
   atomic mass 82
   atomic structure 84–5
   reactivity 68
emphysema 9
endothermic reactions 58
energy
   chemical, in food chain 19
   chemical bonds 58–9
   endo (exo)thermic 58
   and environment 59
   heat 110–13
   kilowatt–hour 102
   kinetic 110, 120–1
   living things 19
   measurements 58
   metabolic rate 31
   radiation 111
   reactions 58–9
   work 120–1
   see also waves
energy saving 111–12
environment, ecology 16
environmental variation 39
enzymes 76
   as catalysts 5
   food, control 77
equations 55
ethane 74
ethene 75
eutrophication 23, 81
evaporation 51,111
evolution 40–1
exam answers 149–56
exfoliation, rocks 65
exothermic reactions 58
eyes 10

F

F_1 and F_2 generations 38
farming
   and animals 23
   intensive 22–3
fats, test 5
fatty acids 4
female reproductive system 36
fermentation 31, 76
fertilisation 36, 37
fertilisers 78, 81
filtration 51
finite resources 23
focusing, human eye 10
food
   absorption 5
   digestion 5
food chains 18
   damage 22
food safety 77
food tests 5
food webs 18
force, moments 123
formula mass, chemical calculations 82–3
formulae 54
fossil fuels 59
fossils 40–1
fovea 10

fractional distillation 51
free fall 122
freeze-thaw, rocks 65
freezing, effects on particles 52
frequency (waves) 124, 125
friction 116
fruit ripening 15
fuels 66
   fossil fuels 59
fungi 20
fuses, electrical appliances 103
fusion reactions 132

G

galaxies 132, 133
gall bladder 4
gametes 36–7
gamma radiation 129, 130
gas exchange 8
gases
   natural gas 66, 74
   noble (Group 0) 89
   properties 52
generator 105–7
genes 37–9
   alleles 38
   variation 37
genetic diseases 37–8
genetic engineering 42
genotype 38
geotropism 14
giant structures
   covalent 73
   ionic 73
glands 12
global warming 23
glucose
   fermentation 31
   in plants 24
   respiration 30
glycerol 4
glycogen 12
gold 89
graphite 73
gravity 122–3
greenhouse effect 23, 59
growth hormone 13
   plants 14–15
guard cells 29

H

Haber process 74, 80
habitat, ecosystems 16
habitat destruction 23
halogens (Group VII) 88
health 34
heart structure and function 7
heat energy
   body temperature 33
   conduction 110
   convection 110
   insulation 13
   radiation 111
   see also infra-red radiation
helium 89
herbicides 15, 22
herbivores 18
heterozygous 38
homeostasis 32
homozygous 38
hormones
   animal 12–13
   plant 14–15
hydraulic brakes 119
hydrocarbons 67
   Haber process 74, 80
hydrochloric acid 55
hydrogen 67, 79
hydrogen chloride 54, 88
hydrogen peroxide 56

I

igneous rocks 64
immunity 34
infra-red radiation 59, 129
insulation
   electrical appliances 103
   saving heat energy 17, 111–12
insulators 96, 113
insulin 12, 42
intercostal muscle 9
iodine 88
iodine solution 5
ionic bonding 72
ionic compounds 70, 72
ionisation, radiation 130
ions 70, 85
iris 10
iron 89
   extraction 69
isotopes 84

J

Joule (J) 120

K

kerosene 66
keys 16
kidneys, function 32
kilowatt (kW), power measurement 102
kinetic energy (J) 110, 120–1
krypton 89

L

lactic acid 30
lamp 98
large intestine 4
laser printer 97
LDR 101
leaf structure 25, 28
LED 98, 101
lenses, eye 10
life, activities 2
light energy, photosynthesis 24–5
light sensitivity, vision 10
light-dependent resistor (LDR) 101
light-emitting diode (LED) 98, 101
lightning 21
limiting factors, photosynthesis 25
lipase 4
liquids 52
   pressure in 119
lithium 87
live wire 102–3
liver 4, 12
lubricating oil 66
lungs 8–9

M

machines *see* power (W)
magma, Earth 62
magnesium 68
magnetic fields and field lines 104
magnetism 104–7
male reproductive system 36
maltose 4
mantle, Earth 62
mass
   and acceleration 116
   formula mass 82
   and gravity 122
mass number 82
meiosis 36
melting 52
membrane
   cell 1

partially permeable 26
menstrual cycle 13
metabolic rate 31
metals
   and acids 79
   alkali 87
   extraction by electrolysis 71
   from rocks 68
   and non-metals 86
   reactivity series 68
   transition 89
metamorphic rocks 64
methane 59, 67, 73, 74, 82
microbes *see* bacteria
micropropagation 37
microwaves 29
Milky Way 132
minerals
   from rocks 64, 68
   for plant growth 14–15, 27
mitochondria 2
mitosis 36, 37
mixtures 50
molecule diagram 54
molecules 50
   giant 73
moments, forces 123
monoculture 27
monohybrid cross
monomers, plastics 75
moon(s) 132
motion, measurement 114
motor 98, 105
motor neurones 11
mountain ranges, formation 63
mucus 9
muscle contraction 4, 11
   breathing 9
muscle fatigue 30
mutations 37

N

National Grid, electricity 107
natural gas 67, 74
   see also methane
natural selection 41
neon 89
nervous system 11
neurones 11
neutral wire 102–3
neutralisation 78
neutrons 84
newton (N) 116, 119
nickel 104
nicotine 35
nitrates 21
   pollution 23
nitrogen 60
   lungs/blood 8
nitrogen cycle 21
noble gases (Group 0) 89
nose 10
Now Do This, answers 139–48
nucleus
   atom 84
   cell 2

O

oceans, origin 61
oesophagus 4
oestrogen 12
ohm (Ω) 100
oil
   alkanes 74
   fractional distillation 51, 66
oils, types in foods 75
omnivores 18
optic nerve 10
optical fibres 127
orbit 131
ores 68